OLD PENINSULA DAYS

Hjalmar R. Holand

Copyright, 1959, by Hjalmar R. Holand
Ninth Edition, May 1990

Designed by
Lakeland Graphic Design
Minocqua, Wisconsin

Cover Designed by
Marathon Press, Inc.
Wausau, Wisconsin

NorthWord Press, Inc.
Box 1360
Minocqua, WI 54548

For a free catalog describing NorthWord's line of
nature books and gifts, call 1-800-336-5666.

ISBN 1-55971-057-8
Library of Congress Catalog Card Number: 59-8387

*COVER ILLUSTRATION
BY ROBERT PENCE*

HEARTLAND PRESS
an imprint of NorthWord Press, Inc.

Old Peninsula Days

ABOUT THE AUTHOR

The story of this unique peninsula and its sturdy pioneers is told by H. R. Holand who has lived here for sixty years. When he came many of the earliest pioneers were still living, so that he obtained his information first hand. Thus we see in this narrative a step-by-step creation of an American community, told by a man who is an expert in this line of research and presentation. It is a story abounding in both humor and pathos. The book is now, with a few changes, in its ninth edition.

Books by the Same Author:

History of the Norwegian Immigration, 1908, three editions

History of Door County, 1917

Coon Prairie, 1927, two editions

Coon Valley, 1928, two editions

The Last Migration, 1930

Wisconsin's Belgian Community, 1931

The Kensington Stone, 1932

Westward From Vinland, 1940, three editions

America, 1355-1364, 1946, two editions

Explorations in America Before Columbus, 1956

My First Eighty Years, 1957

Old Peninsula Days, 1925-1990, nine editions

PREFACE

For more than three centuries the pioneers have been pushing into every part of America, subduing the wilderness rod by rod. In friendly cooperation they have created thousands of small communities, more or less unified. During the first and second of these centuries their progress was slow, but during the third century they moved like a vast army into every state. It was a unique march of millions of people, seeking homes, independence, and the freedom of speech and religion—the greatest migration in history.

In order to understand the growth and spirit of America, it is necessary to get a close-up view of some of these pioneer communities. In the following pages the development of one of these is pictured with reasonable detail. The characters are described just as they were, idealistic or commonplace, but always energetic. The author has lived among them for sixty years and has heard the story of the early settlement from the lips of the original pioneers. The recording of these adventures has been an abiding pleasure, because thus, with local variations, our migrating ancestors for many generations struggled for survival.

This book was first published in 1925 for local consumption. But an ever widening circle of readers has necessitated its reprinting, with some additions, seven times.

HJALMAR R. HOLAND
Big Maples, Ephraim, Wis.

CONTENTS

chapter one

THE DOOR PENINSULA

Though all the bards of earth were dead,
And all their music passed away,
What Nature wishes should be said,
She'll find the rightful voice to say.

WILLIAM WINTER

FAR away, from the thousand hills of northeastern Wisconsin, come the waters of Green Bay. They come purling out of gushing springs, forming little streams which unite into big rivers like the swift Menominee, the somber Oconto and the famous Fox. From cataract to cataract they swirl and flow, until at last they plunge into the Emerald Bay.

More than a hundred miles long is Green Bay, and its width varies from thirty miles at its mouth to two miles at its end. Its bed was fashioned by the glaciers, which a hundred thousand years ago scooped out its basin and spread the former fill of alluvial soil southward over eastern Wisconsin. But on the eastern side the glaciers encountered a wall of limestone which they could not budge. This sturdy ridge which defied the glaciers is the Door County Peninsula.

In most parts of the Middle West there are very few reminders of the physical history of the region. The grassy plains and rolling hills have little to tell of the past. Not so on this Peninsula, for here Father Time has left many footmarks. When we sense their meaning, the Peninsula becomes a place of stirring physical action, of great revelations, from the time when this earth was young, until the Indians came and found it a pleasant place of abode.

Some of the more interesting signs of past events are the ancient shorelines of the Peninsula. They are marked by immense embankments on the sloping hillsides and deep wave-worn notches of the face of the perpendicular cliffs. The highest

shoreline is 95 feet above the present at Washington Island.
Geologists call it the Glacial Lake Algonkian shoreline

But the best thing about this Peninsula is its superb scenery.
There is a sixth sense, dormant in many people, which is beatific.
This is the appreciation of beauty. Here, in the northern half of the
Peninsula, Nature has taken on such forms, shades and qualities
as meet the human eye with perfect approval. It is not merely
good—it is delightful. It is diversified, harmonious, and always
uplifting. The Peninsula has a sinuous shoreline of two hundred
and fifty miles, and every craggy promontory presents a superb
prospect, every indentation of the shore a pleasing panorama.
Along the entire western side of the Peninsula a mountainous
precipice of castellated limestone defies the roaring waves, its bold
crags half covered with clinging cedars. On the east side the land
lies low with deep inlets and dreamy lakes, where the wild fowl
squawk and splash among the reeds of wild rice. Beyond the
rolling combers lie a score of rocky isles, the waters around them
abounding in bass, perch and whitefish. When the pioneers came,
they found the glades of the interior teeming with deer, and the
bear had many a snug winter camp in the hollow trunks of great
basswoods. Due to the fact that much of the soil in northern Door
County is too shallow for farming, there is still an abundance of
woodland, sheltering the homes of the farmers and producing a
glory of autumn coloring which is nowhere surpassed.

Here we have both the great and the small things that please
the eye. I can think of nothing more that is needed unless it be a
lively waterfall. But if one craves to see water in vertical motion,
there are few waterfalls equal in turbulent action to what is seen
at Cave Point when the wind is from the south or east. This is
described in Chapter Twenty-One.

The greater part of Door County is an island because the
Peninsula is cut in two by Sturgeon Bay and the ship canal. Being
thus surrounded by large bodies of water, this northern half of the
county has the most equable climate of any county in the
northwestern states. The mean annual temperature at Sturgeon
Bay is 43°. The winter average is 22°, which is several degrees
milder than any other place in the Middle West, north and west of
Chicago. The summer average is 67°, which is cooler than any
other in the State. A peculiarity of this Peninsula is that here
north is south and south is north. That is, the climate is milder in
the north end. A cold wave registers nine or ten degrees lower
temperature in the city of Green Bay at the base of the Peninsula

than it does 75 miles farther north. This is due to the fact that the land area is much narrower in the north, and the adjacent water area is wider, with a greater modifying effect on the climate.

It is probable that the Indians had little appreciation of scenic beauty, because this seems to be a recently acquired faculty. But the great variety and abundance of food which they found here made the Peninsula a favorite dwelling place for the Red Man. Here were not only wild ducks, deer, and bear, but also beaver—the choicest eating the Indians knew. On one occasion when Nicolet visited the Indians of the Peninsula, a feast was prepared for him, at which 120 beaver were served. The waters around the Peninsula yielded an inexhaustible supply of whitefish and trout, and the herring were considered the best fertilizer for their cornfields. It is therefore logical that when the first white man penetrated into the great West, he found this peninsula in the possession of the most feared and dominating of all tribes of the West. While there may be other regions of equally good advantages, there are none, from the Indian point of view, which have so much recorded history.

Just as it formerly was a haven of delight to the children of the wilderness, so it is now a balm to the pilgrims from the city seeking rest for tired nerves. The perfect harmony of its scenery is like a homecoming to every lover of nature. Many visitors are not content with a few weeks' sojourn. Drawn hither by the peace of its wooded hills and the beauty of its sea-girt shores, discriminating people are leaving their crowded city environs and are here building permanent homes.

The ancient forest has now, to a large extent, been replaced with quite another mantle of trees—a forest of a million fruit trees, stretching for miles over the rolling hills. In blossom-time these far-flung orchards present a vision of floral beauty of unsurpassed magnificence. The pioneers, after conquering the woods, the stumps and the stones, found that the soil was rather shallow, and thought that the rugged uplands of the Peninsula had been niggardly treated by Nature, but these uplands held a potential store of delicious fruitfulness.

chapter two

INDIAN DAYS

In the vale of Tawasentha,
In the green and silent valley,
By the pleasant water-courses,
Round about the Indian village
Spread the meadows and the cornfields,
And beyond them stood the forest,
Green in summer, white in winter,
Ever sighing, ever singing.

LONGFELLOW

IT is a common opinion that the discovery of America was immediately followed by immigration; but this is far from the truth. The Norwegians discovered the American continent in 1003 and later made some attempts at colonization, but they proved abortive. Five hundred years later, the English rediscovered the continent, but more than a century passed before they established their first permanent settlement. To the Spaniards who for a long time were the dominant naval power, America was a vast wilderness whose only value lay in its hidden gold. About 1540 two large bands of robbers, each numbering many hundred men, made simultaneous efforts to find that imaginary gold. Fernando de Soto in the East and Francisco Coronado in the West plunged many hundred miles into the interior slaughtering thousands of peaceful Indians. But their efforts were futile, succeeding only in revealing the grim indecency of their culture.

The stupidity of most of these early Spanish explorers is amazing. De Soto started out with six hundred picked men, two hundred horses, a pack of dogs and a large drove of pigs. He traveled about fifteen hundred miles, lost half of his men, and aroused the Indians to such deadly resentment that no further exploration in that part of America became possible.

One hundred and thirty years later Jolliet and Marquette set out to explore the Mississippi River. They did not have six hundred men—only three Indians to help in paddling the canoe. They started out from Green Bay, crossed Wisconsin and followed the Father of Rivers for two thousand miles to the mouth of the Arkansas. They met with scores of suspicious tribes, made friends with them all and opened the way for future travelers. They returned in safety and no one was hurt.

The first penetration of the great American plain, made for purpose other than robbery, was made in the Green Bay region in 1634. Samuel Champlain, the first and ablest of all the French governors, was a dauntless explorer. He traveled far and wide and won the friendship of the Indians by his frank and friendly manner. On reaching the eastern shore of Lake Huron, he was told that far west beyond that lake lived a people of strange speech called Winnebago, which meant foul or salt water. In the sixteenth and seventeenth centuries, one of the chief objectives of France and England was to find a northwest passage to China and the Spice Islands. To Champlain this mention of a people of strange speech living on the shore of salt water suggested the possibility that perhaps these people were an outlying colony of China, and in 1634 he sent an expedition to visit them and make a treaty of peace.

This one-man expedition of Jean Nicolet is one of the most remarkable exploration expeditions in history. A comparison will illustrate this. In 1870 Henry M. Stanley led a great expedition seven hundred miles into Africa to search for the missionary, David Livingstone, who was temporarily lost. Stanley had almost a shipload of supplies, with hundreds of beasts of burden and a veritable army of attendants, and several books were written about the heroic undertaking.

What was Nicolet's equipment? The Governor had no money and Nicolet had none, so no equipment was possible. But Nicolet had what money could not buy—a self-reliance and resourcefulness of the first quality. So he made a canoe out of birchbark, sewed together with the slender roots of a jack-pine, and persuaded some friendly Indians to help him paddle it. This and some parched corn and pemmican was the sum of his outfit. Then, one single white man, he seated himself in his bark canoe to travel a thousand miles among strange tribes to visit a nation of cannibals, reported to be the most ferocious Indians in America, whom no white man had ever seen before.

What happened to this daring explorer? Did the first group of

Indians that he met kill him and cook him in their kettles? No, Nicolet had lived for years as an Indian among Indians and knew how to deal with them. So he traveled up the great Ottawa River with its forty portages, voyaged over the waters of Lake Huron and Lake Michigan and finally came to the Door Peninsula. Past its rockbound shores he paddled, no doubt charmed with a nature so majestic and different from any he had seen. When he reached Eagle Island (near the village of Ephraim), two days' journey from his destination, he made camp for a few days, while he sent one of his Indian companions to Red Banks, near the head of Green Bay, to tell the Winnebago of his coming, as was the custom among the Indians.

Finally came the day when he reached the great village with its huge stockade on the hill. The Winnebago saw him from afar, and thousands of them crowded the beach when his canoe landed. Most of them were naked savages clutching a stone tomahawk with some vague hope of plunder. But there were also many great chiefs dressed in their ceremonial robes to see this strange white man who had come to visit them.

How was Nicolet to impress these thousands of savages so that they would receive him with respect? They were insolent creatures who had no neighbors because they had made war upon them and killed them. But Nicolet had not only courage but wit. As the canoe touched the shore, he stepped out. On his head he wore a big beaver hat, and he had arrayed himself in a grand robe of Chinese damask, strewn with birds and flowers of many colors, because he thought that he might have reached some outlying village in China. In either hand he held a pistol, but not for defense. Raising one hand aloft, he pulled the trigger and a jet of flame shot out, followed by a thunderous report. Upon hearing this noise, the women and children fled terror-stricken into the woods. And when Nicolet raised his other hand and repeated the miracle, even the warriors forgot their tomahawks and felt constrained to fly. Only a few chiefs, trembling but determined, stood their ground. Who was this strange being who carried thunder in either hand? Was he a friend or a foe?

To answer that question was not so easy, for the Winnebago belonged to the Dakotan group whose language was as unknown to Nicolet as the Chinese which he may have thought that they spoke. But again he found a way. He pushed two crotched sticks into the sand and across these he laid a third. Then he hung upon this stick such presents as he knew would appeal to the Indian mind. These presents said as plainly as words: "See, I come to you as a friend!" Quickly, therefore, the Indians recovered from their alarm, and so winning was Nicolet's personality that soon he won the friendship of all. He stayed with them the following winter, and when he departed in spring, it was with assurances of peace and goodwill which promised to open the doors of the West to French enterprise and business.

But nothing came of it for many years. Governor Champlain died only a few months after Nicolet's return, and his successors in office were not interested in exploration. Meanwhile the Winnebago on the Door Peninsula were reaping the grim harvest of their previous insolence. The ten years that followed were filled with bloodshed, amazing perfidy and unspeakable suffering, and they came to a sudden and disastrous end.

This village stood near the base of the Peninsula, on a hill called Red Banks, twelve miles northeast of the present city of Green Bay. Within its fortifications lived three thousand grim warriors—people not without virtues, but obsessed by a passion for warfare. This pugnacity prevented them from tolerating neighbors, and if emissaries from distant tribes came to visit them, such visitors were often killed and eaten. From this stronghold the proud Winnebago ruled nearly all the present state of Wisconsin. They are the oldest known inhabitants of the West. All their tradition led back to this spot. Even now to this bold hilltop comes from time to time a Winnebago pilgrim from his windswept reservation in Nebraska. From afar he stands, gazing reverently at the broad summit where once the glory of his people was focused. Climbing the hill he stares dreamily across the expanse of whitecapped breakers below. Then he kneels, and with pious hands scoops up a handful of the sacred earth to carry back to his children on alien soil.

After the last wretched survivors of the Winnebago had fled to Lake Winnebago, the Door Peninsula became the domain of the Potawatomi. These Indians were Algonquins, of entirely different stock from the Winnebago, and all the early travelers are unanimous in describing them as the most estimable of the aborigines. Their largest village was Mechingan, at the mouth of Hubbards Creek, a mile north of the present village of Jacksonport. They were very hospitable and liked nothing better than to be praised for their generosity. Thanks to this unquestioning hospitality, they soon played a most significant part in early American history.

During the years immediately before and after 1650, a great

war had been raging in Lower Ontario and the adjoining regions. The Iroquois of central New York, perhaps the most warlike and vindictive tribe in America, had obtained firearms from the Dutch traders in Fort Orange (now Albany), and, thus equipped, determined to destroy all their neighbors for hundreds of miles around. In this they were most fearfully successful, for the French doubted the wisdom of selling muskets to the Indians with whom they traded. In a few years the Iroquois had taken almost fifty thousand scalps, and all the villages east, west, and north of Lake Ontario were laid waste. It was, perhaps, the greatest catastrophe in the history of the Indians of North America. In 1651 the survivors of many of these tribes, such as the Hurons, the Ottawa, the Nipissings, the Amikouek and others, sought shelter on Washington Island and the neighboring shores of Green Bay, while others, fleeing around the south end of Lake Michigan, settled in the Green Lake region of central Wisconsin.

The Hurons on Washington Island feared that not even there would they be safe from the fury of the Iroquois. To guard against a surprise attack, they therefore sent scouts to the Iroquois villages to learn what plans were brewing. One day in 1652 some of these scouts returned with the ominous news that the Iroquois were sending an army of eight hundred warriors into the West to find the fugitives and utterly destroy them. This was only incidental to the main purpose, however. As soon as these fugitives had been hunted down, it was the purpose of the Iroquois to destroy the French and set up a supremacy of their own.

Realizing the futility of making a stand against the Iroquois on Washington Island, the Ottawa-Hurons and other fugitives begged permission from the Potawatomi to take refuge in their village of Mechingan. This was readily granted by the generous Potawatomi, and the population of the village was suddenly raised from fifteen hundred to more than four thousand.[1]

All haste was now made in enclosing the village with the strongest possible fortifications. Hunters scoured the woods in all direction for game, fish in vast quantities were caught and dried, and a large crop of corn and vegetables was grown and harvested. As the Iroquois did not know where their quarry was hiding, they could proceed only slowly while searching the wilderness. By the spring of 1653 when they finally reached the village of the Door Peninsula, the fugitives were sitting well entrenched with storehouses full of provisions.

It was with dismay that the Iroquois found the fugitives so well protected. They had been victors in attacks upon hundreds of villages, but here they found in the triple stockade of green timbers an obstacle which not even their most experienced and reckless warriors could overcome.

Finding that their attacks were futile, the Iroquois finally settled down to a siege, hoping to starve the village into surrender. But soon they found themselves threatened with starvation. The woods seemed empty of game, and they had little fishing tackle and no corn. They finally were obliged to sue for peace. This was agreed to on the condition that the Iroquois give up all their prisoners. As a sign that all enmity was now wiped out, the Ottawa-Hurons, to the delight of the Iroquois, promised to give a pone of corn to every Iroquois warrior on the morning of the departure.

But the Ottawa-Hurons had no intention to befriend those bloodthirsty warriors of the East who without cause had murdered their women and children and almost exterminated their people. Into every pone was mixed a strong poison. This was the proper parting gift, the Ottawa-Hurons felt, for such rapacious wolves.

It happened that among the Hurons was a woman who had been captured by an Iroquois chief many years before. Later she escaped and rejoined her people, leaving an Iroquois son behind her. As this woman was peering through the stockade, she was surprised by seeing her Iroquois son on the outside. Urged by mother love, she forgot all the persecutions that her people had suffered and warned the boy not to taste of the bread, because it contained death. The boy mentioned this strange warning to his father the chief. The next day when the bread was thrown down from the stockade, the famished Iroquois pounced upon it only to be stopped by the barked command of the chief. He fed a piece to a dog which soon howled in agony and then died. With this proof of the implacable temper of their enemies, the Iroquois withdrew in humiliation, followed by the jeers and arrows of the villagers.

Deeply mortified by this defeat and insult, the larger number of the Iroquois now determined to restore their prestige by devastating some less protected tribe of Indians. They turned southward and fell upon the Illinois near the south end of Lake Michigan. The Illinois quickly rallied, however, and defeated the Iroquois so thoroughly, that only a small number of terror-stricken survivors escaped to carry the sad tidings back to their tribesmen in New York.

The other division of the Iroquois had in the meantime turned northward, disconsolately taking the direct road leading to the home cabins. But they were secretly followed by the Amikouek, who set a trap for them and killed them almost to the last man.

Great therefore was the grief and consternation in the Iroquois cantons when it was learned that their proud army of eight hundred warriors had been exterminated. Now was no time to show an aggressive attitude toward the French. Their own safety was in greatest jeopardy. With unctuous servility, based upon deadly schemes for vengeance, the Iroquois made haste to assure the French that the war hatchet had been buried so deep in the ground that it would never again come up in the light of day. An Iroquois defeat on the Door Peninsula had saved Canada for the French.

It was not long before the allied tribesmen in the village of Mechingam learned of the disastrous end of the Iroquois campaign. Knowing that they would now be left in peace for a year or two at least, they scattered far and wide on their fall and winter hunting trips. They collected a huge quantity of furs, and the next spring a large flotilla of Indian canoes carried them to Montreal and Three Rivers. This was not only the first shipment of furs from the distant West, but was also the first important delivery from any quarter for many years due to the paralyzing effects of the Iroquois war. When this large flotilla of several hundred Indians was seen approaching Montreal, its inhabitants feared it was an attack in force by an Iroquois army. But when the friendly shouts of the well-known Hurons were heard, fear turned to joy. The merchants were well nigh ruined by the long interruption of the fur trade, but now plenty and prosperity returned once more.

Among the many curious spectators in Three Rivers who watched the antics of the newly arrived Indians were two adventurous young men by the names of Radisson and Groseilliers. As they saw the big packs of prime beaver, they quickly realized, and, by two hundred years, anticipated Horace Greeley's conviction, that the way to get rich was to go West. Quick in decision, they asked and obtained permission to accompany the Indians on their return to the West. These two men were the first and boldest of the many fortune-hunters who, later known as coureurs de bois, or forest rangers, swarmed through the wilderness, debauching the Indians with brandy, obtaining furs by fair means or foul, and almost always in defiance of the king's orders. Like Nicolet who had preceded them twenty years earlier, they also went first to the Door Peninsula or rather, to Washington Island at its north end, which was the home of the Hurons whose guests they were.

Soon after their arrival they received an invitation to visit the
Potawatomi village at Hibbard's Creek. Pressed by their
hospitality, the two travelers spent the entire winter with the
Potawatomi, thus becoming the first white men who sojourned for
any length of time within the limits of Door County. Radisson does
not tell much of their experience here, but notes that it was a
succession of feasts, and that the time was spent with "a great
deal of mirth." Afterwards they visited many other tribes, being
received with much pomp and ceremony, "as Gods and Devils of
the earth," of which Radisson gives many strange pictures. Many
years later, when Radisson in the peace and quiet of an English
cottage wrote his picturesque narrative of his extensive travels
from Quebec to Minnesota and from Hudson Bay to the Illinois
prairies, he recalls his first wintering place on the Door Peninsula:
"I can assure you I liked no country as I have that wherein we
wintered." Perhaps some day an enterprising hotel will capitalize
this generous testimonial of the first great travelers in the West
and emblazon upon a proper sign a paraphrase of Radisson's
words something like this:

> We travelled far through regions vast,
> Both north and south and east and west;
> But nowhere was its charm surpassed—
> The Door Peninsula was the best.

----

[1] The location of this village is described in H. R. Holand, "The First Mission in
Wisconsin," *Salesianum*, 1954, Vol. 49, pp. 108-111.

chapter three

THE EARLY MISSIONARIES
COME TO THE PENINSULA

*Though I walk in the valley of the shadow of death,
Yet I shall have no fear:
For thy rod and thy staff they comfort me,
And thy word shall be my cheer.*

DAVID

TO this region came also the early missionaries. Their motive was not the growth of empire or the lust of power, but an ardent love which sent them to the ends of the earth to preach a new gospel of salvation to those who sat in darkness. Alone and unattended they came, ready to fight single-handed against what seemed to them a world of iniquity. There were no well-built mission stations ready to receive them, no salary wherewith to buy the comforts of life, and no pensions in store for them to take care of their old age. Indeed, many of them never reached old age, for they perished in the wilderness as martyrs of their faith. They were the noblest idealists of early American history.

In the early dawn of American history, when the pious Catholic missionaries were beginning their labors in the valley of the St. Lawrence and Lower Ontario, the Great West was an unknown region of which they had only the vaguest surmises. With ardent desire they looked toward that mystic wilderness, praying that it might be vouchsafed to them to plant therein the cross of their faith. They had seen the implacable Iroquois annihilate the Hurons, among whom the missionaries had many converts. The big Huron villages had been destroyed by fire, and the few Hurons who had escaped had fled far into the West. Would they ever see them again?

Then one day in 1656 there came to them an exalting ray of light, like a revelation from above, concerning the unknown peoples of that far country. It was Pierre Radisson and Medart

Grosseilliers, two fur traders, who had penetrated more than a thousand miles beyond the French settlements and brought back amazing reports of the vastness of this terra incognita, the variety and abundance of its resources, and the multitude and character of its people. Of surpassing interest was their description of a large Indian village, a veritable city of the heathen with 4000 inhabitants. The bold travellers said that the people of this village were well behaved, intelligent, hospitable to a fault, and invited the missionaries to come and visit them. And there they also had found many Christian Hurons! With uplifted hearts the missionaries felt that the day was near when they could preach the gospel of glad tidings to these worthy people in the West, and in the expectancy of their desires, making the future seem like the present, they called this first inland mission by the name of St. Michael, chief of the archangels.[2]

Nor did they delay in the execution of their plans. Two devoted priests were immediately chosen to return with the Indian flotilla with whom Radisson and Grosseilliers had come. These two missionaries were Leonard Gareau and Gabriel Dreuillettes.

But these missionaries were destined never to reach their appointed field. Even before the flotilla reached Montreal, it was ambushed by the Iroquois and Father Gareau was fatally wounded. The Indians thought this bad luck was due to the presence of the missionaries, and Father Dreuillettes was not permitted to go with them.

The Iroquois were deeply mortified by their great defeat in the West and immediately began preparations for an expedition to annihilate their enemies on the peninsula in the West. This was learned by Father Le Moyne, a capable missionary who had obtained permission to stay among the Iroquois. He sent word by means of a Huron slave in the Iroquois village that an army of 1500 men would soon set out to punish the Indians in the West. In the meantime dissension had broken out among the latter, and they felt unequal to make a united stand—they all decided upon a flight. When the Iroquois shortly afterward arrived, they found only empty cabins and desolation.

After a year or two of restless wandering most of these Indians reunited at Chequamegon Bay, just west of the present city of Ashland on Lake Superior. This was for a number of years a temporary asylum for many tribes, some of whom had not previously seen any of the goods used by the French in barter. Seeing here an opportunity for profitable trading, the Ottawa took the big chance of a trip to Three Rivers to obtain the necessary

trade articles. They were successful and also permitted Rene
Menard, a missionary, to accompany them. But he was a feeble old
man and perished shortly after reaching his destination.

In the meantime a bishopric had been organized in Quebec and
its very energetic bishop, Francois Xavier Laval, was determined
to open a mission in the West. He appointed Claude Allouez "Vicar
General for all the countries toward the North and West" and
instructed him to stay in Three Rivers, fully prepared to go as
soon as a company of Indians carrying furs appeared from the
West.

For several years Allouez waited in vain. But in 1665 a flotilla
of 400 Indians appeared. Six French fur traders were also waiting
for this opportunity. They were immediately accepted, but Allouez
was brusquely told to keep away. The Indians wanted no
"Blackgowns" because an earlier Blackgown (Menard) had had the
"insolence" to rebuke their chief because he had four wives!
However, the French fur traders took Allouez in their canoe

These Frenchmen were poor canoe men, and even before they
left the quiet waters of the St. Lawrence they staved a hole in the
canoe. There was much bungling before the damage was repaired
and it took them three days before they caught up with the
Indians. The canoe now seemed worthless and the Frenchmen
asked to ride with the Indians. They were accepted as passengers,
but Allouez was left helpless on the bank, watching the last canoe
disappear around the nearest bend.

In this dilemma Allouez turned to the Virgin Mary in prayer
and, while thus engaged, he was happily surprised to see the
French fur traders come along the bank. It was too much to leave
him there to perish. They gave the old canoe another overhauling
and finally overtook the Indians at the next portage. Allouez'
reappearance caused much angry talk. One old chief urged that all
the French be left behind, but that did not meet with approval,
being contrary to business prospects. Allouez was left behind with
many angry words, and the flotilla passed out of sight.

Thinking that all was now lost, he went back in the woods to
pray. "I thank God," he writes, "for making me so acutely
conscious of my own slight worth and confessed before his divine
Majesty that I was only a useless burden on earth." Then he
returned to the bank and was surprised to see the same stern
chief who had been so hostile. Brusquely he was told to get into
the canoe, and glowering savagely the old chief brought him to the
main group.

However, that was not the end of his troubles. He was a small man and could not carry his share of the freight at the portages. Moreover, he knew nothing about paddling a canoe. He was therefore the object of a lot of silly jokes, and the Indians took what they wanted of his possessions. But Allouez took it all with a smile and devoted all his energy to become expert in paddling. In this and other ways he gained the respect of his tormentors, and when they after ten weeks' toil reached Chequamegon Bay, the Indians no longer laughed at him, but with him.

On arriving here they found several thousand fugitives of many tongues. They lived in two large villages, some distance apart. Allouez built his wigwam exactly midway between the two. It had two small rooms, one to serve as a chapel with an altar, the other in which he slept and cooked his food. On hearing that a new "medicine man" had arrived, his wigwam was filled and surrounded by an expectant multitude, wondering what wonders he would perform. But they saw or heard nothing that was dramatic, and they went away disappointed. The religion of the stone-age Indians was entirely materialistic while his was spiritual, and the Indians could see no contacts.

As the situation seemed temporarily hopeless, Allouez went on a great exploration journey. Accompanied by a couple of friendly Indians he set out in a birch bark canoe to circumnavigate Lake Superior—a voyage of about 1500 miles. As evidence of this trip he has left us a map which, in view of his lack of modern instruments, is very fine, showing that he was a very good cartographer.[3] This map shows not only all of Lake Superior, but also half of Lake Michigan, Later he added all of Green Bay and a large part of Wisconsin, showing the location of many of his missions.

Four gloomy years passed by with only a few nominal converts. The Indians were fretful because they had been driven from their own hunting grounds and talked big about going to war, without the courage to do so. Finally the big concourse broke up. The Potawatomi were the first to leave for their beloved peninsula, and then the others scattered in different directions. As the Potawatomi seemed the most promising, Allouez followed them as soon as he found a substitute, Jacques Marquette, to take his place.

Early in the Spring of 1670, Allouez found his Potawatomi at Point Sable, near the inner end of Green Bay. They gave him a hearty welcome, and were ready to listen to him. Here, in 1670, he established his first mission, named the Mission of St. Francois

Xavier and marked it with a big cross on top of the escarpment about a mile east of the village.[4] The next year the mission was moved to the site of the present city of De Pere, which was named after him.

This became the headquarters for the missionaries in the West. Allouez was soon joined by Father Louis Andre and they divided the field. Allouez started missions south and west of De Pere, while Andre visited the Indian villages east and north. Like Allouez, he erected great crosses to stand as witnessing beacons of the faith he was preaching. The Indians came to look upon these crosses as symbols of the great unseen God, and brought their offerings and prayers to them.[5] Andre's influence must have been powerful, for almost two hundred years after he departed from that field, the first white settlers were astonished to find in the primeval forest a great cross before which the Indians made their adorations. This cross stood at the mouth of Rowley's Bay, and not far from the site of the ancient St. Michael.

This cross is now gone, but the exact spot where it stood is known. In 1928 the present writer found, directly in front of the spot where the old cross had stood and well hidden in the dense forest growth, six flat stones, black with century-long weathering, neatly laid as a stairway from the beach up to the cross. As this point of land has never been cultivated or occupied by white settlers, these stone steps were no doubt built by the missionary who desired a dignified approach to his place of prayer—the oldest evidence of white man's occupation of the Northwest.

Thus we find that the embryo mission of St. Michael, toward which the missionaries looked with such devout hope almost three hundred years ago, was also the only one which left any physical evidence of their labors.

After weeks and months of pious struggle against superstition and idolatry, it must have been a sweet consolation for the two missionaries to meet together for a brief period of rest, counsel and prayer in the mission house which was their headquarters. Here, in the quiet chapel, the din of the noisy witch doctors was not heard, and the vision of offensive ceremonies was blotted out. The accommodations were most humble, the larder was often empty, and there was no news of their friends—yet, in spite of all drawbacks, this sanctified shelter must have seemed to them "like the shadow of a great rock in a weary land."[6a]

One day there came to this mission house two distinguished visitors. They were Louis Jolliet and Father Jacques Marquette, who stopped here on their great expedition to explore the Mississippi River. The existence of the river was well-known. The Hurons and Ottawa of Father Allouez' mission had traveled a couple of hundred miles on it, and they must have told him much about its greatness. It was also generally known to other tribes, and a report of it had reached Count de Frontenac, the new governor of New France. He commissioned Louis Jolliet to explore the river, and Father Marquette, who for years had been longing to visit the Indian tribes along its course, was chosen to accompany him. On May 17, 1673, they left St. Ignace at Mackinac with five companions, going by way of Green Bay and the Wisconsin River in two birch bark canoes. They descended the Mississippi a thousand miles to the Arkansas River and returned by way of the Illinois River and Lake Michigan. While their journey was rather uneventful, this was due more to good management than to lack of danger. When they reached the mission of St. Francis after a journey of almost 3000 miles, not a man had been killed or lost, either among them or by them, and their birch bark canoes were still intact.

On the return journey the explorers went back by way of the Illinois River where they found a large village of Illinois, called Kaskaskia, at Starved Rock, near the present village of Utica, Illinois. Here Marquette found a promising opening for missionary work, and he promised to return to them the following year. However, an illness that he had contracted on his long voyage confined him to the mission house of St. Francis for more than a year. In November, 1674, he departed in a canoe with two Frenchmen by way of the Sturgeon Bay portage and Lake Michigan to make his visit to the Illinois. His increasing illness prevented him from completing his journey, and he spent the winter in a wretched hut which his two companions constructed on the bank of the Chicago River about five miles from its mouth.[6] In Spring he struggled on, reaching the Illinois village the second week in April. The chiefs received him kindly, and preparations were made for a big meeting on the following Friday which was Good Friday. On that day he expounded the new faith to a concourse of many thousand people. Seated in a semi-circle before him were many chiefs and old men, while behind them stood fifteen hundred warriors besides women and children. His altar was a small flat stone blessed by a bishop and placed on a little platform built of rough sticks, and the reredos was four large pictures of the Virgin Mary suspended behind it. Here he celebrated the Holy Mass. The service was repeated on Easter Sunday, and the missionary was highly pleased with the respectful attention paid by the savages to the holy mysteries. However, feeling that his end was near, he bid them goodby, longing to say a last word to his neophytes in faraway Mackinac. He died on the way.[7]

When Allouez heard of the good beginning that Marquette had made among the Illinois, he applied to Quebec for assistants so that he could personally take charge of Marquette's mission in Illinois. Fathers Silvy and Albanel came, and late in the fall of 1676, Allouez set out in a canoe with two men. They had only paddled a few miles when a storm and drift-ice stopped their progress, and he remained with the Potawatomi in Oussatinoung at Point Sable until well into February. Then, the ice becoming smooth, he fitted two wooden runners under his canoe and hoisting a sail, he made swift progress toward Sturgeon Bay. However, at Chouskouabika (now Pensaukee) he had some converts, and he put in there to visit them. He found the village filled with lamentation because a very promising young Indian, who was one of Allouez' disciples, had been killed by a bear. They determined, as soon as a period of mourning was completed, to avenge the death of the young man. Here we have a most curious instance of how the fear of the wrath of unseen spirits yielded to the Indian wish for revenge. The bear was the most respected of all animals, and whenever the Indian killed one, he always made an apologetic prayer, accompanied with an offering of tobacco, to the spirit of the bear that the killing was "not done with evil intent but because of necessity." Yet here they set out to make a wholesale killing of the noble animal. Allouez remained with them a month during which time the great bear hunt continued, and he writes that 500 bears were rooted out of their winter sleep and killed. Then, after attending a grand feast to the Sun, Allouez hoisted his sail again and glided over the ice to the Sturgeon Bay portage. When he reached Lake Michigan, he found both water and ice, but his canoe was good for both. There was not a village or wigwam on the entire shoreline of three hundred miles, but Allouez did not need them. When night came, he dragged his canoe up on the beach, ripped some birch bark off a tree, and by help of his flint and fire-steel he soon had a fire. After supper he rolled up in his buffalo robes and slept peacefully under the twinkling stars until morning.

Here we have a picture of the masterful man who has

conquered the difficulties of his environment, and thinks so little of it that he without remark starts out on a journey of four hundred miles in the wilderness at the most unfavorable time of the year. At this time Allouez was almost sixty years old.

Allouez became a very successful missionary and was joined by many others. They started many missions and each of these was marked by a high cross placed a short distance from the village.[8] These crosses were venerated by the Indians for a long time, and at least one was rebuilt and maintained by Christian Indians until the white settlers came about 1870. This cross stood on the south side of Mink River at its mouth in the northern tip of the Door Peninsula.

Allouez died in 1689, an outstanding man of faith, humility, and patience, well fit to be listed in the category of saints.

---

[2] This early mission of St. Michael must not be confused with the Mission St. Michael, established among the Menominees by Allouez in 1670. The latter was so called because it was begun on May 8th, the day of the apparition of the archangel Michael. See *Jesuit Relations*, LIV, 227-235.

[3] The map is printed in *Wisconsin Historical Collections*, Vol. 16, opp. p. 80.

[4] As Allouez says he "could see it from afar" while walking along the beach from Fox River, it probably stood just south of the site of the Wequiock Church in the north end of the Bay Settlement.

[5] *Jesuit Relations*, Vol. 59, p. 103; 58, pp. 25, 27.

[6a] Father Andre was an indefatigable missionary. In 1676 he was transferred from Wisconsin to the far northeastern country of the Montaignais where he continued for almost forty years.

[6] This spot, where Damen Avenue crosses the river, is now marked by a monument.

[7] An account of Father Marquette's last days and death, see Father Dablon in *Jesuit Relations*, 59: 185-211.

[8] For a description of these crosses, see H. R. Holand "The Sign of the Cross" in *Wisconsin Magazine of History*, (1933), Vol. 16: 153-167.

chapter four

FOOTPRINTS OF A GREAT EXPLORER

Through hunger, peril, storm and cold
He pushed without a sigh.
His was to blaze the white man's trail
And then lie down and die.

UP to about 1680 the French dominion in America embraced only the St. Lawrence valley with a few scattered fringes of the Great Lakes' shores. But by that time had come a man from Normandy who, without any financial or military aid from the government, added the great Mississippi Valley to this domain. He was the real creator of that vast province later known as the Louisiana Purchase. This man was Robert La Salle. There was in him a breadth of vision, a persistency of endeavor, which we do not see equaled in any of the other French pioneers of America. He was also the most masterful of them all, overcoming alike the hostility of the natives, the treachery of his subordinates, the intrigues of jealous men in high places, and the stern opposition of relentless Nature.

In his extensive journeys he is said to have penetrated to more than a hundred Indian tribes which never before had seen a white man. This is an exaggeration. But so ingenious and masterful was he in winning the respect of the aborigines that, wherever he blazed the trail, other men could follow without molestation. He is of special interest to readers of this narrative because he chose this fair Peninsula to be the spring-board for his greatest undertaking.

This great explorer—"A man of iron, if ever there was one," as John Fiske so aptly characterizes him—spent several weeks on the Door County Peninsula in 1679, while on his first expedition to explore the Mississippi. To this threshold of the Great West he came, finding here the means to finance his great enterprise. His stay here was marked by some of his highest flights of hope. But this hope culminated in tragedy, and just one year later the few and famishing survivors of his first futile endeavor returned to this Peninsula, seeking only a warm campfire by which to die.

René Robert Cavelier, Sieur de La Salle was born in Rouen, Normandy, in 1643. It is quite probable he was a direct descendant of those indomitable Northmen who so masterfully had conquered the city and province of his birth seven hundred years before his time, because he was much like them both in physical characteristics and mental traits. In 1666 he came to Canada and secured a large tract of wild land near the frontier post of Montreal.

But La Salle had no intentions of settling down as a country gentleman. After some years of struggling to get his bearings, we see him devising a vast scheme of exploration. Other men had done some probing into the mystic West, but none had attempted the project of opening up the whole continent. He is said to have been the first to explore the course of the Ohio River which is doubtful. But he was the first to undertake the exploration of the Mississippi from its source to the sea. This great waterway he prepared to mark with a string of forts, which would enable France to hold the whole continent (except the Atlantic seaboard) for herself.

To carry out this vast enterprise required money or credit. Upon the recommendation of Governor Frontenac, whose protegé he became, he went to Paris and laid his plans before King Louis XIV. That epicurean king was only mildly interested in La Salle's visions. But he graciously permitted this eager young knight-errant to undertake the doubling of the dominions of France—but strictly at his own expense. He also condescended to give him exclusive trading rights with the Indians in the new regions which he planned to discover. As there were no means of protecting this monopoly, it was really an empty phrase.

At first sight it would seem that La Salle had not obtained enough from the king to pay for his journey, but he was satisfied. He had the papers to show that he was the king's official representative both in the exploration of new regions and in trading with the Indians, and that gave him credit with the merchants of Montreal.

This credit being secured, the next thing was to earn the money necessary to finance his journey of exploration. To earn this he resorted to fur trading. Almost every spring he had seen a large flotilla of fur-laden canoes manned by hundreds of Indians float past his home at La Chine Rapids. These riches of furs came mostly from La Baye des Puans (Green Bay), and were brought by the friendly Potawatomi who were the jobbers and carriers of the furs from the Wisconsin area, just as the Ottawa were the factors in the trade of Lake Superior. La Salle decided to seek his fortune in the same distant region, but he saw an opportunity of greatly improving the transportation methods then in vogue. If the business paid a profit with the enormous expense of paying hundreds of men for months of toil in transporting the furs, it should be much more profitable if this transportation expense could be almost eliminated. Accordingly he set to work to build a large sailing vessel, in the hold of which he could carry a larger cargo more safely and expeditiously with a half dozen men than could be transported in a couple hundred Indian canoes. This vessel of sixty tons burden, the first to sail the interior waters of America, was appropriately called the Griffin, being both in speed and strength like the fabulous griffin of old. It was built at the mouth of Cayuga Creek above Niagara Falls and launched August 7, 1679. Its beak was adorned with a flying griffin surmounted by an eagle, and it had five cannon. La Salle embarked with thirty-four men which constituted not only the crew of the vessel but also his army for the conquest of the regions to be discovered.

As it was necessary to proceed slowly and take soundings all the way, it took twenty days to reach Mackinac. The night before they reached this place they were overwhelmed by a sudden gale, and the vessel was driven furiously through the turbulent waters in the darkness. Panic seized the whole company and brought them all to their knees in prayer—all except the captain, a grizzled Scandinavian salt water sailor by the name of Luc, who stuck to the wheel and swore loudly at the unspeakable tricks of these fresh water lakes.

The expedition was planned partly as a missionary enterprise, for there were three priests on board—Father Gabriel Ribourde, Zenobe Membré and Louis Hennepin. The last wrote a long account of it and mentions that the Indians of Mackinac Island were greatly alarmed at seeing the Griffin, fearing that it would mean the end of their business as traders between the Indians of the East and the French of the St. Lawrence. "They took such jealousy to our ship," says Hennepin, "that they endeavored to make our expedition odious to all the nations about them." We shall soon see how well their plots worked.

At Mackinac La Salle was detained six days owing to the

desertion of about half of the men. These fellows decided they would rather be soldiers of fortune in the woods than sailors of fame on these uncharted lakes where danger lurked in every boat length. La Salle was finally obliged to depart without them, leaving to his trusty lieutenant, Henry Tonty, the difficult task of winning them back to their duties. On September 2nd the Griffin departed from Mackinac bound for the Potawatomi, on the Door County Peninsula.

The preceding year La Salle had sent some men to this place to barter with the Indians and thus secure a cargo for the Griffin. These men, presumably on the advice of La Salle, who seems to have been there before, had selected Detroit Harbor on the south side of Washington Island, where there was a village of Potawatomi, as their headquarters. Here was not only the safest harbor on Green Bay, but the island was also large enough to provide good hunting during their long and uncertain stay. Here the Griffin put in and lay anchored for about ten days. Hennepin mentions the exact place of her anchorage, being, he says, "in the Bay, about thirty paces from the furthermost point of land." This would be in the passage between the west point of Detroit Island and Lobdill's Point, about a hundred feet from the latter.

Many Indians were encamped here, eagerly waiting to see this remarkable sight, the floating fort about which the fur traders had told them wonderful stories. Among these Indians was Onanguissé, the head chief of all the Potawatomi, whose village was on Sturgeon Bay. He had previously been to Montreal and Quebec where he had gained the friendship of La Salle and the Governor, the great Frontenac. Of these two men he had the highest esteem, and it was customary for him to say that he "knew but three great captains—Frontenac, La Salle and himself."

The fur traders had been very successful, and a vast quantity of pelts was obtained which was estimated at a value of forty thousand livres (having a probable purchasing value of about forty thousand dollars now). In exchange for this, the Indians received thousands of inexpensive but useful articles such as fishhooks, needles, awls, knives, hatchets, combs, kettles, beads, and brightly colored coats gaudily ornamented with gold braid. Never before had they made such a satisfactory trade, and that right at home—no laborious and dangerous canoe journey of four or five months to Montreal and back this time. The barter was therefore concluded with a great feast accompanied by much fervid oratory and the smoking of the Calumet with all ceremonious dignity. As a climax they placed La Salle, the great chief, on a red blanket, which, lifted by innumerable hands, was raised high and carried with deafening shouts around the campfire.

No doubt La Salle, too, fully shared this exultation because this trading venture had fully satisfied his expectations. In a few weeks now these furs would reach the storehouses of his creditors in Montreal. With such returns they would cheerfully fill his long order for new supplies which soon would reach him at the south end of Lake Michigan. Everything would then be in readiness to carry out the main object of the expedition—to follow the Father of Waters to its unknown outlet and thus add a new province to his country. Thankfully he waved goodby to the crew of the Griffin as it glided out of the harbor, and benignly the stars seemed to shine as he retired to his tent that night, the 18th of September, 1679. Visions of speedy success and glory floated before his eyes.

But if La Salle had been gifted with second sight, he would have seen a sight that night which would have chilled his soul with horror. He would have seen the crew of his vessel cruelly murdered in their bunks, and the proud Griffin, the apple of his eye, a burning wreck.

As already mentioned in the statement quoted from Hennepin, the Hurons of Mackinac took offense at the sight of the Griffin. When they saw this huge but graceful craft with its tall masts and bulging sails, so vastly superior to a canoe, glide smoothly through the water, unaided by the hand of man, they were first amazed and then alarmed. They conceived the idea that it had come, not for beaver-skins, but for slaves. Their neighbors, the Ottawa, were easily persuaded to share their alarm, particularly as the Ottawa realized that the Griffin could quickly put them out of business as the traders and transportation agents between Mackinac and Montreal. Filled with jealousy and evil forebodings, they took steps to prevent the success of this new enterprise. A delegation of Ottawa and Hurons was sent to the western tribes to warn them against La Salle.

The *Griffin* had proceeded only a short distance on the first day after leaving Washington Island owing to contrary winds and had put into a small harbor, probably near Point Detour, for the night. Here it was found by the Ottawa-Hurons who were returning from their incendiary mission among the Wisconsin tribes. They feigned friendship and were kindly received by the unsuspecting crew of the vessel and invited on board as some of the Indians were recognized from the visit at Mackinac. During the night the crew was murdered and the vessel burned. This done the Ottawa proudly returned to Mackinac feeling that they had acquitted themselves like able warriors.[1]

But Robert La Salle knew nothing about this and probably slept well. The next day, having bought five canoes from the Indians, he departed with fourteen men for the south end of Lake Michigan.

Between Washington Island and the end of the Peninsula is a strait about five miles wide, known as Death's Door because of its frequent storms and dangerous currents. When the canoe party was half way across "the Door," a strong wind from the northeast threatened to upset the canoes, but they finally made land in safety. At this place, now known as Northport, La Salle for five days sat imprisoned by the ceaseless surge of the sea that boomed thunderously at his feet. He must have been alarmed for the safety of his beloved ship and searched the sea with anxious eyes. But nothing appeared but the mist shrouded islands of the passage—Plum, Pilot, Detroit and Washington—rising murkily over the frothing waves. This poor beginning was an ill omen to the success of his journey.

In order to identify the location of La Salle's successive campsites, his own very clear description of this part of the journey will here be cited. He says:

> On the 25th (of September) he continued his voyage during the whole day and a part of the night, rowing along the coast favored by the moonlight; but a rather stiff breeze having sprung up, he landed with his men. They encamped on a bare rock, where they tried to shelter themselves from rain and snow with the help of their blankets and a small fire which they fed with wood cast up by the waves.[2]

The term *bare rock* indicates that they landed on a treeless rocky island. This conclusion is supported by the fact that they mention no difficulty in landing. Any "stiff breeze" which would compel them to land would also make a landing on the shore of the peninsula difficult. But if they landed on an island, there would be a safe side where they could land in quiet water. The conclusion that they landed on an island is also supported by the statement that they made a fire with wood cast up by the waves. If they had landed on the mainland they would have made fire with dry twigs of evergreens which are much more inflammable than beach wood.

There are two such formerly bare rocky islands on the east shore of the Peninsula, both of which in their location fit the description of La Salle. One is the extreme point of the small peninsula outside of Baileys Harbor where the lighthouse was built. The other is Cana Island, a little to the northwest. As the first day's journey apparently was a little longer than the second, the Baileys Harbor point is more likely to be the location of the camp. But the weather conditions may have been more favorable the second day, so the time element is not a conclusive factor.

> On the 28th, toward noon, they got into their canoes again and rowed a good part of the night, till a cyclonic wind forced them to land at the point of a rocky summit covered by shrubs.
>
> There they stayed two days, consuming the last of their provisions, that is to say the Indian corn and pumpkins they had bought of the Pouteatamis and of which they had not taken in a greater store because their canoes were already overladen and they hoped to find more on the way.

The only rocky summit on the shore south of Cana Island is Cave Point where the precipice rises about thirty feet. At the extreme point of this elevation the landing is not difficult as there is no precipice there. This precipice is the last rocky formation toward the south and lies about midway between the previous campsite and the next.

> They left October 1st, and after rowing ten leagues on an empty stomach, they arrived at another village of the Pouteatamis. The coast was high and steep, and exposed to the northeast wind which was then blowing . . . . The Sieur de La Salle in order to land safely had no choice but to throw himself into the water with his three men and all together lift the canoe with its load and carried it on shore. . . ."[3]
>
> As he did not know the savages of this village and feared they were hostile, he first prepared all his arms and then placed his camp on a height where he would be able with a few men to defend himself against a larger number. He then sent three of his men with the peace pipe which Chief Onanguissé had given him . . . to the village, which was distant about three leagues, to buy food.

We see from this that the Indian village was not at the place where La Salle fortified himself, but about three leagues farther north. This village is described by Henry Tonty as being three or four miles south of the Sturgeon Bay portage (where now is the Sturgeon Bay Ship Canal).[4] The campsite, where La Salle with his fourteen starving companions sought shelter, was therefore about seven or eight miles south of the village. At this place there is a narrow pointed ridge, its two sides almost perpendicular, where La Salle "would be well able with a few men to defend himself against a larger number." This he fortified by building a barricade of green timber. La Salle estimated the distance from the "rocky summit" to the new camp at about ten leagues. The distance from Cave Point to the new camp is twenty-two miles, which agrees well because the distances are uniformly overestimated.

La Salle and his men were here in a very precarious situation, because not only were they completely without food, but soon it was discovered that a band of twenty Indians fully armed were steathily approaching the camp. Throwing discretion to the winds, La Salle with four men went down from the redoubt to meet them. With more gestures than words he endeavored to explain that his mission was friendly, meanwhile scanning the beach to the northward for signs of his three men. The Indians seemed highly suspicious of all this pantomime and they, too, narrowly watched the beach. But when eventually the three men appeared, one of them carrying the calumet of Onanguissé, all suspicions faded away and the Indians became most friendly. Some of the natives were sent back to the village for provisions, and the white men were given more food supplies than they could safely carry away in their canoes. These gifts saved the lives of La Salle and his men because he mentions that they were unable to find any game during the next two weeks.[5]

The weather becoming settled, La Salle and his men were now able to make better progress toward the head of the lake. The Chicago portage was evidently unknown to them for they passed this and rounded the south end of the lake to St. Joseph River, where now lie the cities of St. Joseph and Benton Harbor.

Tonty had been successful in rounding up the deserters and arrived at St. Joseph River a few weeks after La Salle. They then ascended this river to the vicinity of South Bend, Indiana, where a portage was made to the headwaters of the Kankakee River. This route was about three hundred miles farther than if they had come by way of the Chicago portage, and they almost perished of starvation while descending the Kankakee which flowed through a region of endless swamps. The winter was well advanced when they were finally obliged to stop near the site of Peoria, Illinois, because of the cold weather. Here they built a camp which they named Crevecoeur (i.e., Heartbreak) because, as Hennepin says, "the difficulties we labored under were almost heartbreaking."

Their stay at Fort Crevecoeur was so wretched as to amply justify that dismal name. Loyalty seems to have an almost unknown virtue among La Salle's retainers, and several of them deserted after first putting poison in La Salle's food. He survived this attempt to take his life, but his days were filled with gloom while vainly waiting for news of the Griffin. Despairing at last of her return, he set out afoot on the first day of March 1680 to make his peace with his creditors in Montreal, a thousand miles away, and find some way to obtain new supplies.

He departed with four Frenchmen and one Indian, but without any provisions for the journey, sleeping in snowdrifts, fording swollen rivers of icy water, leaping from one cake of ice to another. By the time they reached their destination his companions, French and Indian alike, were shorn of all strength and helpless, but La Salle's indomitable courage carried him on and he brought his sick companions to safety.

Meanwhile his trusty lieutenant, Henry Tonty, in the Illinois wilderness was endeavoring to cajole his surly crew into turning the trees of the riverbank into boards and planks by means of a whipsaw. The purpose was to build a vessel to carry the expedition down the Mississippi. Slowly this work proceeded, and the vessel began to take shape. But not for long. Tonty was called away on a journey, and when he returned after some days, he found that nearly all his men had deserted. They had wrecked the fort, burned the vessel and taken with them all guns, ammunition and food supplies, leaving behind them scratched on a board the quite unnecessary information: "We are all savages." Out of the original expedition of about forty men, there were left only Tonty, the two priests, Gabriel Ribourde and Zenobe Membré and three young men newly arrived from France.

Tonty and his companions now sought refuge in a nearby village of Illinois Indians, hoping to enlist some of them in his enterprise. But in so doing he jumped from the frying pan into the fire. A party of six hundred Iroquois warriors suddenly appeared and attacked the Illinois. Tonty fearlessly tried to act as peacemaker, but was almost killed for his pains. He and his companions were taken prisoners by the Iroquois, but were finally permitted to depart. Dejectedly they set out, on September 16, 1680, without supplies or weapons except one damaged musket and a leaky canoe.

It was a retreat full of the greatest hardships, toil and danger. On the first day of the journey as they stopped to make some repairs to the canoe, Father Ribourde went some little distance away to make his devotions. While thus occupied he was captured and murdered by a wandering band of Kickapoo. His companions disregarded their own safety and searched for him for two days. Despairing at last of finding him, they departed in great sadness, for Father Gabriel Ribourde was a noble-minded, pious old priest, the most beloved member of the whole expedition.

They reached Lake Michigan by way of the Chicago portage and then turned northward to paddle their way along the forest-clad shore which stretched somber and silent for hundreds of miles. Being the time of autumn gales, they were continually compelled to seek the land to escape the turbulent waves, and their progress was very slow. As they were short of food and clothing, their condition was very wretched indeed.

After having proceeded slowly northward for about five weeks, their canoe was wrecked at a point near the present Two Rivers, November 1st, 1680. Here they all went searching the woods for something to eat, and in so doing one of their company by the name of Boisrondet got lost. They were finally obliged to leave him and the dilapidated canoe and set out afoot along the shore. After dragging wearily for fourteen days more, they came in sight of the friendly village about four miles south of the Sturgeon Bay portage. With joyful exclamations they hastened forward feeling that their sufferings were over. But, alas! When they reached the village they found it deserted. All the inhabitants had gone on their winter hunting trip. They searched the cabins for food, but found nothing at all. Bleakly discouraged, they went out into the cornfields of the village and searched among the dead weeds for a stray kernel of corn that perchance might have escaped the eyes of the crows or the field mice. By diligent searching they were able to pick up an average of two handfuls together per day for future consumption and also some frozen squash. These gleanings they laid aside in a cabin near the shore to serve as provisions on their journey to Mackinac.

Meanwhile Boisrondet had wandered for many days in the deep woods, subsisting principally on an occasional root of garlic which he had dug up under the snow. He had a flintlock gun, but the flint was lost. Nor did he have any shot or bullets. But necessity is the mother of invention. He had a pewter cup which he melted and made into shot. Carrying with him a smouldering firebrand wherewith to fire his gun, he discovered a wild turkey which he was fortunate enough to shoot and kill. On this he lived for many days. Finally returning to the shore, he found the canoe which had been abandoned as useless. He managed to partly repair this and paddled northward along the shore. Finally he reached the Potawatomi village and entered the first cabin near the shore. Here he was overjoyed to find a substantial heap of corn and squash which Tonty and his men had gleaned in the field. Boisrondet supposed that they had left the food supplies for him and sat down to make such a meal as only a lusty young fellow with a three days' hunger could devour.

Here Tonty and his companions, returning from a weary day's work of gleaning in the fields, found him. They were very glad to see him, but their joy changed to dismay when they saw what havoc he had made in the provision pile which they had intended for their journey to Mackinac. As there was not another kernel of corn to be found in the fields around the village, they embarked in the canoe to go as far as they could. They had gone about four miles, when they were forced to land owing to a rising wind. Here they found a well-trodden path. It was the Sturgeon Bay Portage. They crossed this, taking their canoe with them, and turned to the right where they found a big village at the head of what is now called "the Cove," just south of the present city of Sturgeon Bay. This village was named Nahmamequetong and was the home of Onanguissé, the principal chief of the Potawatomi. Tonty and his men found plenty of dry wood in the cabins, but here also the inhabitants had gone away for their winter hunting.

Wearily they embarked again, following the shore of Sturgeon Bay and came out to Green Bay. About thirteen miles from their last stopping place in the village on the creek, they were detained by a northwest wind for five days. This place must have been at or near Horseshoe Bay. Here they consumed the last of their provisions. Being in November, the air was filled with rain, snow and sleet, and they were unable to make a fire. Utterly discouraged, starved and chilled to the marrow, they all had but one desire—to return to the village on Sturgeon Creek where there was dry wood so that they might once more feel warm before dying. "Everyone asked," writes Tonty, "to return to the village since there was dry wood there, so that we might die warm."

When the storm ceased they paddled back to the cove at the

head of Sturgeon Bay. Here they passed the night with nothing to eat but some old pieces of leather. The next morning they intended to proceed to the village on the other side of the cove, but this was now covered with ice and they could not use the canoe.

Tonty now urged his men to proceed on foot to the village, but this had to be postponed. Their supper the night before of bits of old leather disagreed with one of them so that he was unable to get up.

In this extremity they were surprised to see a group of Indians suddenly appear before them.

These Indians were on their way to Chief Onanguissé, had plenty of food with them, and treated the famishing explorers with every kindness. When they were ready to move, they took Tonty and his men in their canoes and, proceeding down the bay about "three leagues," they reached Onanguissé's winter camp, probably in the vicinity of the present Idlewild. Here they found some French fur traders, and the Potawatomi chief received them very kindly. They remained as guests of Onanguissé during the following winter with the exception of Father Membré who spent the winter at the Jesuit Mission at De Pere. The next spring they proceeded to Mackinac where they met Robert La Salle.

Such was the futility, the suffering and the weariness of La Salle's first attempt to explore the Mississippi. Twice the Potawatomi of the Green Bay region had saved the lives of the travelers, and they had also by their furs furnished the considerable capital needed to carry the expedition through. But that capital was lost with the staunch *Griffin*, a year of fruitless toil had been spent, and many men had perished. But notwithstanding all these disasters, La Salle remained indomitable in his determination to reach the mouth of the Mississippi. The next year he and Tonty set out again and accomplished their purpose. A vast region, later known as Louisiana, comprising almost half the territory of the present United States, was added to the French domain, but La Salle met his death at the hands of a French assassin.

---

[1] La Potherie in Blair, *Indian Tribes*, I, 351-353. See also Le Clerq, *Estab. of the Faith*, II, 115. We have no certain information as to how the *Griffin* was lost. But as Perrot, who spent much of his time with the Ottawa at this time, was told the above and accepted the narrative without question, it is probable that it states the truth. The French fur traders at Mackinac who may have heard of this probably connived at it for their enmity was aroused at La Salle for trading with the Potawatomi. In so doing, La Salle, perhaps unwittingly, violated the patent granted him by the king which expressly forbade him to trade with the "Ottawas and 'others' who bring their beavers and other peltries to Montreal." (See the king's patent in Le Clerq, *ibid.*, II, 126-127.)

[2] This and the next two descriptions of La Salles's journey are from Pierre Margry, *Decouvertes et Establissements des Francais*, Paris 1876, I: 450-461, and are recognized as being in the main verbatim copies of La Salles's own notes.

[3] Father Hennepin mentions that Father Gabriel, who was sixty-four years old, was unable to withstand the buffetings of the waves and would have perished. But Father Hennepin, seeing his perilous condition, took him on his back. Here, feeling safe, the old friar quickly recovered and chuckled happily under his cowl as his rescuer staggered wearily over the slippery stones.

[4] A map of 1673 also shows a village at this place. Its name was Mechihegahning. See Chief Kahquados in *Wisconsin Archeologist*, 19: 51.

[5] A county park comprising ten acres has been created at the spot where La Salle and his men were rescued from starvation by the Indians. The Door County Historical Society has put up a monument in memory of La Salles's visit. The spur, on which he built his redoubt, is just south of the monument on the other side of a small ravine.

chapter five

A FORGOTTEN COMMUNITY

There is a pleasure in the pathless woods,
  There is a rapture on the sounding shore;
There is society where none intrudes
  By the deep sea, and music in it roar.

BYRON

THE very successful missionary work of Father Allouez and his associates together with Joliet's and Marquette's great exploration of the Mississippi in 1673 produced wide publicity for the Green Bay region. This was greatly augmented by La Salle's and Tonty's explorations. The French became conscious of the vast possibilities of the inland plain. Green Bay (or rather La Baye as the settlement was known) became the first business center west of the Appalachian Mountains. Here was the outfitting station for fur traders throughout the Middle West, and the traders in Milwaukee and Chicago were obliged to paddle their canoes to Green Bay for their goods until well into the Nineteenth Century.

And now the Green Bay region became famous for something else besides furs. The new attraction was fish, and for more than a century it held the reputation of being the best fishing area in all the Great Lakes.

Beyond the tip end of the Peninsula lies Rock Island, containing almost 800 acres. It is situated in the middle of the mouth of Green Bay, storm-lashed by all the heaving seas of Lake Michigan. On the north and west its limestone ramparts rise in perpendicular grandeur from the lake to the height of a hundred feet and more. On the south and east, however, its shores slope gently down until their sands blend with the lapping waves of the inland sea. From shore to shore the interior is covered with a majestic mantle of forest green, shrouding a solitude which was unbroken by human habitation. Only upon the northern cliff sits a watchful lighthouse, its gleaming light turning throughout the night upon the dark waters to warn away the wind-swept mariner from the dangerous coast it is guarding.

More than a hundred years ago this isolated little island, now ruled over only by the "murmuring pines and hemlocks," was the home of an energetic community of about a hundred people. Their snug homes lined the eastern shore and their sailboats ventured far out to sea for fish and fun. Up on the hillside a number of early Wisconsin pioneers are laid away to rest, and in a log schoolhouse whose very site is forgotten many worthy citizens of this state and Michigan have learned their A B C's.

Rock Island is the first place in Wisconsin visited by white men. When Jean Nicolet in 1634 passed through the Straits of Mackinac, the customary Indian route was along the shore of the northern peninsula of Michigan until the present Point Detour was reached. There the natives crossed the mouth of Green Bay to the north shore of Rock Island and Washington Island and then followed the west shore of the Door County peninsula to the Winnebago capital at Red Banks.

The first white settlers on Rock Island were John A. Boone, James McNeil, George Lovejoy, David E. Corbin, Jack Arnold, and Louis Lebue. They were fishermen and trappers who came from the island of St. Helena in the Straits of Mackinac in 1835 or 1836. As they were the first settlers in the northeastern part of the State outside of the settlement at Green Bay, a brief mention of their personalities will be desirable.

John A. Boone was a quiet, apt-spoken man who, without thrusting himself forward, was always looked upon as the leader of the community that grew up on the Island. He had evidently spent his entire life on the frontier, as he spoke the Chippewa dialect like a native and fully understood the Indian character. These accomplishments later served him well when he was the means of averting a threatening Indian war. He was a married man when he settled on the Island, and lived there until his death in 1866, when he was fifty-two years old. A little white-painted cedar cross still marks his grave on the Island.

George Lovejoy had been a sergeant in the United States army, having seen five years' service at the frontier post of Fort Howard. He was a hunter of fame in many parts of northeastern Wisconsin and an eccentric bachelor of remarkable capacity for almost anything he undertook. He could beat an Indian on a trail, and he astonished the sailors by personally building a schooner with which he traded along the shore. His commercial qualities were crude, however, and barren of success. He was an expert with the violin and a master ventriloquist. Sometimes he would go out on the ice where an Indian was fishing and make the trout talk back to its captor in the most approved Potawatomi dialect, to the poor Indian's terrorized amazement. This, with his reckless bravery and easy skill in every undertaking, made the Indians look upon Lovejoy as a veritable demon, and they were always most anxious to gain his favor by gifts of all kinds. In one direction, however, Lovejoy was anything but brave. That was in his attitude toward the fair sex. When suddenly confronted by a woman, he was struck dumb with embarrassment and often fled precipitately. This failing of his was the cause of many broad jokes played on him by mischievous young folks of the little community.

To James McNeil belongs the honor of being the first taxpayer in Door County. He owned the entire south shore of Rock Island. He was an old bachelor of a penurious disposition, with a failing for whisky. He was very close-mouthed about his own affairs except when the jug arrived from Chicago. Under its stimulus he would become confidential and would prate with tipsy garrulity of his "yellow boys," which, he confided, would support him in comfort when he should retire. By "yellow boys" he referred to his store of gold coin, which, unfortunately, became his undoing instead of his support. One morning the poor old man was found beside his chicken coop, wounded and unconscious. When he came to, he shouted, "Boone! Boone!" in agonized appeal. Boone, who was justice of the peace, was quickly summoned, but by the time he appeared, McNeil had passed away, taking the secret of his murder with him. For some time there was much hunting in the potato patch and among the crags for the old man's treasure, but nothing was found.

Both David E. Corbin and Jack Arnold were old soldiers who had been sergeants in the War of 1812. Corbin was the first lighthouse keeper in Wisconsin, being in charge on the Rock Island lighthouse (the first in Wisconsin) from its construction in 1836 until his death in 1852. Arnold stayed with Corbin in the lighthouse because they were such inseparable cronies. They rarely ever conversed but were apparently able to read each other's thoughts. When finally Arnold sickened and died in 1848, Corbin watched by his bedside with ceaseless vigilance, caring for him with the greatest tenderness.

Of all these men Louis Lebue is the only one from this section whose name is mentioned in the territorial census of 1836. In 1843

he had the misfortune to lose his wife, who was buried on the
Island. This unsettled him, and he departed for Chicago, the rising
metropolis of the West. On Calumet River, near Chicago, he made
the acquaintance of some men by the names of Miner and Luther.
Henry D. Miner was the son of a clergyman who, as early as 1828,
had settled at Kaukauna as a missionary among the Indians. The
following year he died of fever at this place. His boy, Henry, who
was then eight years old, returned to his relatives in New York. In
1842, however, he returned to the West accompanied by his
brother, T. T. Miner, and Job, Seth, and Brazil Luther. In the
spring of 1844, Lebue met these men and told them of the easy
living that could be made on Rock Island by fishing. He showed
them how to repair and knit twine and initiated them into the
mysteries of the piscatorial art. As a result he sold them his outfit,
whereupon in June, 1844, they moved to Rock Island to become
the forerunners of a steady advance of settlers to this distant
region. Job Luther had a vessel and at intervals he freighted fish
down the lake and fishermen up, until after three or four years
there were upwards of fifty men, many of them having families,
living on Rock Island. Nearly all of these people came from
Lemont, near Chicago, and were known as the Illinois Colony.
Among them were a number of well-known pioneers by the names
of Chauncey Haskell, Robert, Sam, and Oliver Perry Graham,
and, last but not least, old Father Kennison.

Old David Kennison was for a while the most famous character
of Rock Island, entertaining its denizens with tales of stirring
events in the infancy of the Republic in which he had personally
taken part, for he was more than a hundred years old. He could
say with Tennyson's Odysseus:

> Much have I seen and known; cities of men, and
> manners, climates, councils, governments, and drank
> delight of battle with my peers—

Kennison was the last surviving member of the Boston Tea
Party. He had participated in several wars and smelled blood in
many battles. Now, after a century of toil and trouble he had come
to Rock Island, satisfied to ruminate in peace upon a busy life.

He was born in 1736 in one of the frontier settlements of New
Hampshire. Of his youth and early manhood we know nothing.
Very likely he carried a musket in the French and Indian War and
had his share of fighting against the Indians in the region of the
home of his youth.

At the outbreak of the Revolutionary War we find Kennison right in the midst of things. He was a member of the Boston Tea Party, a participant at Lexington and Bunker Hill and many other battles of the Revolution, surviving them all. Keenly loving the strenuous life, he later went west and in 1804 enlisted at Chicago, serving for eight years at Fort Dearborn until the massacre of the post drove the surviving members of the garrison east.

Having a charmed life and net yet sated with fighting, he then served through the War of 1812, escaping as before without a scratch.

Being eighty years of age Kennison now settled down to a quiet life, but here his expectations miscarried. He should have remained in the army, for he discovered that a civilian's life was vastly more dangerous. "A falling tree fractured his skull and broke his collar bone and two ribs; the discharge of a cannon at a military review broke both of his legs; the kick of a horse on his forehead left a scar which disfigured him for life." Trouble thickened fast and thickened faster.

In spite of all his public and private tribulations, Kennison succeeded in marrying four times and becoming the father of twenty-two children. The records are silent about these successive broods for they faded away, until Kennison in his old age had only one son to lean upon. With him, at the age of one hundred and ten years, he went to Rock Island to repair twine and clean fish.

Kennison found life on Rock Island very pleasant. The big sea surging all around him from beyond the skyline spoke to him of other days and events and was soothingly companionable. Up at the lighthouse were David Corbin and Jack Arnold, two other veterans of the War of 1812, with whom he now and then swapped reminiscences.

It is pleasant to contemplate this veteran of many wars, seated on the front steps of the lighthouse on Rock Island. Behind him rose the tower of the first lighthouse in the Middle West—a symbol of the watchful care of the beneficent government, for which he had risked his life many times. Before him was spread one of the grandest panoramas on earth. Blue and clear, the waters of Lake Michigan shimmered in the sun far below him, its surface broken only by the occasional thrust of a frisky trout. Not far away lay St. Martin's Island, a big rocky flat, covered by giant timber yet uncut. Beyond this could be seen other green islands, stretching northward to the hazy line of the northern peninsula of Michigan. It was—and is—a perfect vision of peace and beauty. Here this weary old man must have found true contentment.

But not for long. After some years the twenty-second son got tired of the island and joined the other twenty-one renegades in deserting their father. When the winter came, the fishermen scattered, as was their wont, to different cities to spend a part of their earnings in having "a good time." Old man Kennison was obliged to leave and secured free passage to Chicago, hoping to eke out a meager existence on the paltry pension of eight dollars a month which the government doled out to this last surviving champion of her liberties.

As the pension was insufficient, he was finally constrained to enter a public museum and obtain a small pittance by exhibiting himself as a curiosity. Finally he died February 24, 1852, one hundred and sixteen years of age. At last his troubles were over.

Then, at last, when he was beyond the reach of knowing it, came recognition and honor. On the day before his death, in response to a request presented in his behalf that he be saved from the potter's field, the city council with patriotic energy voted that a lot and a suitable monument by provided for him in the city cemetery. A grand funeral was held from the Clark Street Methodist Church, and many clergymen assisted in the services. The procession moved in two divisions from the church to the cemetery with cannon booming at one-minute intervals. In the procession were the mayor and city council, a detachment of the United States army, various military companies and bands of the city, companies of firemen, and a large part of the population of the city. The cemetery at that time occupied a portion of the ground which later was included in Lincoln Park. When this area was added to the park, the bodies interred in it were removed, but Kennison's was left undisturbed. In 1905 several patriotic societies joined in marking his grave by placing upon it a large granite boulder to which is fixed a bronze tablet containing an appropriate inscription.

Here old David Kennison will probably forever lie, in unique dignity, in Chicago's most beautiful park. He was greatly honored in his death, but his declining years were suffered to be spent in cleaning fish and later in being gaped at by the idle and curious multitude.[1]

Nearly all these people lived along the sandy east shore of Rock Island where they constituted the first community on the Peninsula. And a very contented community it was. The fish were plentiful and very large, often only ten to fifteen being required to fill a half-barrel. In the woods was game, and in the little garden

patches of the settlers potatoes and other vegetables grew
luxuriantly. Apples, plums and berries in abundance grew wild in
the woods, and there was no lack of firewood with which to keep
warm in wintertime. It was a free and easy life to lead, somewhat
indolent and uncouth, without taxes or sociological troubles of any
kind. Their chief handicap was their distance from any post office
through which to learn the news of the outside world. The most
accessible one was Chicago, three hundred miles away. Mail
intended for the settlement was usually directed as follows: "H. D.
Miner, Rock Island, care of X. Y. Williams, Chicago, Illinois." On
his occasional visit to the metropolis, Job Luther would get the
little bundle of Rock Island letters and newspapers, often many
months old. On such visits he would also lay in ample stores of tea
and tobacco, boots and biscuits, soap, sugar and soda, coffee and
calico, and all the other staples which T. T. Miner carried for sale
in his little store on the Island, Besides these things he was also
entrusted with a multitude of private requisitions, such as a
mouth organ or a fowling piece for a young hopeful, or a bonnet or
a brocade for one of the fairer sex. Such fineries were needed to do
honor to the occasional weddings, funerals, and other events of
importance. Weddings were of rare occurrence and, while of
transcendent interest, were usually not attended with any
ceremonial, being in the absence of church and organized state
only "common law marriages." Now and then a contracting couple
was found who felt the need of the blessing of the church upon
their union. This, however, was difficult of attainment. On one
such occasion H. D. Miner was drafted into service to tie the knot.
The cause of his selection was that a certain faint glow of
sacerdotal dignity was attributed to him by reason of the fact that
his father had died as a missionary to the Indians. Miner
complied, and with all the unction he was capable of, joined
together Henry Gardner and Elizabeth Roe, the first marriage
ceremony to be performed in Door County.

Another wedding is recalled by the old pioneers with much
relish. It was a big affair in which two Norwegian couples were
joined in wedlock, and fishermen from many shores had gathered
to celebrate the double feast of love and liquor. As usual, there was
no clergyman to officiate, but a humble visiting evangelist was
drafted into service. He had no license to perform a marriage
ceremony, but he was anxious to please his prospective converts
and consented to officiate. It was a new undertaking for him, and
being nervous and not knowing the contracting parties, he made

the unfortunate blunder of marrying the two men to each other and then the two women. The two Norwegian bridegrooms on their part had but little knowledge of the English language, and only a very dim notion of the procedure at an American wedding. They, however, had a vivid impression that it was their part to answer "yes" when spoken to. When therefore Ole Olson was asked if he would take Halvor Johnson for his wife and vice versa, an energetic "yes" was the response to the uproarious acclaim of the assembled guests. It was not until the young exhorter was similarly joining together the two brides, who by the way, were sisters to begin with, that the officiating witnesses rallied their wits and interposed, whereupon a fresh start was made.

Dependent on the lake as these people were and exposed to all its squalls, hairbreadth escapes on the water were quite frequent. While thrilling adventures were common, the fishermen were so used to Neptune's whims that comparatively few fatalities occurred. Now and then, however, one would be caught unawares and go down to his watery grave. A notable instance of this was the drowning of the Curtis family.

Newman Curtis joined the Illinois Colony in the late forties. In the summer of 1853, he went with his family, consisting of his wife, daughter, and newborn baby, to St. Martin's Island to fish. After a successful season he prepared to return in the fall to a newly built home on Washington Island. He was accompanied by his nephew, W. W. Shipmen, and Volney I. Garrett, two young boys.

As Mr. Curtis had a quantity of household goods and freight, he rented an old and clumsy schooner, which in early days had outridden many a storm, but was now considered too unwieldy to be safe. But as it is only eight miles between the two islands, the little party started off without fear. All went well until the vessel was drawing quite near to Washington Island, where its occupants could almost see their little white cottage among the trees on shore. By this time the fair wind that had favored them had gained in force until a storm was blowing and the creaking old schooner began to roll heavily. In doing this she took in a great deal of water as the top seams were quite open. The pump was kept going but in spite of this the vessel settled fast and soon was so water logged as to be quite unmanageable. When just outside of Indian Point, on which the seas were rolling terrifically, those on board realized that in all probability the schooner would sink before she would be dashed on the rocks, not a hopeful alternative.

Curtis and Garrett, therefore lowered the yawl while Shipman went down to fetch the baby who was still sleeping in an upper bunk oblivious to her peril.

At this juncture a heavy sea dashed over the vessel, tearing away the frail grip of the Curtis girl on the cabin to which she was clinging, and washing her overboard. This wave was followed by another which tore loose the yawl, throwing it into the sea endwise and pinning Curtis underneath it. When he finally came to the surface he was so overcome by his exertions and bruised by the blows he had received that he was unable to swim the few feet that separated him from the yawl which floated away filled with water. Upon seeing sudden death thus overtake her daughter and husband, Mrs. Curtis for a moment forgot her own peril and stretched out her arms to them, screaming in anguish. Instantly she, too, was washed overboard.

By this time Shipman, drenched with water, had emerged from the cabin with the baby in his arms. He made for the remaining hatch, reaching it simultaneously with Garrett, who also seized it. "Who takes the hatch takes the baby," shouted Shipman, thrusting the baby toward his companion. Garrett, however, refused this handicap. The next moment they were all thrown into the water. Clinging to the hatch, Shipman and his charge made land safely, where they were soon joined by Garrett, clinging to the submerged yawl. The next morning the battered bodies of the Curtises were found on the beach and were buried on Rock Island.

Besides the Illinois Colony and other white settlers, there were about fifty wigwams of Chippewa Indians on Rock Island, living under the leadership of their renowned chief, Silver Band. The two communities got along very well together except on one occasion when open war was threatened. It happened in this way. Among the whites was a widow by the name of Oliver. She had three boys, one of whom, Andrew, was a half-grown fellow. Widow Oliver was much broken down over the loss of her husband; but was nevertheless in great demand for nursing the sick, at which she was very capable. Her boy one day took her place in the kitchen where he was peeling cold boiled potatoes. Some of the Indian urchins noticed this through the partly opened window, and soon there was a group collected, their noses pressed flat against the glass, making grimaces at the white youth and calling him "squawman." This was too much for the willing Andrew, who suddenly threw a cold potato at the leader of the band of mockers. He, however, dodged the missile which, with splinters of glass, struck an innocent little bystander full in the eye—the seven-year-old son of Chief Silver Band. The screaming sufferer, bleeding profusely, was hurried to his father's tepee, and soon the Indians were seen rushing excitedly back and forth. The white settlers, on hearing what had happened, felt that a crisis was imminent, and sent Henry Miner to parley with the chief. He was met at the door and gruffly told to go away. Others attempted to interview the Indians, but without gaining a hearing. The situation was alarming for they knew that any moment a signal could be sent to the Indians on Washington Island, and they would have no chance against the overwhelming numbers that might be brought against them.

In the midst of this hubbub John Boone arrived. He would talk Chippewa fluently and was highly esteemed by Silver Band. Taking the weeping Widow Oliver by the hand he made his way to Silver Band. In well-chosen words he reminded the chief of their earlier associations. He called up one picture after another of the chief's greatness in war, and cunning in battle, and mighty prowess in hunting the bear and the buffalo. He told of how wisely Silver Band had conducted the affairs of his people as chief, keeping them out of trouble of all kinds, showing magnanimity to his foes, and gaining the esteem and confidence of the white people. He concluded:

> And now I am glad that so magnanimous a chief as Silver Band rules his people. Children play, children quarrel, children get hurt. It is easy to be magnanimous when another's child is hurt, but not so easy when your own child, the pride of your eye, suffers. Another chief, less noble than Silver Band would let rage master him, and thus bring everlasting trouble upon himself, his people, and his neighbors. Not so with my brother, the great chief Silver Band, the lord of the Chippewa. He suffers, but he forgives.
>
> And now I bring you this woman to be your handmaiden. She is weak of body and crushed with grief that her son should unwittingly have brought this evil upon his little playmate, your son. But her hands are skilled in the mixing of potent medicinal herbs, and she can nurse your child to health.

Soothed, complimented, and gratified by the skillful discourse, the chief sat silent. Finally he rose, extended his hand to Boone, and led Widow Oliver to the couch of his suffering boy. There she remained nursing him unremittingly until he was able to go about again, blind, however, in one eye.

Little by little the fortunes of Rock Island declined. In the fifties and early sixties when other parts of Door County began to be occupied, the exodus from Rock Island began. The Island's lack of good harbors, and the inconveniences attendant upon its isolation, more than outweighed the greater profits derived from its fishing. One by one the old-timers slipped away to seek their fortunes in other parts. Some of the buildings were removed while others mouldered away. It is now long since the Island's last loyal denizen bade good-by to his romantic habitation. Where once stood the village of the Illinois Colony wild roses now grow, and the rabbits and chipmunks frisk undisturbed over the knoll that marks the site of the old schoolhouse. Up on the hillside lie the bones of John Boone, Silver Band, Newman Curtis, and all the other worthy men who played a man's part in their day; the moss of the forest has garbed their graves, and their aspirations and their deeds are alike forgotten.

Among the sons of these early pioneers, there should have been one who, upon gaining wealth and vision in public life, returned and converted this magnificent island into a grand baronial estate. But he never came. Instead, the island lay unnoticed for a half century, subject only to the nibbling of occasional woodchoppers who picked up some unpaid tax certificates and tried their luck in shipping out forest products. Fortunately, the transportation of these products was such a problem that most of the timber was permitted to stand. Each year most of its million trees gained in girth and height. It was a treasure not yet discovered by seeing eyes.

But finally came the island's redeemer. He was C. H. Thordarson, an Icelandic inventor and manufacturer of electrical appliances of outstanding fame. Learning that there was a large colony of Icelanders on the adjoining Washington Island, he went up there to call on his countrymen. From them he learned of Rock Island, and he (about 1920), straightway bought the whole of it, with the exception of the lighthouse reserve. To this genial scientist the island was the grandest possession on earth.

There followed many years of planning and incidental construction, such as building cottages for his many workmen and visiting friends. This was only preliminary. His main thought was to make the island the perfect workshop for the study of botany, sylviculture and related sciences. The first building erected with this end in view was a fireproof assembly hall, 80 x 100 feet in size. There are no pillars or other obstructions within the building, the roof being carried on immense steel joists 80 feet long. The building was planned for educational and social gatherings. To give cheer to the latter purpose, he built a huge fireplace, so big that on one occasion he served dinner to six guests sitting around a large table within the fireplace. Beneath this hall is a vast boathouse protected from the waves by ponderous iron gates operated by machinery.

Perhaps his absorption with these idealistic plans was too great for his own good, because competition in the production of electrical appliances is very keen. New inventions appeared, making his own obsolete, and old age was also a most serious handicap. Eventually he became bankrupt. He died in 1945, 77 years old.

Mr. Thordarson was a noted bibliophile with a library of many thousand volumes. It contained one of the most complete collections of Icelandic literature in existence, and also many rare works on botany and ornithology with hand-painted illustrations of rare beauty. All, or most of these 25,000 volumes, were bound in England at big expense. Finding the climate of Chicago detrimental to the bindings of his books, he moved the entire collection to his assembly hall on Rock Island. Thus we had on this little island one of the finest private libraries in America. A New York expert appraised the value of the collection at $250,000. It is now in the possession of the University of Wisconsin.

------

[1] For further information on David Kennison, see *Chicago Democrat*, Nov. 6 and 8, 1848 abd Feb. 25-27, 1852; *Chicago Daily News*, Dec. 19, 1903. His grave is about one-third mile north of North Avenue near the Clark Street edge of the park.

chapter six

THE FIRST PIONEER

Not for us delectations sweet,
Not the cushion and the slipper,
Not the peaceful and the studious,
Not the riches safe and palling,
Not for us the tame enjoyment,
Pioneers, O pioneers.

WHITMAN

THE north end of the Peninsula and its islands have always been famous as the best of fishing waters. But the fishermen were not interested in farming, and they had very little to do with the later development of the county. Fishing is a form of gambling, and luck plays a large part. Farming on the other hand is 99 percent hard work, but it is the most important of all occupations for the common man. When the farmers began their hard toil, the first small beginning of prosperity, order, and culture was made.

The first of these farmers was Increase Claflin. However, being a Yankee he was only a fifty percent farmer. The other fifty was a craving for barter and adventure.

He was born September 19, 1795, at Windham, N. Y., and was a descendant of a long line of sturdy Yankees who, centuries ago, conquered the forests of New England. His father, also named Increase Claflin, was a member of the Hopkinton Company of Minutemen who responded to the Lexington alarm. He served with honor throughout the Revolutionary War.

His grandfather, Cornelius Claflin, was a soldier who had served in the French and Indian War. Later he also served throughout the Revolutionary War as lieutenant in the same regiment in which his two sons were privates.

Like his father and grandfather, our Increase Claflin was also a soldier. In 1812, when less than seventeen years of age, he enlisted and served through the war with Great Britain. But, unlike his ancestors, Increase Claflin was of an adventurous, roving disposition, and about 1820 we find him spending a few years among the fragrant magnolias of New Orleans. Ten years later he is chasing the redskins of southwestern Wisconsin in the so-called Black Hawk War.

Some time before this he was established as a fur trader at Kaukauna, Wis. Here he must have had a number of men in his employ, for the census of 1830 gives the number of people in his household as thirteen.

That large, nameless peninsula to the northeast of Green Bay, with its bold promontories and mysterious coves, which the Indians described as their original paradise, soon attracted him. After visiting it, he decided that here was the most attractive region he had seen in his many thousand miles of wanderings. On March 19, 1835, he set out to blaze a new trail for civilization to follow. A trackless forest jungle of forty miles lay between him and his destination, but Claflin found an easier way. Old Jack Frost had prepared a smooth highway for him on the ice of the bay. On one sleigh was a load of hay. On another was his sailboat in which were stowed his family, his furniture, tools, grain, provisions and other necessaries, while behind followed his cattle and some breeding horses. Thus equipped he made his way to Little Sturgeon Bay. On the point of land at the mouth of this bay, on the west side, he built the first white man's house on the peninsula.

Here Claflin lived an independent, masterful life. He produced on his farm practically everything that his family ate and more. Emergencies, such as sickness, fire and protection of his homestead from prowlers, he met for himself. Besides this he exported large quantities of food supplies and other things needed in the world he had left behind. He paid no taxes and he needed none to help him provide peace, order and progress in his own field of activity.

Little Sturgeon Bay was then as even now a most idyllic spot, abounding in all kinds of fish and game. Along the west side of the bay stretched miles of grassy marshes and meadows affording good forage for horse raising, which was Claflin's principal purpose. On the opposite side of Little Sturgeon Bay, on what is now called Squaw Point, was a village of four or five hundred Menomini. Claflin got along very well with these Indians, as he treated them fairly and generously. Two or three years later, however, serious trouble broke out between them, brought on by Claflin's son-in-law, Robert Stevenson.

This man, originally from Pennsylvania, came to Little

Sturgeon in 1836, and was employed by Claflin in various capacities. The next year he married Claflin's oldest daughter, but continued for a time to make his home with the Claflins. He was a capable, energetic man, but domineering and tricky in dealing with the Indians. His usual procedure was to get the Indians drunk, whereupon he would obtain their peltries at prices ruinous to the poor redskins. This greatly displeased Claflin, who was as fair to the Indians when they were drunk as when they were sober.

One day, when Claflin returned from a round-up of his horses, an alarming sight met his eyes. A band of Indians in war paint were scurrying around his cabin. Stevenson was engaged in a hand to hand fight with several redskins and was felled to the ground with several knife stabs. Another white man in the employ of Claflin lay dead in the doorway, and a couple of Indians were dragging out his daughter, Mrs. Stevenson. Dashing his horse into their midst, Claflin scattered the Indians who were dragging away his daughter, and hurried her into the house where he found the other members of his family safe, but trembling with fear. Turning to the Indians he demanded the meaning of the attack.

A stalwart Indian, their chief, stepped up and spoke:

"You are our friend and we wish you no harm. You may take your squaw and your papooses and go away in your boat. But we shall kill your son (pointing to Stevenson), and burn your house and let no white man stay here among us. Our young men bring their furs and our daughters their robes and blankets to your house and he (Stevenson), makes them drunk with firewater and gives them nothing in return. We shall kill him and give his squaw to our young men for our daughters to laugh at and spit upon. Go, while we remember your good deeds!"

In vain Claflin tried to reason with them, but a hubbub of excited Indian outcries and threats broke out. Claflin then said:

"Well, if I have to go, let me treat you before I go. We have always been friends and let us part in the same manner."

The Indians grunted their approval of this and seated themselves in anticipation of their feast.

Claflin entered his storehouse, and returned with a keg and a tin cup. He carried it into their midst and poured a little of the contents into the cup. To their amazement the Indians saw not whiskey, but gunpowder trickle into the cup. Then he took his flint and fire-steel, ignited a piece of tinder and threw it into the cup. There was a flash, a loud report, and the cup was gone!

Apprehensively the Indians looked at each other and fidgeted in their seats. The chief then said, "Wh-what is my white brother going to do with the keg of powder?"

"Do!" exclaimed Claflin, "I am going to blow you all to hell! Either you smoke the peace-pipe with me or not a man leaves this spot! I have always treated you Indians fairly and squarely and now you turn upon me like wolves to kill my children and drive me from my home. If my son Robert has misused you, you have punished him enough. Now let us be friends and smoke the pipe of peace."

Filled with mixed feelings of admiration and apprehension at Claflin's audacity, the Indians assented. Claflin filled his pipe and lit it, whereupon it was passed from Indian to Indian with all proper solemnity. A monument beneath a gigantic elm near the shore at the mouth of Little Sturgeon Bay now marks the spot where this eventful meeting took place.

The Indians made no further trouble for Claflin and his household, but the strained relations between Claflin and Stevenson increased. Finally, like Abraham of old, Claflin decided to leave his son-in-law in possession of the favored land, and with his family go elsewhere to seek a home. In 1844 he went twenty miles north and settled on a promontory immediately north of the present village of Fish Creek. This promontory now embraced in Peninsula Park, is still known as Claflin's Point, and is the most popular camping ground in the state park.

Increase Claflin was a splendid type of pioneer. He was reliable, fearless, resolute, loyal, and self-sacrificing. In the rare quality of his ancestors as well as in his own sturdy manhood, Door County could ask for no truer type of American virtue. There is a familiar painting of fine conception typifying "The Spirit of 'Seventy-Six." Three figures of martial bearing are seen advancing at the head of a body of troops. In the middle is the grandfather, white locks flowing in the wind, playing on a flute. On one side is his son, a drummer in the prime of life. On the other side is the grandson, not yet fully grown, but catching inspiration from his elders and keenly beating his drum. Advancing onward they make a soul-stirring picture.[1]

In the history of the Claflin family there are events that are just as soul-stirring as this famous painting. As a parallel we see Increase Claflin's grandfather, the Revolutionary lieutenant, charging the breastworks of Crown Point, closely followed by his two sons. By such was America freed! And as a climax we see

Increase Claflin, the Door County pioneer, now old and weary of days, standing in the doorway of his Fish Creek cabin, speeding his three sons to war for the preservation of his country. In the summer of 1862, when the President called for troops to save the Union, Claflin sent his three sons as volunteers, saying, "If I had twenty more, they should all go!"

---

[1] The painting referred to is by Archibald M. Willard. The picture is now in Abbot Hall, Marblehead, Mass.

chapter seven

THE OLDEST VILLAGE IN DOOR COUNTY

'Tis here that Nature tried her hand,
To make a wild romantic lands,
And spread her streams and bays and lakes,
In all the forms that Beauty takes.

ALLEN POWERS

BAILEYS Harbor enjoys the distinction of being the first place on the Peninsula that was selected for a village site. Not only this, but it was officially selected as the county seat several years before Door County's actual organization was effected. The genesis of this early Baileys Harbor boom is as follows:

On a windy afternoon a hundred years ago (1848) a Captain Bailey was piloting his storm-tossed vessel back to Milwaukee. He had been to Buffalo with wheat and was now returning with a lighter but more troublesome cargo of immigrants bound for the West. After he had passed the Straits of Mackinac and turned southward, a fresh northeast wind began to blow which soon developed into a fierce gale. He was now skirting the shore of Door County and was thinking with gloomy misgivings of the 200-mile journey up the lake to Milwaukee without a harbor or an island or a lighthouse to ease him on his way. His top-heavy schooner, almost stripped of canvas, was rolling about in the heavy sea in a fashion which promised little hope of her safety in the approaching night. Finally as the wailing of the frightened immigrants was threatening to drive the worthy captain frantic, he saw a small harbor opening into the land on the west. He did not know whether the water was deep enough for his vessel or how the passage was into it, as his faulty charts said but little of the harbor at this point. However, fearing shipwreck if he continued, he determined to take a chance on the harbor and turned in. He found the passage deep and easy, and in a few minutes his vessel lay snugly anchored under a protecting wing of pine trees that shut out all evidence of the storm that raged outside.

As it continued to blow for several days, the captain had time to explore his surroundings. He found the harbor was deep and well sheltered, while the shores were covered with a splendid growth of mixed timber. Back from the shore a short distance he found a ledge of buildingstone. Up among these crags grew the most luscious raspberries which were eagerly picked by the immigrants, weary of a diet of salt pork and dry bread. No human occupants were found.

Pleased with his discovery, Captain Bailey took with him several cords of buildingstone and firewood and proceeded on his way to Milwaukee. Here he gave such an enthusiastic account of the harbor he had discovered, that among the other captains of the line "Bailey's Harbor" at once became a famous place. The owner of the line, a Mr. Alanson Sweet, also became interested in the samples of stone and wood that Captain Bailey had brought. Mr. Sweet was doing an extensive shipping business and owned a dozen large vessels. These plied between Milwaukee and Buffalo. On the way east there were large cargoes of grain to be carried, but the return freight was scant and uncertain, consisting chiefly of salt and immigrants. In Captain Bailey's discovery he saw a chance to increase his profits by adding another freight to his return trips. Buildingstone, cordwood and lumber were in much demand in Milwaukee, and at "Bailey's Harbor" they were all easily accessible. In the summer of 1849 he therefore purchased 125 acres where now lies part of the village of Baileys Harbor.

The same summer he sent a crew of men to build a pier and sawmill and to open a stone quarry. During the following winter the pier was completed, being the first to be built in Door County. The men also cut and banked 2500 cords of wood which were shipped to Milwaukee in the summer of 1850. Six comfortable log houses were put up in the vicinity of where now stands Brann's Store, and a road was cut across the Peninsula from this point to the Green Bay shore. This was the first road cut in Door County and is the one which leads out of the village in a northwesterly direction (County Trunk F).

Mr. Sweet had great hopes of his colony at "Bailey's Harbor." He went to Madison and persuaded the state legislature to set off Door County as a separate county with its present boundaries. This being accomplished, the next thing was to choose a site for a county seat. Mr. Sweet persuaded the lawmakers that "Bailey's

Harbor" was the best harbor—not only in Door County—but along the entire west shore of Lake Michigan. It was therefore bound to become a place of great commercial importance. In contrast to this he claimed that the entire western shore of Door County consisted of steep, unapproachable cliffs, affording no natural shelter for shipping. He also showed that the proposed site for the county seat was halfway between the northern and the southern extremities of the county and therefore most centrally located. Finally, Baileys Harbor was the only village or claimant for the county seat in the entire county. All this was more than enough for the legislators. The county seat was therefore established at "Bailey's Harbor," but under another name. Mr. Sweet felt that the name of Baileys Harbor—named after one of his own happy-go-lucky captains—was not sufficiently sonorous for the future metropolis. As the principal characteristic of the place seemed to him to be stone and rocks, he was reminded of Gibraltar, the great rock of the Mediterranean. He therefore suggested this name which was adopted as the official name of Door County's capital. This new name did not, however, stick with the people as did the old name of Baileys Harbor. This was accomplished February 11, 1851.

Mr. Sweet must have been a most enterprising man. To transfigure a little sawmill camp on a previously unknown cove on a deserted lake shore into a county seat with the accompaniment of an organized county to pay it tribute, all in less than two years, was some achievement. But even this did not satisfy Mr. Sweet. He felt that now that the State had done all it could do to promote the prosperity of his little sawmill, the Federal government should also step up and lend a hand. He therefore petitioned the government to erect a lighthouse for the purpose of conducting the mariners to the docks of the new metropolis.

Up to this time only two lighthouses had been erected in the northern part of Lake Michigan and these were both for the purpose of marking the dangerous passages between the lake and the waters of Green Bay. No lighthouses for local ports had been built, and Sturgeon Bay did not secure any such aids to navigation until in 1880. But Mr. Sweet's arguments were so persuasive that his petition was granted at once. In fact, he was personally given the contract to erect the lighthouse, which he did the same year, 1851. This was the only lighthouse on the Peninsula for many years and stood on the point opposite the village.

If Mr. Sweet had continued as the guardian angel of Baileys

Harbor, there is no telling what heights of fame his protegé might have reached. But, due to business reverses or other reasons, his connections with Baileys Harbor suddenly terminated. His mill burned down, his pier went to ruin, his cottages crumbled into decay, and the hopeful county seat expired in its infancy. Only the lighthouse continued under the undeviating course of a conservative government to light up the passage to a deserted port, hemmed in on every side by a trackless forest.

Legally, however, this Rip Van Winkle among villages was still the county seat, and this situation could only be changed in a legal way. In 1857 the energetic hustlers of the thriving village of Sturgeon Bay therefore took the necessary steps to have the county seat removed to the latter village. Notices were posted in the brush-grown lanes of Baileys Harbor and elsewhere, chiefly inspected by chipmunks, stating that an election would be held to learn the wish of the people as to the location of the county seat. A cigar box was then accommodatingly carried around to the scattered fishermen and few dozen farmers in the county with the invitation to vote for the new metropolis, Sturgeon Bay, which they obligingly did.

But no sooner had its glory departed than Baileys Harbor began to show signs of returning consciousness. That same year, 1857, a stranger by the name of A. K. Sea, chanced to visit the deserted village and, like Alanson Sweet of old, straightway fell in love with it. He built six lime kilns under the bluff and planned to burn and ship lime in vast quantities. Confident that he had struck a bonanza, he also erected a very large dwelling house, "with a cupola from which one could see clean across Lake Michigan," on the site of Wm. Brann's house. He succeeded, however, in making only one shipment of lime when he failed in business. Shortly afterward his big house also went up in smoke like the material of his toil.

Mr. Sea was succeeded by a long line of village fathers, but the above brief narration of his experience epitomizes theirs. They came with a little money and abundance of pluck, and for a brief space wrought wonders of destruction in the nearby timber, only to fail in business. It seemed to one and all that a splendid tract of virgin timber, purchased for a pittance, ought to prove a short cut to wealth. But almost invariably it became a quick road to ruin. Their big cargoes of pine logs would sometimes fail to bring enough to pay the freight to Chicago, and their thousands of cords of wood would strike glutted markets yielding scarcely enough to pay the wood-choppers. Numerous other hazards made the timber operator's life a nightmare of uncertainty.

But this matter of failing in business was all in a day's work with those old fellows. One season they would be proudly bossing a crew of scores of wood-choppers and speculatively estimate their earnings at a hundred dollars a day. The next year, they would be constrained to humbly act as a fisherman's helper. Soon, through luck and daring, they would again grandly operate and ship out cargoes of wood products almost every day. Life in Door County has from the beginning been so stimulating and healthful, that whether they failed or flourished, it was a joy to be alive.

Such was the experience of Cooley Williamson, Thomas Severn, Fritz Woldtman and Joseph Smith. The last was known as the "Cedar King of Door County." For many years he did a business of $150,000 a year. His wood-choppers were everywhere, and there was hardly a day in summer that a schooner did not leave Baileys Harbor or Jacksonport with one of his cargoes. Yet, when the timber was all gone, he had scarcely enough left to buy a stony eighty of land near Jacksonport where he spent his declining years.

Such also was the experience of the indomitable Moses Kilgore. He came in 1860 and built a pier. In 1869 he built a long extension to this pier at a reported cost of five thousand dollars. The following winter 800 cords of green maple wood were piled on this extension. The load was too heavy for it, and in January it collapsed with a total loss of the pier to Mr. Kilgore. It was also a great loss to the farmers who owned the wood, for when the ice went out in spring, it carried the wood with it, scattering it to all the shores of Lake Michigan.

After having had sufficient ups and downs in the timber business, Mr. Kilgore became a stage driver. As such he soon became famous because of his quaint and uncensored vocabulary. It is said that he had a greater command of strong language then any man in the county. A rare lot of picturesque profanity perished when he finally passed away.

Mr. Kilgore was one of those unusual men who believe in heralding their vices and hiding their virtues. Superficially, he, like David Harum, appeared vulgar and blatant, but at heart he was kind, capable, and the soul of honesty. Many who knew him well considered him the most energetic and efficient man in the county for procuring public improvements. He was the first to urge the creation of a highway from Baileys Harbor to Sturgeon

Bay, and he personally staked it out. But it led through an uninhabited region, ten miles long, including a vast swamp. As there was no tax money in sight, the idea seemed chimerical. But Moses Kilgore was not daunted. He got himself elected to the state legislature, and there his irrepressible energy and spicy language was so compelling that he returned with a sizable appropriation. Then he personally supervised the construction of the road which is now known as State Trunk 57.

Generous and enterprising, he had many friends. Among these was an old crony, Adam Hendricks by name, the owner of the local hotel, with whom it was a relief to drink a glass of beer. These two companions agreed one day that the usual style of conducting funerals was unsatisfactory. They pledged each other that whosoever of them died first was to have his obsequies signalized by the energetic music of a brass band to be furnished at the expense of the other. Moses Kilgore was the first to pass away and true to his promise Adam Hendricks imported a brass band to do honors to his worthy friend.

Baileys Harbor in the seventies was a much more lively place then it is now. There were several piers, and schooners were coming and going with timber products every day. The farm lands in the neighborhood were rapidly being settled by prospective farmers and a lively business was done in building material, farm machinery, and general merchandise. There were six saloons, and at night when several score of thirsty wood-choppers came into town, they did a roaring business.

There was a physical fitness about these old pioneers which seems almost impossible in these days when automobiles are rendering the lower limbs of man almost useless. Their endurance in toil and hardships was only equalled by their capacity for food and drink. The explanation of this physical heroism lies in the fact that life on the frontier would appeal only to the most rugged and self-reliant.

There was, for instance, William Jackson—small, but quick and fierce as a wildcat in a fight—who came at a very early date to join the big fishing crew of the Clark brothers. The latter came from Cleveland in 1838 to engage in extensive fishing operations at Whitefish Bay, south of Clark's Lake. After many years of fishing and bear hunting the others left, but Jackson stayed to become in his old age a shrewd pettifogger and respected county squire. Early in the fifties he had been on a prospecting tour along the unsettled shore of Lake Superior. When the Christmas holidays came and went, he felt very lonesome for his friends the wood-choppers of Baileys Harbor. There were no boats to carry him around by Mackinac, but Jackson determined to find a way home nevertheless. Like the wild geese that honked southward on their flight to the tropics, he also struck a beeline for the south. His course led him through a wilderness of snow-covered forest of more than a hundred miles without a single human habitation. But with his gun in his hand and his blanket on his back he trudged on, finding his food in the game of the forest and his bed on the snow-covered ground. Finally he emerged at the mouth of Cedar River on the northwest shore of Green Bay. Here he shot a deer and after taking what he needed he hung the carcass up in a tree for the benefit of another possible traveller. Then he set out to cross the ice of Green Bay, a distance of about thirty miles. He had not gone many hours before he was enveloped in a raging blizzard. He tried to keep his course by the direction of the wind, but as this changed he lost his way. After struggling for hours against the fury of the storm, during which he circled around, he was surprised to find himself again at the mouth of Cedar River. Completely exhausted he was now very glad to hack off a few fragments of the frozen venison he had had the forethought to hang up, and soon with his feet to a blazing fire he was asleep while the falling snow gently spread a protecting blanket over him. The next day the weather was clear and he crossed the bay in safety. Another day brought him to the snug camp on Baileys Harbor, feeling quite fit after his long journey of almost two hundred miles on which he had not seen a single human being, either white man or Indian.

Back of Baileys Harbor is beautiful Kangaroo Lake, the largest lake on the Peninsula. This was the first of Door County's many beauty spots to invite the appreciative onlooker to song. Among the friends of Jackson in Baileys Harbor was Allen G. Powers, a man of considerable culture. When Sweet's camp in 1852 broke up, he made the first clearing on the shore of Kangaroo Lake and lived there for a number of years. Although a hermit in the wilderness, he was evidently quite happy there, as is indicated by the following respectable poem on Kangaroo Lake written in 1857:

> *This wild northwestern land I love,*
> *As 'mongst its bays and lakes I rove.*
> *Nor wish for other home than this,*
> *To give me all home can of bliss.*

I love this beauteous inland lake,
Whose tiny waves in ripplets break
On pebbly beach, begirt with trees
All murmuring in the gentle breeze.

And when my restless spirit craves
A stormy scene and wilder waves,
Within one mile, an inland sea
Rolls its surf on a rocky lea.

I love to stand on that rockbound shore,
And hear the mighty waters roar,
And feel the earth beneath me quake,
As the foam-capped waves in thunder break.

I love its skies so deeply blue,
Its stars so brightly shining through,
Where Luna holds her nightly sway,
And Sol's refulgence lights the day.

Where Orion's belt with its triple clasp,
And the heavy club in his mighty grasp,
With radiant beauty nightly shine,
Unknown in stars of southern clime.

'Tis here that Nature tried her hand,
To make a wild romantic land,
And spread her streams and bays and lakes,
In all the forms that Beauty takes.

The waters of Kangaroo Lake reach Lake Michigan by means of
Hein's Creek. This is now a very small stream, but old settlers say
that in the early days before the land was cleared, it was quite a
large watercourse. At the mouth of Hein's Creek was once a large
Indian village as is shown by the abundance of Indian chippings
that have found there. North of this is one of the most picturesque
beaches in Door County. A short distance south, Hibbard's Creek,
a much larger stream, empties into the lake. In old times this was
a small river, draining the peninsula as far north as Peninsula
Park. Archeologists say that at the mouth of Hibbard's Creek must
have been the largest Indian village site in the State, as the
ground is covered with flint chippings for a long distance. This was
the village of Mechingan where was enacted one of the most

stirring incidents in the history of the Indians of the West as is briefly told in Chapter Two.

Baileys Harbor was the first important shipping port on the Peninsula, but many years went by before it shipped anything but forest products and lime. Many men came looking for work, and if they could cut cordwood they were welcome. Most of them also wanted to get a tract of land and become farmers, but the forest stood dense and unbroken except for the ruthless slashing of the woodchoppers. Cordwood cutting yielded only enough for a very humble living and left no opportunity for turning the wilderness into farming land. This was the situation up to the end of the Civil War.

After the war there was a large immigration of Germans from Poland, and they took land on the west and northwest sides of Baileys Harbor. At the same time came also many Irish who settled southwest of the village. They cleared land around beautiful Kangaroo Lake. Before long these two groups created one of the most pleasing farm areas on the Peninsula.

Many hopeful young men and women are each year leaving their farm homes to go to the cities where they think there are better opportunities for success. Most of them make good and a few—very few—even become rich or famous. Some of them come back occasionally and look with pride on the fields their fathers had wrested from the wilderness. But they seldom realize that it is very difficult for rural districts to meet the obligations of providing up-to-date schools and hospitals, churches and libraries and forget to lend a helping hand to the home communities.

Baileys Harbor was most fortunate in having a son who did not forget the needs of the old home community. He was Michael W. McArdle, born in 1871, the son of James McArdle who came from County of Louth in 1866 and singlehanded cleared a farm a couple of miles southwest of Baileys Harbor. Michael was an indomitable young fellow who worked his way through high school and college by selling books and graduated from the University Law School. Later he was hired to straighten out the books of the Flexible Shaft Company, It had no money to pay him but gave him some stock in the company. He saw the vast possibilities of this concern and made four trips around the world to introduce its products. Now they are seen in all kitchens.

But in spite of this whirlwind business, he did not forget the old community. He planned to spend his old age in his father's old house and bought the old farm. He also bought several hundred adjoining acres and built a first class golf course and a number of cottages to provide proper hospitality for his friends when they came to visit him. Many plans were germinating in his mind.

But then came bad news. He was told that he had cancer and had not long to live. This necessitated a drastic revision of his plans. Instead of long range planning, certain necessities demanded immediate attention. About a month before he died he wrote a letter to the members of the congregation, part of which is printed below:

> "Fifty years ago I served on this very spot as altar boy. More than once I tumbled over in a faint from the bitter cold for I was of delicate constitution.
>
> "Even then I had an ambition to see a nice, warm, comfortable Catholic church here, but I didn't dream that I would ever take part in it. But I am glad to say that all is now ready to go ahead. You will have a larger lot to build on—plenty of room to build a church and rectory that will be extra nice.
>
> "This new church and rectory are coming to you a few years earlier than I had intended, but my health has changed so much that I find it necessary to change all my plans for what I intended to do for Baileys Harbor."

He also left ample funds for a new town hall and a public library. All of these buildings were designed by a competent architect and built of stone. Altogether he spent several hundred thousand dollars to make his boyhood home a better place to live in.

The memory of Mike McArdle will long endure because his townsmen were proud of his business achievements, grateful for his benevolence and charmed with his friendly personality.

Baileys Harbor has gained much favorable publicity because there is a tract of land adjoining the village on the north on which grow many rare flowers. This is known as The Ridges. This land containing about forty acres, was a U. S. Coast Guard reservation on which stood the old lighthouse which had been succeeded by another. About twenty years ago when I was chairman of the Door County Park Commission I went to Milwaukee and asked the Coast Guard Superintendent to give this land to the county for a county park. As we had a very good record for creating county parks, he kindly promised to see that it was given to the County.

Since then the park has been considerably enlarged by gifts of adjacent tracts.

Mr. Jens Jensen, the well-known nature lover and landscape architect, suggested that the park be called the Ridges Sanctuary. This was adopted, and Mr. Jensen for many years was its principal patron and spokesman. Thousands of people will recall with pleasure their visits to this park made rich and glowing through his eloquent interpretation.

Baileys Harbor has still another rare gift of beauty. This is the little chapel built by Mr. and Mrs. D. S. Boynton on their property south of Baileys Harbor. It is patterned after the quaint and ancient Norwegian Church in the Lillehammer folk museum in Norway, and as such is pleasing enough. But the interior is a revelation of fine art. The walls are covered with beautiful scriptural paintings and all the woodwork, such as the doors, the pulpit, the baptismal font and the pew ends, are ornamented with most skillful carving. Altogether this chapel is a thing of loving beauty unlike and superior to anything of its kind in the State and far beyond. This interior decoration is principally the work of Mrs. Winifred Boynton who is an expert with the brush as well as with the carving chisel. For almost ten years she and her husband labored here with pious hands, and produced a work of rare spiritual beauty. She is also a capable writer, and in her fine book, Faith Builds a Chapel, she makes the reader a participant in all the many problems that arose and were conquered as the work progressed. She spared no pains to make her work thorough and truly beautiful. In her book she writes:

> "The desks and tables in the Studio were stacked with reference books covering a wide range of religion, arts, symbols, birds, flowers and animals. . . . Manual work can be done with a certain number of interruptions, but ideas have to develop in quiet. For me, this came only between dawn and the family breakfast hour. There were no distractions to disturb the stillness everywhere. . . . As the earth, shrouded in darkness, waits expectantly for the light of a new day, so I (in the studio) waited for the dawning of an idea."

On every Wednesday afternoon during the summer brief vesper services, many times repeated, are held and conducted by local clergymen, sometimes with Mrs. Boynton at the organ. This is the only church I know of where a continuous queue stand waiting to be admitted.

chapter eight

WASHINGTON ISLAND

And now for scenes where Nature in her pride
Roared in rough floods and waved in forests
wide—
Where men were taught the desert path to trace,
And the rude pleasures of the wildwood chase—
With light canoe to plow the glossy lake,
And from its depths the silvery trout to take.

ANON.

FAR out amid the white-crested waves of Lake Michigan lies Washington Island. It has a shoreline of twenty-six miles with rocky beaches, deep bays, towering headlands and rolling contours. When the pioneers came it was covered by a dense primeval forest, but now the sun shines on more than a hundred well tilled farms. It is a little land of amazing thrift and co-operative enterprise.

In historic memories and archeological remains Washington Island is the first in all Wisconsin and the Middle West. No doubt Jean Nicolet camped here on his way to Red Banks near the site of Green Bay in 1634, but his narrative is lost. Nowhere else can be found so many Indian village sites, cemeteries, mounds and cornfields as here. There is such a wealth of Indian remains that, as one archeologist says: "there is little left to desire." The entire shoreline around Detroit Harbor shows remains of village sites. So also do the shores of Little Lake and Jackson Harbor.

The earliest known name of the island was Huron Island because the survivors of the great Huron nation sought refuge here after being almost exterminated by the rapacious Iroquois. Here Radisson and Groseilliers found them in 1654 and spent a winter with much pleasure. Somewhere in the interior of the Island was then "a great field," and here the two travelers joined with the Hurons in vanquishing a small Iroquois war party who had discovered their hiding place. This Island was also the destination of the first ship to sail the Great Lakes, the Griffin, which Robert La Salle built at Niagara Falls and sailed into the West to find a cargo of furs wherewith to finance his expedition to explore the course of the Mississippi.

Washington Island is almost an ideal place in which to live. It is big enough to check any feeling of isolation and confinement, yet small enough to promote a sense of solidarity and cooperative effort. In the latter its thousand inhabitants have made remarkable progress. In everything except in church work the island is perhaps the most cooperative community in Wisconsin—the prejudice of creed is the only obstacle to complete fellowship.

The Island is also a place of delightful scenic charm. With twenty-six miles of water front there is a great variety of water views. Prominent among these pleasing vistas is Washington Harbor which cuts into the land about one and a half miles, its steep surrounding slopes covered by beeches and low-spreading cedars. On its west side Bowyer's Bluff rears its perpendicular mass of limestone to a height of more than two hundred feet, looking at a distance like the crumbling ruins of some gigantic Yucatan temple. The cliff is seamed with caves and fissures, and carved into fantastic figures by the storms of bygone ages; but now the clinging cedars are weaving a drapery of green for its rugged sides.

Many thousand years ago there was, just south of this imposing bluff, a cove or small bay extending eastward for about a half mile between wooded hills. But the crumbling rocks of the bluff falling into the waters of Green Bay were pushed southward by the waves driven by the prevailing northerly winds, and eventually the mouth of the bay was closed by a broad belt of polished cobblestones. The little bay became a little lake, and the stormwrought belt of beach stones that closed it in became a dense belt of woodland. Now the little lake lies peacefully embosomed by steep hills and sturdy woods, looking quite like a mountain lake, although separated by only a few rods from the turbulent waves of Green Bay. Among all the scenic delights of Door County this little lake is well toward the top.

Here, at the southwestern corner of the lake, is a pleasant little glade of flat land. This spot was the long occupied home of Indians, for their remains are here very abundant. The owner, Jens Jacobsen, cleared some land on the borders of the glade, and in so doing he made a most interesting discovery. In clearing away a thick growth of cedars, he uncovered a large cross trenched in the ground near the shore of the lake. This cross lies directly north and south, with its head or top a few feet from the beach. Between the head of the cross and the beach is a small mound which apparently is artificial. The trunk of the cross is twenty feet long, twenty inches wide and about eight inches deep. The cross arm is fourteen feet long, twenty inches wide and about eight inches deep. From the center of the cross where the arms intersect, it measures about seven feet to the end of each transverse arm and also to the head of the cross.

There is a possibility that this cross is a memorial of the work of an early missionary. To him the representation of the cross was an ever present appeal and refuge. Father André who preached to the Indians of Washington Island was quite an unusual type of a missionary. Resolute and ingenious, he made use of many expedients to turn the Indians from their idolatrous ways. As an illustration may be mentioned his religious songs written in the language of the Indians but sung to French airs to the accompaniment of a flute. These songs he taught to the Indian children. With a band of "these little savage musicians," he went about the villages "to declare war on Jugglers, Dreamers, and those who had several wives." It therefore does not seem at all strange if this missionary with his flair for the dramatic cut the symbol of his triumphant faith into the very ground of the village. The soil that he excavated he perhaps heaped into the mound at the head of the cross. Here he and his "band of musicians" perhaps stood, while with glowing zeal he painted the greatness of his God, the Indians meanwhile sitting mute and spellbound around this mystic symbol, amazed at the antics of this new "medicine man" and the wonderful accomplishments of their own children. When there were converts—and he made many—the water was at hand for baptism immediately at his rear.

The most probable significance of this cross is therefore that it is the memorial of the valiant and eloquent missionary, who, almost 300 years ago, ignoring hardships and sufferings and defying torture and martyrdom, preached a new gospel to a strange and idolatrous people. Carved in the ground, it was more enduring than a cross of wood, because it could not rot away, and surrounded as it was by waters of the lake and the green cedars, there was no dust to obliterate its sanctified excavation.

More than a hundred years ago the first white man settled on Washington Island, attracted by its rich fishing. The fish then were very abundant. Whitefish could be seen leaping into air, and sturgeon were so plentiful that they were often stacked like cordwood on the shore, there being at that time no market for them. Trout were incredibly large. Some time later a record was kept which will illustrate what huge fish were caught. In the spring of 1860 Joseph Cornell caught a seventy pound trout off Rock Island. In 1862 William Cornell, a fourteen-year-old boy, caught seven trout, the smallest weighing forty, the largest forty-eight pounds. In the spring of 1882 two trout were caught on Fisherman Shoal weighing fifty-eight and sixty-five pounds. They were sometimes just as numerous as they were large. In 1869 Godfrey Nelson caught two hundred and twenty trout in two days. In the winter of 1875 Charles Sloop caught one hundred and twenty in one day, and one hundred and forty the next. Sometimes it required perseverance, but the results were usually satisfactory, as was the case with Silas Wright, who fished for eleven days without a bite and then caught a boat load on the twelfth. These were all hook-and-line catches of authentic record.

With such generous returns for the labor expended, there was the usual extravagance which goes with easy money. To make up for the restrictions in the life and diet imposed upon them by their surroundings, the fishermen were lavish in their expenditures whenever an opportunity presented itself. A dollar was a very small coin in those days. Canned goods, fancy toys, laces, and costly furnishings were imported in reckless quantities. Ranney, their easy going merchant and fish buyer, was also their banker, and handed out liberal quantities of cash without any formality of notes or securities.

These hardy pioneers of the deep for many years constituted a sort of fisherman's aristocracy, who looked with pity upon the poor fellows coming in as wood choppers and farmers. They esteemed the land of little or no value except to supply the potatoes they needed with their finny diet. Their thoughts and plans were of the sea, and its vagaries were a constant subject of conversation with them. The land was dull and dusty, but the sea was fresh, and full of riches, sparkling with sport, and full of thrilling adventures.

While nearly all these fishermen were seasonal visitors, returning to their homes in Illinois late in Fall, there were a few who planned to be permanent settlers, In 1850 these men "organized" the Town of Washington. They elected a chairman, clerk, and justice of the peace. As they elected no assessor or treasurer, they evidently had no thought of taxes. This was the first organized town north of Green Bay.

The next step in Door County's political history was an act

passed by the Legislature in 1855 organizing Sturgeon Bay into an election precinct. In November, 1856, a town election was held and A. G. Warren was elected chairman. There was now quite a demand that the county board should meet and levy taxes for needed improvements. As Mr. Warren did not know where the county seat was, he struck a bee line through the woods to Green Bay to get legal advice from the district attorney. He was given a written opinion that the county seat was Gibraltar, supposed to be located in section 20, town 30, range 28, where now lies the village of Baileys Harbor. He also authorized Mr. Warren and two other men to act as a board for the canvass of returns. These three men late in November set out afoot through the swamps and along the shore to discover "Gibraltar," Door County's legal county seat. They did not know which piece of timber constituted the capital of the county, but finally they found the ruins of certain shanties built by Mr. Sweet's men. Of human life there was none. Here on some fallen logs they sat awaiting the arrival of Mr. Nolan, chairman of the town of Washington, who had been properly notified. But no Mr. Nolan appeared. They killed and ate some ducks and the next day they killed and ate some more, but Mr. Nolan did not appear. The three men then elected Ezra Stevens, member of the Assembly, Joseph Harris, Register of Deeds and County Clerk and A. M. Iverson Superintendent of Schools. They then returned to Sturgeon Bay hoping for the thanks of their fellow citizens.

But instead of thanks they got jeers. How could a one-man board take any action or elect anyone? Mr. Warren was the only qualified member of the county board who was present, and he could take no legal action alone. This was clear, and the imprecations hurled at the callous Mr. Nolan did not help any.

Winter was now coming on and nothing more could be done that year. The next year the Town of Sturgeon Bay elected Henry Schuyler chairman and Joseph Harris clerk. They sent notice to Mr. Nolan that the County Board would meet on a certain day in Sturgeon Bay, but, as expected, Mr. Nolan did not come.

It was now clear that if the County Board was ever to meet, it would have to be on Washington Island. After many postponements the two officials started out one day in November on a long walk to Fish Creek. This was before any road or trail was made through the woods. At Fish Creek were some fishermen and they hired a sail boat and arrived at Washington Island safely.

Eventually, after nosing around for a half day, they found Nolan on the other side of the island, and here in Nolan's fish shanty the first meeting of the County Board was held. Nolan was a man of few words with a tantalizing manner and he was busy with his nets all through the meeting.

First Schuyler suggested that they levy a tax to build some roads, but Nolan said no: he did not feel it would be right to tax the fishermen on Washington Island to build roads for the Sturgeon Bay people. Then Schuyler proposed that they raise some money for schools and teachers, but Nolan said no: he thought they ought to raise the kids first. Then Schuyler asked for a little money for a ferry across Sturgeon Bay. It would promote immigration because it would save sixteen miles of hard walking around the head of the bay. But Nolan said no: he did not think the fishermen on Washington Island cared to spend any money to save shoe leather for the people of Sturgeon Bay. Then Schuyler got mad and asked Nolan what in hell he wanted to do, and Nolan said he did not want to do anything in hell—he was satisfied with the way things were in Washington Island.

On the return trip the two men were caught in a gale while crossing "the Door." They were tossed about all night and in the morning found themselves within sight of the saw mills in Escanaba. It took them two days to get back to Fish Creek half starved. Then came a twenty-five mile tramp through the woods to Sturgeon Bay.

A way was found to get rid of Nolan. Two or three new "towns" were organized, and then it was possible to hold County Board meetings without going to Washington Island.

For thirty years the fishermen ruled Washington Island alone. The land was considered too far north for farming, the woods too formidable, the soil too stony. But in 1868-70 came some groups of stout Norwegians, Danes and Icelanders who secured homestead rights back in the timber. They did not expect to do much in the way of agriculture. Their main hope was in cutting cordwood. This they set to work with great energy to do. Soon the mighty maples swayed and fell, and were then split and cut into four foot lengths with an axe, for cross cut saws had not yet come into common use. The price, delivered at the pier, was two dollars per cord, an immense amount of toil for a pittance. Yet it was better than nothing. Frequently there was no sale for cordwood and they were obliged to roll huge logs together and burn them. When a little field was finally cleared, the stumps stood immovable for years, an obstacle to cultivation. Meanwhile they had nothing to sell, and their distress was great. With small pastures and little hay, their cows dried up in winter and gave no milk.

Unexpected difficulties also developed, chief of which was the difficulty of securing water. The story is told that one of the Danes set to work the first summer to dig a well. He got down only a few inches when he came to a flat rock. He dug and dug on every side to get around this stone, but it seemed to stretch out indefinitely. He told his neighbors about the trouble he was having with it. They came and inspected the difficulty. Then one of them started to dig on the other side of the cabin. Only a few inches down the same stone appeared. Filled with evil forebodings they hurried home and began to dig around their own huts. The same stone appeared also there, for it was the solid rock which underlies all of Washington Island only a foot or two below the surface.

Since they could dig no wells, they were obliged to carry water from the lake, in pails, in kegs, on wheelbarrows and in barrels on wagons with oxen. As it was so laborious to get water, they were obliged to be very saving with it.

But outside the borders of their island lay the water, a hindrance to communication with the outside world, and especially so in fall and the first half of the winter when navigation ceased and "the Door" had not yet frozen over. They felt like stranded mariners a thousand miles at sea. L. P. Otteson recalls how they once went for seven weeks without word from the outside world. This was bad, but what was worse was that the whole island had run out of chewing tobacco. All possible substitutes were tried, such as willow bark, juniper twigs, cabbage leaves, etc., but without relief, and further abstinence was intolerable. Finally, Henry Miner consented to go to Green Bay. It was his last trip on the ice. A long and dreary week followed. At last a large party of young fellows walked out on the ice to meet him, or rather the quid, half way. When he appeared in the distance they broke into a run and soon were eagerly pulling at the strappings of his sled. The tobacco was found and immediately passed around, each one snapping off a generous allowance with intense relish. There was a minute of silent bliss, wherein the movement of many jaws was faintly audible. Then they all turned homeward, staining the ice an odorous brown and feeling that all was well with the world.

Undismayed by the many obstacles of nature, these Scandinavians stuck to their task and, in spite of all evil prophecies, turned this formerly unproductive island into beautiful farming land. The stumps were blasted with dynamite, the deep, dark woods were turned into sunny fields, and well drilling machinery was found which pierced that solid layer of limestone a hundred feet deep and found waterbearing strata beneath. Even the innumerable rock fragments which everywhere littered the ground were finally turned into good use, because they were crushed into first class road material, giving the island smooth and excellent highways.

Washington Island now exports thousands of tons of food-stuffs annually, such as potatoes, butter, grain, fish and fruit of all northern kinds. Few places in America have such a diversity of export products as this island. It is as progressive and enlightened a community as can be found anywhere.

Among the oldtimers on Washington Island was Jens Jacobsen, a man of poetic vision. He owned an Indian village site on the south side of Little Lake. Finding here a large quantity of Indian artifacts, he built a neat little museum to house them. It has a superb setting and has already become a very creditable Island institution.

chapter nine

A MAN OF IRON: A TALE OF DEATH'S DOOR

He was a man; take him for all in all,
I shall not look upon his like again.

SHAKESPEARE

PORT des Morts the French called it—the Door of Death. This was not an invention of the French, for the Indians had learned its treacherous nature and so called it long before the white men came to visit them. The French merely translated the Indian name into their own tongue after learning by personal experience how well it applied.

It is not long, this door of death, nor wide. It is merely a passage between the tip end of the Door County peninsula and the islands beyond. But in this strait are often met strong currents and fierce winds running counter to each other, which baffle the seaman's skill and drive his craft on the rock–bound shores. Hundreds of vessels have here been flung ashore and wrecked. One week in September, 1872, no less than eight large vessels were wrecked or stranded here. The summer before almost a hundred vessels suffered shipwreck in "the Door."

The most vivid legend of Indian days is not the recital of a great war, nor the exploits of a dominating hero. It is the memory of an overwhelming tragedy which befell the Winnebago when they tried to cross The Door for the purpose of exterminating a small tribe of Potawatomi who were living on Washington Island. Filled with insolence and self–confidence, the Winnebago set out, 500 strong, in canoes from the north end of the Peninsula. Halfway across, they were caught in a sudden wind which ran counter to the current in the strait. The round–bottomed canoes were unmanageable in the short, choppy waves, and all the 500 warriors perished. This happened shortly after Jean Nicolet's visit in 1634, and was the chief cause of their later almost complete annihilation.

Just as turbulent as are these straits in summer, just as
treacherous are they in winter. The ice forms late and breaks
early. Never is it entirely safe. Shifting currents undermine the ice
unceasingly. Where the ice may be two feet thick in the morning,
the waves may wash in the evening.

Many stories could be told of terrible adventures in crossing
this treacherous bridge of ice. Many a man and horse have had a
desperate battle with death while plunging through the perilous
ice, and more than one man has seen his last hope of life perish as,
clinging to a cake of ice, he has been driven out into Lake
Michigan where soon his frail craft would break up.

As an illustration let us recount the story of Robert Noble's
experience in "the Door," not because it was the worst, but because
he lived to tell of his icy battle. Also because in human endurance
it is almost unique among the tales of suffering.

On December 30, 1863, Robert Noble left Washington Island
after having spent some happy Christmas holidays in visiting the
girl of his heart. He was a splendid young fellow physically, was
twenty–five years old, weighed two hundred and twenty pounds
and stood more than six feet in his stockings. He had a
flat–bottomed skiff, and for a while had little difficulty in making
his way among the broken ice floes in "the Door." Abreast of Plum
Island, however, he struck a large field of thick ice through which
it was impossible to force a passage. With some difficulty he
finally made a landing on Plum Island, hoping that the wind
might clear a passage for him to the mainland a couple of miles
away. It was now getting dark, snow had begun to fall, and the
weather which had been mild was getting very cold.

While groping about on the shore of the deserted island, he
came to an abandoned fishing hut which had neither roof, doors,
nor windows. Here he made a fire, but had difficulty in keeping it
burning because of the falling snow. Toward morning it went out
altogether. Ice was now forming all around the island. When he
saw that he would have to remain there for some time, he
thoroughly explored the island. He found that the only other
building was a ruined lighthouse, of which only the cellar and
chimney remained. Here was a sort of a fireplace and he managed
after much trouble to light a fire, but not before his last match had
been used. He heaped this fire with such fuel as he could find, and
became more hopeful as its warmth began to be felt. But suddenly
his hopes were blasted. The chimney was full of snow. It began to
melt and soon there was a rush and tumble and his fire was
buried under a heap of snow. It was a most depressing blow, since

it was now getting dark and the weather was becoming bitterly cold.

He had a revolver with him and made a number of attempts to start a fire by putting strips of lining from his coat over the muzzle, hoping that the explosion would cause the cloth to catch fire. But this was all in vain. Yet he managed to hold out in the little cellar all night without food, sleep or heat. Through the interminably long hours of that bitter night he paced about in his prison, keeping from utterly freezing by all kinds of exercise, moving stones and logs about and otherwise exerting himself. Finally the gray dawn of January 1, 1864, appeared.

January 1, 1864! Old settlers have not yet, after a lapse of almost a hundred years, forgotten the intense cold of that day. Tales are told of water freezing by the side of the heated stoves, of the impossibility of keeping warm in snug beds, of cattle freezing to death in their stalls. It is remembered as the coldest day in the history of Door County.

Robert Noble did not know anything about this. He only knew that it was fearfully cold, that he was starving and that he had gone for two nights without sleep. He realized that his only hope was to leave that deserted island at once. The wind had now broken up the ice which was bobbing about in a slushy formation. He launched his boat and for a quarter of a mile managed to row his boat toward Washington Island. Then he encountered solid ice and could make no further progress with the boat.

As the ice was not very thick, he tore out the seats of the skiff, and by help of some ropes fastened them to his feet in the shape of rude snowshoes. He hoped in this way to distribute his weight on the fragile ice. For a few steps this worked satisfactorily, when suddenly the ice broke and he was plunged into the water. Fortunately he had a long pole with him, which saved him from going under the ice. He tried to kick the boards from off his feet, but could not. By hanging to the pole with one hand he managed to secure his pocket knife and, reaching down, cut the ropes that held the boards to his feet. Finally he managed to get out of the water and back to the boat.

He was now extremely cold, his wet clothing had frozen to his body, and his arms and legs were encased in an armor of ice. Yet such was his splendid vitality that by stamping and tramping about in the boat he once more got circulation through his limbs. As soon as this was obtained again, he took his two boards and, lying down on them so as to distribute his weight over as large a surface as possible, he attempted to pull himself, snake fashion, toward the shore of Detroit Island, about a mile away. He had not gone far, however, before the ice broke again and he went down head first. By the time he could turn over in the water the current had carried him under the ice. Then followed a terrible struggle, hampered as he was by his heavy and frozen garments. In youth he had accustomed himself to diving and remaining under water a long time. This now saved his life. After an interminable struggle against the current and the ice, he finally regained the surface through the hole he had fallen into.

He now gave up the attempt of gliding over the treacherous ice by means of boards or otherwise. Instead of that, he stayed in the freezing water, using his ice–encased arms and hands as sledge–hammers to smash the thin ice and open a passage. He slowly moved forward, like an animated iceberg, half swimming, half crawling, by help of his elbows. When he came to a floe of heavy ice, he pulled himself on top.

This incredible struggle against the merciless elements continued for hours. Time after time he believed himself lost, but again and again he conquered, smashing, plunging, rolling and swimming, with the temperature at forty degrees below zero.

Thus he continued until late in the afternoon, when he reached the shore of Detroit Island. Here he encountered a high barrier of ice made by the freezing spray of the waves. Loaded down as he was with such a burden of ice, he was not able to pull himself over this obstacle. Finally he found a tunnel in the barrier, such as is sometimes formed by a spiral of spray, and wormed his way through it to the land.

By this time his feet and hands were frozen and senseless, but yet he was able to keep on his feet. He crossed the ice of Detroit Harbor without further accident, and came about dark to the house of a fisherman. He was met in the door by the owner who stared amazed at this bulky apparition of ice in the shape of a man. Quickly Noble explained what had happened and begged him to provide a tub of water in which he would put his feet and two pails for his hands. This was done and immediately the poor sufferer, who had had no food or sleep for three days and two nights, fell asleep.

Unfortunately for him a meddler just then appeared upon the scene. A neighbor came in who insisted that cold water would not help. He told of kerosene, the new mineral oil, a shipment of which had shortly before reached the island, and of which exaggerated stories were in circulation. This, he claimed, would take the frost out. The kerosene was found and the poor man's hands and feet were soaked in this oil. But the kerosene was bitterly cold, far below the freezing point of water, and, instead of taking the frost out, it effectually prevented the frost from leaving the affected parts. When Noble awoke, he found his limbs were frozen beyond remedy.

Then followed months of bitter suffering for poor Noble. There was no physician on the island. The nearest was at Green Bay, a hundred miles distant. Nor was there any means of getting him there. There was not a horse or an ox on the island, and most of the able bodied men were off to southern battlefields. Bert Ranney, the Washington Harbor storekeeper, ever ready to help a sufferer, took Noble to his home and gave him as good care as possible. Here for month after month, Noble sat, as helpless as a child, enduring agonies of pain, and in dreary idleness. One by one his fingers dropped off and little by little the flesh of his legs peeled away. After a while only the white, lifeless bones of his feet were left, while his system with never ceasing pain and agony strangely adapted itself to the changing conditions.

Finally, in June, 1864, an opportunity presented itself to send Noble away. A Doctor Farr, from Kenosha, was temporarily in Sturgeon Bay while negotiating the purchase of a saw mill. He was willing to perform the needed operations, but he lacked the necessary surgical instruments. He obtained some from Green Bay; but the only saw available was an ordinary butcher's saw. With this rough tool, Noble's legs were amputated below the knees.

The operation was successful, and in due time Noble once more felt able to work. By the help of friends he obtained artificial limbs, and soon was back at his business of drilling wells. In spite of his lack of fingers, he developed a remarkable dexterity in handling the tools of his trade, and he was never one to ask for favors because of his physical handicap. Later on he operated a ferry between Sturgeon Bay and Sawyer for many years.

Such energy, such extraordinary endurance, such fortitude in suffering, should have been rewarded with a pension and public honor. But unfortunately the keen competition of the later years drove this sturdy pioneer to the wall, and his reward was finally a "home" in the poorhouse.

Many years later, a man named Sam Newman, from Algoma, had a somewhat similar experience, but was more fortunate. He and a friend drove up to Washington Island to buy a horse. The

deal was made, and they started back. The day was clear, the ice
was smooth, the horse, tied behind the sled, was worth the money,
and all was well. Then, as they were within a half mile of the
mainland, there was a sudden crash, and the ice broke beneath
the sled. The momentum sent them safely over the crack, but the
new horse fell in. Quickly the two men threw off their fur coats
and tried to pull the horse up on the ice, but in vain. On looking
around, Newman saw that he was on a large floe which was
moving rapidly toward the open water of Lake Michigan, only a
mile away. There was already an open lane of water along the
shore of the mainland, so he tried to return to Plum Island, but
the crack was now ten feet wide. He drove back toward the
mainland, hoping to find some projection of the shore that would
help bridge the open water between them and safety, but saw that
in a few moments the floe would pass a point where the shore
curved sharply to the south, thus greatly widening the opening
between the floe and the beach.

The only thing to do seemed to be to drive the horse at full
speed into the water with the hope that its momentum would
carry them some distance toward land. But would not the horse
balk on reaching the edge of the ice? To guard against that danger,
Newman tore off his coat and tied it over the head of the horse,
jumped into the sled, and started the horse toward the open water.

On seeing this, his companion was terror stricken and tried to
grab the lines, but Newman gave him a push with his elbow and
sent him tumbling over the seat and into the box behind. With
bitterness he saw that he was now past the last point of land and
all hope seemed gone, but sharply lashing the horse, he sent him
on a run into the water. There was a tremendous splash, and then,
to his surprise, Newman felt the runners of the sled strike a stone
ledge only four or five feet deep.

Unwittingly, he had timed his plunge just right. If he had
succeeded in leaving the ice opposite the point as he tried to do,
they would probably have perished because the water there is
deep, and they would have had little chance to overcome the
current, laden as they were with heavy winter clothing.[1] But just
a few feet south of the point is a flat shoal with water only waist
deep stretching out from the shore for several hundred feet, and
here the horse was able to walk ashore.

---

[1] The point mentioned above is called Northport, and a steamboat pier is now
built there.

chapter ten

"THE MARIT BUCK"
OF CHAMBERS ISLAND

Full thirty feet she towered from waterline to rail,
It cost a watch to steer her, and a week to shorten sail;
But, spite all modern notions, I found her first and best—
The only certain packet for the Islands of the Blest.

KIPLING

THE largest island within Green Bay is Chambers Island. It is about eleven miles in circumference, and its straight shore lines do not present an inviting appearance to the passing traveler except on the northwest side, where a large bay indents the land. About a quarter mile from the head of the bay lies a beautiful lake about a mile long and half a mile wide. It has two small timbered islands with reedy shores, and the fishing is excellent. The lake is separated from the east shore of the island by a high wooded ridge only a few rods wide.

Chambers Island received its name in 1816. In August of that year, Colonel John Miller was sent to Green Bay to establish a military post. While the territory embraced in the State of Wisconsin had been ceded to the United States by the treaty of 1783, England did not relinquish her hold upon it until July 1815. Now Colonel Miller, with 500 men, was sent to take possession of this distant western region. This military force with ample supplies was conveyed to its destination in four large sailing vessels. This party named many of the localities, and these names still remain. The largest island in the mouth of the bay they called Washington Island in honor of the father of this country and also because the flagship of the fleet was named Washington. The next largest was named Chambers Island in honor of one of the officers of the expedition.

To most people on the Peninsula, Chambers Island is only vaguely known as a timbered island where the deer roam unmolested through the forest arches. There was a time, however, when Chambers Island was not only a settled community, but an organized municipality, where the voters once a year gathered in solemn conclave to discuss the need of schools and highways, distribute political honors, and grumble at the state tax. It had a full list of town officers with no less than three Justices of the Peace, three constables, and even a "Sealer of Weights and Measures." It also had a public school and a post office, farms (a few), orchards, livestock, sawmill and a shipbuilding plant. It had occasional religious services and a sewing circle. There were no taverns, but tea parties met frequently. The little island was in nearly all respects a well ordered community.

Eventually the work of these people, which was timber cutting, came to an end, and they moved elsewhere. Their schoolhouse and their dwellings fell into decay. So also did the countless heaps of brush and rubbish, and Chambers Island is once more reverting to the sylvan dreamland it was when the troops of 1816 first saw it.

But this is not the whole story. Among the men on this island who long ago toiled, planned and dreamed of better things, only to pass away and be forgotten, was one of such unusual energy, such tireless perserverance, and such constructive ability under unfavorable circumstances, that he holds a unique position even among the outstanding pioneers of all regions who have led the way in blazing a path to civilization. It is to his memory that this sketch is dedicated.

He was a keen–eyed young man in his later twenties, a sailor from Norway. He had about him an air of dashing fitness such as we are wont to associate with heroic knights of old, but like them he had one serious limitation—he could neither read nor write. Since he was ten years old he had spent his time following the sea, both in the English and the Norwegian marine. Now he was married and had promised his wife to find another livelihood. Eventually he and his wife reached Green Bay, where he soon found a job.

His name was Johannes Bukken, but when he came to Green Bay, he was told that that name would never do. His employer was another Norwegian, his big, pompous uncle whose name was Jeremiah Meraker. This he had changed to the more euphonious Jasper Morefield. He assured his newly arrived assistant that he must change his name to John Buck.

"Oh, all right!" said John, "if that is necessary, let it be. But what about my wife's name? Her name is Marit."

"Hm," said the man of experience, "I'm afraid that name will never do."

"Oh yes it will," replied John, "for a better name is not to be found, either in America or Norway. And Marit shall be her name as long as she is mine!" He was tempted to add that neither was a better wife to be found, but Marit with the sky–blue eyes and the deft gentle hands occupied a sacred place in his heart, and he did not wish to reveal such tender sentiments to his rather cynical employer.

One morning John was sent out to look after a fish net quite a long distance down the bay. He had a flat–bottomed boat with a center–board, called pound boat, which was in general use by the fishermen. Just as he arrived at the net a very strong wind from the southwest sprang up. Before he was through with his work, the bay was foaming with whitecaps. He had already found that these flat–bottomed boats were no good in heading into the wind and he therefore took in the main sail, but let the jib stand, and coasted down the bay.

It was a glorious trip. By help of the jib he had no difficulty in holding the boat straight before the wind. For long intervals the boat would rush forward, perched on the crest of a big wave, with the bow hanging over the hollow in front. Then the boat would glide gently down into the smooth trough below, while the greenish white foam vainly snapped after him like wild dogs. There his speed slackened until another wave again hoisted him up on its foam–lathered crest. It was like riding wild horses.

Late in the afternoon he came close to a large island. But the waves were raking the beach with such force that landing was impossible. Finally he rounded a high point and came into a large sheltered cove. At the head of it he saw a dim light from a cabin blinking in the gathering dusk. This was a comforting sight, especially as he was now very hungry, and soon he landed in front of the cabin.

This was the home of Dennis Rafferty, a good–natured Irishman who was the only occupant of the island. John Buck was his first visitor, and he gave him a boisterous welcome. The fishing was very good, and less than ten miles away sawmill operations on a large scale had been started in what is now the cities of Marinette and Menominee. Dennis needed a helper very bad and John seemed to be the ideal man for the job. After a lengthy discussion the two men finally agreed to form a partnership. The next morning John returned to get his wife and baby boy and a plentiful supply of household necessities.

Dennis Rafferty was an impulsive person, boisterous and full of loud laughter. He was highly pleased with John's efficiency and Marit's cooking and spotless housekeeping. However, he had a small boy's love of practical jokes which led him to play whatever pranks he could on John, which from time to time were repaid with interest. When they were not occupied with fishing, they spent their time in enlarging their clearing, where they grew potatoes and other vegetables. They also had a flock of chickens. Dennis' love of minor excitement caused him to separate the chickens in two flocks, so as to see who was the better poultry man.

A couple of years after they had settled on the island, Dennis was able to send money to his mother in Ireland so that she could come to America. In preparation for her coming a house was built for John and Marit, and they had just moved in when she arrived. Among other things she brought a small bag of wheat with her from a small hamlet in Ireland. These kernels of wheat Dennis was as fond of as if they had been gold. He immediately brought them over to John to show them.

"Here is wheat, my boy, which it is worth your while to look at. This is something quite different from the chaff they grow in this country. This wheat my father and my grandfather and their ancestors have grown ever since the holy fathers of Shandon Abbey received it by a miracle from heaven a thousand years ago. Three years they were without a crop and there was no more seed wheat left. Then the holy fathers prayed to the Virgin Mary to relieve the need of the people and she commanded them to turn the mouth of the abbey bell upward. They did as they were told, and the next morning they found four bushels of wheat in the bell. Half of it they used for the holy wafers and the rest of it for seed. Since then there has always been fine wheat in Ireland. Now you will see how it will grow, and what excellent bread we will have."

He immediately set to work on a new clearing which he burned and cleared most carefully. Then he made a harrow with heavy wooden teeth which he dragged back and forth between the stumps until he managed to get the soil quite well stirred. Then he sowed his wheat and covered it well by more harrowing. Warm showers came and soon the young wheat stood green and promising.

When midsummer came and the wheat was ripening, Dennis was in constant excitement lest something should happen to it. He shouted at birds and chickens if they approached the field, and swore until he was black in the face if a rabbit dared to hop through it. Finally, he shut up his hens and asked John to do likewise. John promised to do so, but the next morning his chickens were out as usual. Then Rafferty became angry and shouted:

"Can't you keep those pesky hens of yours shut up a few days, John? They will ruin that wheat yet."

"Yes," said John, "I will see that they are shut up. I forgot to tell my wife last night."

"Well, see that you don't forget it again, John, or I will kill every hen that comes near that field."

Now it happened the winter before that Dennis had played one of his little jokes on John. One day he had suddenly come into John's cabin with an old newspaper, wherein he had read aloud the important news that the Legislature of the State had just passed a law requiring all immigrants who had not become citizens to present themselves before the nearest sheriff on St. Valentine's Day, the 14th of February. Whoever neglected to do so was liable to thirty days in jail.

Of course, nothing like this was printed in the paper. It was only a joke of Rafferty's. But John did not know this, for he could not read English. He naively thought that if such were the requirements, it was up to him to meet them. When the time came, he got up early one morning and travelled off on his skis sixty–five miles to Green Bay, where was the nearest sheriff. To this official he presented himself timidly and awkwardly. The sheriff, whose mind dwelt on evil–doers, thought John was a repentant criminal, and took him before the district attorney. Here John was given a searching examination, but as the vocabulary of the prosecutor was new to John, it was rather slow work to get at the supposed criminal's confession. It was necessary to get an interpreter, and finally the matter was explained to the amusement of all except John.

This foolish trip to town was no serious matter to John, as he needed to go anyway. Still he felt that he owed something to Dennis for it. The morning after Dennis' explosion about the chickens, John got up early. He shut up his chickens as he had promised, and went over to Dennis' chicken coop and opened a window.

After a while Dennis awoke and as usual went to the window to take a glance at his beloved wheat field. How yellow it was becoming! He must surely go to Increase Claflin and borrow his "cradle" so that he could cut it. Then suddenly his joy was changed to bitter wrath: "If there ain't those doggoned chickens of John's again. I will fix them, I will—." Anger left him speechless, but he seized his gun and began to shoot chickens with deadly vengeance. Little did he think they were his own. Soon quite a number were dead, while the others, broken–winged and lame, cackled and hopped off to the woods as best they could.

During this episode, John had come out of his house yawning and stretching, and approached the battle field. Dennis poured a flood of abuse upon him. Finally he threw the dead hens in front of John and said with a chilling voice, "Here, take your damn hens. Tomorrow you will get the rest if they show up."

John picked them up quietly and meekly said, "It is too bad, Dennis, that you are bothered this way. I would do the same myself."

It was not until late in the evening that Dennis returned from his trip to Claflin's home. Then he learned from his mother that he had been slaughtering his own chickens. That was the last straw for the honest Irishman. Without waiting to eat, he marched out to have a settlement with John. Nothing short of a downright licking would atone for this. Nothing less.

In the meantime, John was keeping a lookout from his house. When he saw Dennis coming toward the house with quick steps, he extinguished the candle. Just inside the door was a trap door leading into the cellar. This he opened and withdrew into a corner to await developments.

Dennis' steps were soon heard on the porch outside. He did not stop to knock, but kicked the door open. He would take the knave right out of his bed, that was what he would. He stepped in, when the floor suddenly disappeared beneath him and he shot down the cellar steps with terrific noise and many bruises. Immediately he heard the shutting of the trap door. Then a heavy trunk or a cupboard was pulled over the opening and all became quiet. In spite of all his shouts, threats and exertions to get out, he could not hear a sound above.

The next morning John called down to Dennis.

"Good morning, Dennis!"

"Good morning, John!"

"Did you go down to the cellar to look for chickens, Dennis?"

No answer.

"Will you promise to be a good boy if I let you out?"

"Yes, John," came the humble answer. "You win this time."

This incident made no break in their friendship. On the contrary, after Dennis had cooled his wrath by sitting on a potato bin all night, he laughed heartily when he came out. That John should get him to shoot his own chickens and then trap him like a rat in a box, answered so fully his own Irish conceptions of humor that he respected John more than ever. But he meditated revenge, nevertheless.

At this time John was occupied with a great undertaking. He had started to build a schooner. For some time he had realized that there was not much to look forward to in fishing. Although there was an endless abundance of fish, the profits were small on account of low prices. Often it was impossible to sell, and much of it had to be thrown away after it was cleaned and salted. To own and sail a trading vessel was something quite different. Settlers were pouring into Green Bay, Milwaukee, and Chicago, and the great sawmills were turning the pine forests into lumber. Ships were needed to carry all this freight, and John decided that there lay his opportunity. When he first mentioned his project to his partner, Dennis was enthusiastic about it. He thought the idea was simply to build a large sail boat. But when he found John preparing to lay out a huge oak keel eighty feet long, he stared at the shipwright in amazement. "Are you crazy, man? Are you thinking of crossing the Atlantic?" And thereupon he attempted so many jokes about "John's Noah's Ark," that John became quite disgusted and determined to build his vessel alone without any help from Dennis. He would show this Irishman what a Norwegian sailor could do!

John was not as inexperienced in this sort of undertaking as Dennis thought. He had followed the sea for fifteen years, and was as familiar with the smallest details of a ship as a farmer is with his stable. Moreover, he had worked sufficiently long in the shipyard at Stavanger to know the nature and use of the different tools employed, and the usual manner in which the ship's timbers are joined together.

He went to work with quiet resolution. The massive oaken keel was laid in place on rollers near the shore. The ribs were of tamarack roots which had the desired shape as they converged to make the trunk of the tree. For all other purposes he used pine, of which there was an abundance on the island. To be sure, he had no sawmill to cut them up; but he rolled the logs up on high trestles, and then he and Marit sawed them with a whip saw. Up on the log stood John, and Marit below, sawing their way to fame and great achievement through hundreds of logs. As bolts and nails were expensive, he did not use many of these, but pinned his vessel together with wooden trummels. They had the advantage of not rusting, and they made the vessel lighter. The greatest labor was to raise the masts. But with block and tackle, much ingenuity and many failures, but with indomitable persistence, he finally got these also in place and wedged fast. Finally came the many sheets and shrouds, blocks and halyards. Here the work went fast and also the money.

All this took a long time, more than three years; but the two, John and Marit, did it all alone, built the vessel from stem to stern, from keel to truck. Finally the great day came when she floated in the harbor, a three masted schooner, shining in her new paint, with swaying sails which Marit had sewed. High up on the peak of the main–mast, a blue pennant with a white star was fluttering,—this was from Marit's wedding dress. There the vessel lay, graceful, imposing, fit to battle with the tumbling seas, carved out of the primeval forest by two pairs of hands.

Only one thing now remained, and that was the name. She was to be called *The Marit Buck*. Since this name was to be her crowning glory, John wanted it to be painted by an artist. As this task was not among his gifts, he induced Dennis to help him sail the schooner to Green Bay. There it was to be registered, insured, the name to be painted, a crew hired, and a cargo obtained.

Arrived at Green Bay, the proper official was soon found to inspect the vessel and make out registration and insurance papers. When he was filling out the blanks he inquired:

"What is the name of the vessel?"

"*The Marit Buck*," answered John in his stiff English.

"How do you spell the name?"

John scratched his head. To spell in English was Greek to him.

In the meantime Dennis was ruminating on what seemed to him a brilliant idea. Ever since the affair with the chickens he had looked for an opportunity to repay John for his humiliation, but no adequate chance had yet presented itself. Now he suddenly lifted his head with a serious mien and said: "I will write it for you."

The agent looked at the paper which Dennis handed him. "*The Married Buck*." That was a queer name! But thus it had sounded from the owner's mouth. The officer filled it in and said:

"It is well that you came this morning, because I am off for Milwaukee and will not return for two weeks."

As John had much to do in selecting a crew and finding a cargo, Dennis undertook to buy the provisions, dishes, and cooking utensils, and to find an expert painter.

Toward evening John came back in splendid spirits; a cargo of wheat for Buffalo had been secured and most of his crew had been found. He had also obtained the necessary sailing charts. He needed only a dependable mate who could also help him with the accounts. He would rather have Dennis for this, but Dennis was unwilling to leave his mother.

As he approached the dock, he saw quite a crowd of men gathered on the pier and looking at the schooner. John's heart swelled with pride. They had reason for admiration, he thought, for a trimmer schooner had not been seen in the harbor. And he had built her from the flying jib to the spanker boom. Tomorrow she would be filled with wheat, and then off to Buffalo with himself as captain. Captain Buck! It had a fine sound. It was the proudest moment of his life.

But, alas, it is truly said that pride goeth before a fall. When he reached the pier he saw among the crowd his uncle, Jess Morefield, pompous and grave as ever. They shook hands, and with ill–concealed exultation John asked: "Well, what do you think of the schooner?"

"Oh, I guess the schooner is all right" answered Jess, "but it's that queer name we are looking at." He pointed to the bow where, in large, richly ornamented letters were painted

THE MARRIED BUCK

"Why, what is wrong with that?" inquired John. "That is my wife's name."

A boisterous laugh of derision broke out around him. "Ha, ha, ha!" Even the very sedate Jasper was in danger of losing his dignity, because his sides heaved with merriment and a crude grimace indicated that he was laughing.

"No , my boy, I don't think that is your wife's name. Don't you understand that *The Married Buck* means 'the buck that has found a mate?' Of course, I understand you're tickled because you found a wife; but that you're so silly about it as to advertise it on the bow of your schooner, that is too much. I told you long ago that her name would not do."

John turned on his heel in disgust and met the grinning Dennis.

"Now, you rascal, what have you done? You must have spelled the name wrong?"

"Spelled the name wrong!" answered Dennis. "I spelled it as you spoke it. Isn't it right?"

"You know very well it isn't right, Dennis," said John sadly. "To think that you, my best friend, would make a laughing–stock of me like this."

"Hm," said Dennis thoughtfully. "I guess you are right. It was a fool trick. I wonder if I got a little rattled in the head when I fell down those cellar steps." he added with a sly side glance at John.

John walked off.

"Where are you going, John?"

"To find a painter who can fix this mess."

"But that won't do, John. There is a big penalty for changing the name of a registered vessel. Moreover, if you were to have a shipwreck or fire you couldn't collect any insurance money if the name of the vessel is changed. The law is very strict about that."

"But this wretched name, I can't stand it."

"Oh, let it go for a year, John; then we can fix it when you renew the papers. And if you will forgive me for this, I will sail with you and help you as well as I can in writing and in business accounts. You will need that if you don't want to get fooled worse."

A few days later the local weekly had a long account of the new vessel which had been built by a single man without bolts or irons. It was the first vessel built on the bay and it was greeted as a great event. Dennis had given the editor a long account of John's persistence and ingenuity, and told how he had literally sawed and planed his vessel out of the primeval forest. This account was reprinted by other papers and John at once became a famous man. But he did not know this, for when it was printed he was far out on Lake Michigan, absorbed in the study of elementary business methods.

It was a dark September night and a schooner was drifting with reefed sails in a great storm on Lake Erie. It was John and his schooner. For almost a year he had sailed the Great Lakes and had become an expert skipper. He had visited many ports, and the schooner with the queer name had attracted much attention. Now, he was on his way from Cleveland to Port Huron with sand ballast to take on a cargo of salt. But evil luck struck him. Outside of Belle Island he was overtaken by a furious gale. As the vessel was running very light, it was a mere plaything for the waves, and John saw himself drifting helplessly toward the shore where the waves were dashed to flying spray. He felt the vessel waver in the shifting current of the undertow and expected to be instantly crushed against the rocky shore. To his amazement, just as the crash was to come, the vessel was lifted by an unusually big wave and thrown like an eggshell clear over the stony beach and into a marsh beyond.

Dazed by the tremendous shock, and with many bruises, the crew crawled out to take an inventory of their injuries. Fortunately, not one had been seriously injured.

But the schooner? There she lay on her side in the slimy ooze, her rigging entangled in the brush, safe, to be sure, from the fury of the storm, but apparently doomed never again to ride the waves.

That at least was the opinion of the insurance company, whose nearest agent after inspecting her reported her a total wreck, and John at once received the insurance money.

John sat on the bowsprit and ruefully inspected the plight of his schooner. In retrospect, he saw the sturdy oaks and tall swaying pines on Chambers Island. He thought of how he and Marit with ceaseless energy and hard labor had felled those ancient giants, and with axe and saw, plane and auger, had changed them into a ship. That vessel was to be a monument to all his wife's virtues, to her cheerful fortitude in the wilderness, to her hopeful endurance in toil, to her youthful grace and her abiding love. He loved that vessel like a home and fireside, yes, like a part of his own flesh, partly because it was his great accomplishing, but mostly because Marit's share in its construction was to him like a constant benediction. The planks of the deck that he walked on she had helped to saw, the bulging sails were her handiwork, the waving pennant high up at the top of the mainmast spoke to him of her love and the children at home. Probably she was at this moment sitting in the lonely island cabin telling the children that father was on his way home in father's and mother's own schooner. And here lay the schooner half submerged in the slime of a swamp, her deck smeared with black mire. Was this the end? Was she to lie there, a hive for hedgehogs and water snakes, soon to be covered with green moss and trailing creepers? No, never! Let her meet her end, if need be, in the floods which were her element, but he would never suffer his vessel to sink out of sight in the mud of a nameless swamp. To Marit's honor he would make her float again.

There was a shallow bayou or slough in the swamp where the vessel had been tossed. The captain found that after it had meandered through the swamp for some distance, the slough communicated with Lake Erie, about a half mile away. At that point it was obstructed by a broad gravel bar rising above the lake

level. The captain decided, however, that if he could get his vessel
to that point he could cut a channel through the bar.

The problem was how to get his vessel to the bar. There was a
little water in the bayou, but quite insufficient to float the
schooner. But John set to work with his usual determination.
First, he purchased the vessel from the insurance company for an
insignificant amount. Then he procured several large
kedge—anchors and also some big blocks and tackle. With the help
of his crew of six men and some nearby Indians, the
kedge—anchors were securely fastened a couple of hundred feet in
front of the schooner. The pulleys were fastened to these and the
ropes then carried through them back to the windlass on the deck.
The entire crew then manned the windlass and the vessel was
heaved forward inch by inch through the slippery muck. Some
days they could make a hundred feet or more, while on others, it
took hours to work to budge her a foot. But John always found
some way to move her forward. Finally, after a month's toil, he had
the vessel nosing against the bar. To dig a channel through the
reef was easy. Then the captain waited for an east wind to raise
the water. It came and the vessel glided smoothly out. Its injuries
were slight.

The first thing John did when he was once more under sail, was
to bring out a box full of large shiny brass letters. "Now that the
schooner is born again," he said, "she ought to have a new name."
Then he laid the letters out on the deck until they spelt the words

THE MARIT BUCK

"Put these on the bow and stern," he said to Dennis, "and since
you are so interested in that name, you will have the job of
keeping them polished until we get to Chambers Island."

On the first anniversary after John's departure from Chambers
Island, a chubby little boy with his dog stood on the
northern—most point of the island. He had posted himself there as
a lookout early in the morning. Now in the middle of the forenoon,
he saw a black speck rise above the horizon toward the northeast.
He watched it for more than an hour as it grew in size and took
the shape of a vessel. Finally, he saw it was a schooner with every
sail spread, churning the water to foam with its prow as it came
directly toward the island. Then the boy ran as fast as his short
legs could carry him down the woodland path to the house. "Ma,"
he shouted when he was still far from the house. "Ma, here comes

pa and the schooner." And wild with joy he rolled over and over on the ground. Quickly Marit came out of the house, a little girl clinging to her dress, another little one on her arm. At the same time the schooner sailed into the cove and hove to with a proud sweep so close to the shore that the little girl jumped with fear, but Marit smiled happily. She waved her hand and quickly was answered with a roar from the little brass cannon in the vessel's stern. Thereupon the cheerful rattle of the anchor chains was heard. John stood by the rail, looking with shining eyes upon the silent forest island and upon the woman on the shore. Blue were her eyes, blue was her starched dress, and blue was the sky above her head.

chapter eleven

A MAN OF VISION

Words pass as wind, but when great deeds are done,
A power abides transfused from sire to son;
Men's monuments grown old forget their names,
They should eternize, but the place where shining
Souls have passed imbibes a grace
Beyond mere earth.

LOWELL

THE history of the average American village has very little of epic quality. In general, it represents only materialistic impulse guided by chance. A hopeful grocer puts up his booth at the corner of a crossroad; a blacksmith places his anvil on another corner, and in due time they are joined by the butcher, the baker, the candlestick maker and others of their kind until the village is a fact. There is very little of historical import in such chronicles.

But the history of Ephraim is different. It is not only the oldest community on the Peninsula, but in its inception we see a noble quality of dignity and brotherly love. Such motivation is rare in any colonization attempt, and although it failed through stupidity and groundless suspicion, the hopes and record of its founder is a rare and worthy memory of former times.

In the southeastern corner of Norway, near the little city of Halden, lies the estate of Röd, the patrimony of the Tank family for many generations. Its spacious park and ancient game preserves tell of its pleasures, and its dignified manor house, filled with treasures gathered through many centuries, speaks of the luxuries. Within its walls Royalty often found a comfortable resting place, and many cabals of state have here been constructed or unraveled.[1]

In the beginning of the nineteenth century the owner of this estate was Carsten Tank, a lumber baron of great wealth. He owned vast forests of pine and scores of farms. He had mills and factories, and his large fleet of ships carried his produce to many foreign countries. But his chief interest was politics.

As a result of the catastrophic disturbance caused by Napoleon, Denmark–Norway became an ally of France. Later, when Napoleon was defeated, England and her allies decided to punish Denmark by giving Norway to Sweden as a province. There had previously been considerable sentiment in Norway in favor of a union with Sweden. But this high–handed proposal to treat the Norwegian people as feudal vassals aroused the greatest opposition, and in open defiance of the great powers Norway declared her independence and chose a prince of Denmark for king. It soon developed that while this prince was a charming man, he did not have the stronger qualities of a monarch. The final compromise was that Norway and Sweden united as two equal and sovereign countries under one king. In these negotiations Carsten Tank held the position equivalent to prime Minister (Chef for det Förste Statsraad).

He had one son, Nils Otto, who was born in the year 1800. He was a gifted young man and an ardent idealist who was given the very best education, supplemented by leisurely visits to foreign universities and centers of culture, where he found a ready welcome through his father's letters of introduction.[2] It was the chief aim of the ambitious old statesman that his son become a worthy successor of his distinguished ancestors who for centuries had carried the name of Tank with dignity.

The Tank family consisted of five members: the father, mother, Nils Otto, his sister, and an adopted girl. The mother was a very pious woman who was sympathetic toward a small pietistic sect called Moravians. The adopted girl was a beautiful young woman, and it was natural that Otto (as he was called) should fall in love with her. After much travel in foreign centers he, in 1825, returned home, proposed to her, and was accepted. Filled with happiness the two lovers went hand in hand to tell the glad news to the mother. But the latter, on hearing this, staggered as if about to fall. "No—no!" she exclaimed. "That can never be!"

"But why?" asked Otto. "We are both of age."

His mother led him aside. "It cannot be, Otto, because she is your own sister."

"What! Sister?"

"Yes , the result of your father's indiscretion."

This was Otto's first great disappointment in life, and it was a staggering blow. He became physically ill and was almost out of his mind. He refused to see his father, but his mother's tender love and pious teachings calmed him.

After a few days he packed his trunks and departed. He told his mother he would have nothing to do with his father's business or associates. Nor would he go to the influential men in foreign capitals whose acquaintance he had made. Instead he went to the little groups of Moravians in Denmark and Germany whom his mother knew, and where he was known only as the son of a very devout and generous sister in the Faith. Bitter indeed must have been those years when hatred of his father drove him out among strangers.

He remained in Denmark and Germany for many years, esteemed as an excellent schoolteacher and gaining a reputation for good business management. Eventually he married, and later, in 1840, he was asked to go to Surinam in South America to take charge of the mission there. Henceforth for many years we see Otto Tank, who had been reared amid the bon mots of brilliant salons, humbly and patiently teaching the gospel of salvation to dark–skinned natives in the tropics. His wife fell a victim to the enervating climate and died within a year, but Tank labored on with dauntless energy. He was six feet four inches in height, with a body and constitution to match.

The Moravians are famous for their zeal in missionary work. In former times their missionaries received no salary, but were supposed to earn their own living by some handicraft. The Surinam mission was more than a hundred years old, but had made no progress. When Tank and his wife arrived in Paramaribo, they found the two missionaries sitting cross-legged on a table making pants and shirts for the freed slaves in the city. As it is so hot down on the low-lying plain of Paramaribo, close to the equator, that clothing is a torment, the work of the two former missionaries was not greatly appreciated.

Tank had other ideas. Instead of pious platitudes, he believed that the best way to gain the goodwill of the natives was to make himself useful to them. He therefore looked about to see what was most needed. He found that the management of the food supplies was very bad. There were no modern bakeries and there was a lack of other staples. He therefore built a bakery, bought flour by the shipload, and soon the natives were able to buy the best bread they had ever eaten at a lower price then if they did their own baking. This was followed by other enterprises, and Tank became the most popular man in town. When he built a large meetinghouse and invited the freed Negroes to come and join in the singing, the hall was filled with an eager throng whose emotional temperament quickly responded to the story of a persecuted and crucified Christ.

Back in the foothills of the Surinam River, in what was known as "the Dead Country," was another large group of Negroes known as Bush Niggers. They were the descendants of slaves who from time to time had broken their fetters in bloody uprisings. Eventually their status as free men had been officially recognized, but their hatred of the plantation bosses who had so cruelly oppressed their parents resulted in periodic acts of violence, and they were often shot at sight.

When the work with the Negroes in the city was well started, Tank turned his attention to the "Bush Niggers" in the Dead Country. But here he found it more difficult to make an opening. He made some journeys to their vicinity, but he always found the district apparently deserted. From afar they must have seen him and hid in the jungle, watching him with venomous eyes, thinking he was a spy. Under the circumstances, Tank thought they showed great self–restraint in not shooting him. But finally came an unexpected opportunity to befriend them.

One night his bakery was broken into by a band of thieves. It so happened that just as they came out, each with a sack filled with bread, a company of plantation overseers returning from a night's carousing chanced to turn the corner. They immediately gave chase and caught two of the thieves while the rest escaped. They were Bush Niggers.

The next morning the two thieves were arraigned in court. Tank was also there, but although he was the injured party, he refused to make complaint. Nevertheless, the overseers who were present as witnesses demanded that the culprits be hanged as an example to their fellows. The session was noisy and informal. Finally Tank got an opportunity to speak.

"Gentlemen, inasmuch as these men broke into a bakery to steal bread, it is highly probable that they were starving. If so, they obeyed a law more urgent than any law made by man—the law of self–preservation. You would not severely punish a drowning man carried away in the current of the river for seizing a plank that did not belong to him. These men were probably prompted by the same desperate urge to save their lives. It seems to me this is an offense which calls for kindness rather than severity.

"I am aware that the Bush Negroes are looked upon as hopeless criminals to be shot at sight. But this attitude is foolish. You know that if these men come to harm, it will not be long before their friends will come and take life for life, and bloodshed will continue indefinitely.

"It seems to me you have tried brute force long enough. Why not try gentleness for a change? As I am the injured party in this instance, I will ask the judge to let me have the prisoners and settle this case in my own way. I promise not to violate the law in doing it."

This appeal did not at all agree with the overseers' sense of justice and was greeted with a babble of scornful comment. The judge, who in private life was an apothecary, rapped for order and, prompted chiefly by curiosity, asked Tank what he would do with the prisoners if they were turned over to him.

"Your honor, I shall send them back to their own people as a sign of our friendly attitude toward them. As long as these people are treated like savage wolves, they will continue to snap their teeth at us and will never settle down to peaceful occupations. They will continue to be a menace to the town. I have a bakery and I don't want my shop looted. If these people could be induced to settle down and cultivate the soil, I and the other merchants of the town would be glad to take their produce in exchange for our merchandise, and business would increase."

This argument appealed strongly to the apothecary side of the judge and he said: "The prisoners are entrusted to your care."

Tank took the two Negroes to the bakery where their two bags still lay in a corner. He filled the bags with fresh bread, gave them to the men and told them with a smile to go home. It is doubtful if these men had understood much of what had been said at the trial, but Tank's smile and his gift of bread they fully understood.

When Tank about a week later made another journey to the Dead Country, he did not have to search for the inhabitants. It was not long before the poor Negroes gathered around him patting his back and giving every expression of pleasure at seeing him. He had become their hero. He stayed with them several days and explained his new plans for them. He assured them that if they would clear some land and grow produce, they would not be molested. He would personally provide them with a few plows and rent them some mules. He would also make arrangements to have their food products exchanged for other necessities in town. With amazement largely mixed with incredulity they heard this proposition, but there were several among them who were eager to act on his suggestions.

His next step was to build a school in their midst, and he installed some of his newly trained Negro assistants as teachers. This school was largely an experimental school in agriculture. Religious services followed, and churches and more schools were built. Before many years the formerly dreaded Bush Niggers were well on the way to becoming a contented and civilized community. In eight years the Surinam mission grew from two tailors to twenty–nine missionaries and more than a hundred lay workers. The congregation in Paramaribo counted more than four thousand members, and there were a number of other small congregations in the vicinity.

Strange as it may seem, some of the mission elders were not satisfied with this rapid progress. It was not the traditional way of winning converts. They thought that Tank was too much concerned with the material welfare of the Negroes and too little with their spiritual salvation. This fear was supported by the fact that he did not wear his religion on his sleeve, and in the testimony meetings he was far from eloquent. There was, therefore, grave doubt among some of the mission workers whether he was really a converted child of God. They sadly whispered their doubts that perhaps after all he was at the bottom a proud man of the world seeking worldly fame instead of heavenly glory.

Nor was Tank satisfied because he was unable to help the slaves on the big sugar plantations. Thirty thousand wretches toiled here in the greatest misery, watched over by brutal overseers with a whip in the hand and a gun in the belt. It was useless to talk to these slaves of a loving Father in heaven because, if there was one, why did he not set them free? No, he was evidently not the god of the Negroes but of the white men, and the poor black people would have to suffer until their guardian spirits awoke and came to their rescue

Tank was so distressed over the conditions of the slaves that in 1848 he went to Holland to urge the abolition of slavery. He presented his plea so eloquently that the King and court were much impressed, and many men and newspapers supported him. But among the wealthy Hollanders there were many who had big incomes from these slavery plantations. Their spokesmen claimed that Tank's charges were probably without foundation because there was no supporting evidence. The plantation overseers had prepared for this. They told the missionaries in Paramaribo that they would be given every opportunity to preach to the slaves, provided the "visionary" Mr. Tank's "misrepresentations" were checked. If not, the gates would be closed against all missionary work. Confused and fearful, these elders compromised with evil, sacrificed Mr. Tank, and sent reports to Holland that the plantation owners were giving the slaves every opportunity of hearing the gospel of salvation.While slavery, they said, had its dark sides, it was recognized in the Bible as having a respectable standing, and God was the Lord of free men and slaves alike.

This seemed to prove that Tank was a sensation–monger, and his recommendations were filed away. But over in Surinam the sufferings of the slaves continued and the cause of liberty was retarded for many years. Tank could not, under these circumstances, return and the great mission quickly went to pieces.

During his long stay in Holland, Tank was a frequent guest of a very distinguished clergyman and scholar, the Rev. J. R. van der Meulin of Amsterdam. He had a daughter whom Tank admired very much, and this culminated in a wedding. Van der Meulin was a descendant of a long line of prosperous art collectors and bibliophiles, and his house was filled with a wonderful collection of antique furniture of most artistic workmanship, choice plate and paintings, rare bric-a-brac, and thousands of ancient books and manuscripts of great value. Great wealth had also come to him through his wife, formerly chief lady in waiting at the court of Holland, and daughter of the famous general, Baron von Botzelaar, who had repulsed Napoleon at Willemstadt in 1797. For this service the Baron had been munificently rewarded by the Crown.

When Tank and his wife visited Norway on their wedding journey, they spent a few days in the little city of Stavanger. One Sunday afternoon they passed a house, through the open windows of which came the sound of singing. It was an old familiar Moravian hymn, and it was delightful to Tank to hear it sung in his mother tongue. They were invited in and found a group of Moravians with whom they spent a pleasant afternoon. They learned that about half of this Moravian congregation had emigrated to a place called Milwaukee in Wisconsin. A letter had been received from them in which they said that there were no Norwegian ministers in Milwaukee, and they asked for someone who could be their pastor. Fortunately there was a promising young man in a Bible School in Stavanger, and he, accepting the call, was already on his way. The letter also mentioned that the times in America were hard, and they hoped that a way might open for them to leave Milwaukee and become farmers.

When this letter was shown to Tank, he saw in it the finger of Providence. Together with his wife and daughter he sailed for America and reached Milwaukee in the spring of 1850. A newspaper of the city reported that he had with him a million and a half in gold.

When he found that the conditions were as stated in the letter, he set out at once to find a suitable place for the colony to settle. For six weeks he traveled over a large part of Wisconsin, and finally selected a fertile stretch of land on the west bank of Fox River. Here he made a preliminary purchase of 969 acres of land, much of which is now included in the city of Green Bay. He made a further purchase of nine thousand acres lying a little farther south on the same (west) side of the river. Thereupon he invited the entire congregation in Milwaukee to come there and settle, and promised free lands to all. It was his plan, he explained, to build a fellowship colony on the pattern of the one at Herrnhut in Germany, which Count Zinzendorf, the first great leader of the Moravians, had established.

His offer was received with great joy by his countrymen in Milwaukee, and in August, 1850, the pastor, Rev. A. M. Iverson, and the major part of the congregation, forty-two grown persons besides children, moved to Green Bay. A Rev. Fett, a German minister of the same faith, who was sent to take up the work among the Germans in Green Bay, also accompanied them.

Tank's first work was to lay out a number of building lots on both sides of what is now State Street, near the present Green Bay Junction railroad station. Surrounding these, ten-acre lots were laid out for farming purposes. These tracts of land were then apportioned among the colonists by lot, according to Moravian custom. A park covering about two acres was also laid out on the bank of the river: this was to be the site for the church. In the meantime, the north room of Tank's cottage was consecrated as a place of worship. The congregation was formally organized, which, together with the village, received the name of Ephraim, that is, "the very fruitful."

There was a large two-story building in the vicinity which had been erected by eastern Episcopalians as a mission for the Indians. This building was vacant at the time. Tank fitted it out with the necessary furniture, and here for six months the entire congregation dwelt in comfort and fellowship. The housekeeping was managed on the communistic plan. At five o'clock in the morning the matin bell aroused all. At half past five another bell called them to prayers. After breakfast the men separated and went to work at the various occupations which Tank found for them: some to clear land, some to build houses and ships, while others went out on the bay to fish. Being a man of education, Tank also made immediate arrangements for a school. One room was fitted out for educational proposes, and here five of the young men were enrolled as a students' class. Tank taught history, English, and science, while Iverson taught religion. This was the first Norwegian academy in America. It was Tank's plan to expand this school into a college where his immigrant countrymen could study medicine, law, theology, and science, and thus become fitted to take an active part in building up the new land of their adoption.

I have spoken with old men who followed Mr. Tank from Milwaukee to their new home in the wilderness. They have told me of their joy in their new–found rural liberty, of the ardor which animated them as they entered upon their work of building their homes, and of the great hopes they had for the future of their communistic colony. It was, they said, a continual song of rejoicing, with each new day a stanza of bliss.

The founder entered into his communistic plans with enthusiasm. He meditated on them as he wandered through the serene silence of his woods, and pondered their ultimate fulfillment as he sat in his cottage on the banks of the placid Fox River. He thought of his extensive travels in many lands, of his father's political dreams, of his own long service as missionary in tropic Surinam, and felt that here, in the primeval wilderness of a new continent, the Lord had shown him his true field of work.

Perhaps, he thought, he was here to be permitted in some slight measure to emulate the shining example of that man of God, Count Zinzendorf, who had founded the religious community he supported, and whose influence had gone to the uttermost parts of the earth. His countrymen were every year coming to America by the thousands, destitute and friendless: he would help them from the bounty with which the Lord had blessed him. There was no established church to minister to their spiritual wants: in his community they should find a well–ordered service and sanctuary. Their young people needed education and religious training: in his schools they should be amply provided with both.

In imagination he saw the timbered solitudes give way to well–tilled sunny fields. He saw thrifty villages, merry with the

laughter of romping children, and busy factories filled with
contented workingmen. He heard the full–toned hymns of praise
from crowded churches, and saw devout young men in his Bible
school studying the word of God, preparatory to a missionary life.
And as plan and prospect opened before him, it seemed to him far
greater to be the steward of God for the relief and help of the
needy in a faraway land, than to be the envied and uneasy head of
a petty temporal principality.

Almost a year passed in brotherly co–operation, the colony grew
in numbers and resources, and the school started by Mr. Tank was
highly appreciated. But then misunderstandings which had been
brewing for some time began to be manifested. The German, Rev.
Fett, was a taciturn, suspicious person, who had been skeptical (or
envious?) about Tank's plans from the beginning, and he
frequently voiced his suspicions to his colleague, Mr. Iverson. The
latter was an impulsive young man of great piety, but because of
wide temperamental differences, it was difficult for him to
understand the broad character and lofty aims of Tank. Probably
it was also irritating to the young Iverson to occupy a secondary
place in the colony. Under the circumstances it was easy for Mr.
Fett to drop seeds of discord into his restless mind. Fett had told
him that Tank had greatly embarrassed the missionaries in
Surinam, almost wrecking their work there. What was the real
motive that made this great millionaire bury himself in this
wilderness? Was it a gigantic speculation, or something worse?

These and other insinuations from Fett were communicated by
Iverson in confidential conversations with the members of the
colony, and Tank noticed that they began to regard him with
apprehensive doubt.

Finally Iverson, feeling his responsibility as pastor, decided to
put Tank to a crucial test. He went to him and demanded that the
colonists be given deeds to separate tracts of land. Tank replied
that the fellowship plan of the colony made this impossible. He
had not left the busy activities in Europe to become a land agent
in the wilderness, but to carry through a great plan of brotherly
love and co-operation.

This was enough for the impulsive, inexperienced Iverson. He
went to his flock and said: "He intends to make tenants of you!"
This was chilling news and caused much disturbance. The
Norwegian tenant system was just as obnoxious to the colonists as
slavery. To be sure, they had an uncertain impression that they
lived in a free county; but what can one not do with money? It was

best to get out of such a doubtful situation without delay. To most of them the whole experience had seemed like a dream. That a strange man from the upper class of European aristocracy with fabulous wealth at his disposal should suddenly appear among them and give them land, church, school, and other things, seemed too good to be true. Somewhere in the scheme, they thought, there must be a snare. The result was that the congregation was disrupted and the members scattered. Not until almost fifty years later did Iverson begin to realize the great idea which he in his impatience had assisted in frustrating. A great man had appeared among them, but they knew him not.

Almost fifty years later I was sitting in Iverson's house listening to his account of Tank's fellowship colony. He was biased in his viewpoint, but evidently desired to be fair. When he finished his story, he sat for a while in silence, then added with sadness: "I suppose I was much to blame. I was young and did not understand him. How different things might have been if we had not been so blind!"

It was most unfortunate that Tank's community corporation was frustrated. Down in Paramaribo Mr. Tank had shown that he was a most capable businessman as well as a good missionary. With his abundant funds, the colony could have been self-supporting from the start and might have been followed by other similar corporations whose aim was not merely pecuniary profit, but also culture and Christian fellowship.

---

[1] I visited this beautiful manor in 1911.

[2] In the Wisconsin Historical Society library there is a fine painting of him in his early twenties, painted by an artist in Dresden.

chapter twelve

EARLY DAYS IN EPHRAIM

Yea, the sparrow hath found a house
And the swallow a nest for herself,
Where she may lay her young!
Even thy Altars, Oh Lord of hosts,
My King and my God!

PSALMS OF DAVID

WHEN the little colony of Ephraim, at Green Bay, lost its unity of purpose as well as its leader, it quickly disintegrated. Most of the members moved to other parts. Some of the men took the sailboat which Tank had given them and went northward, prospecting for land. At the head of Sturgeon Bay they found a broad valley of good soil, watered by a stream called Big Creek. Highly pleased with this land, six families in the old colony decided to settle here, and they begged Iverson to join them. He therefore went up to inspect this land. However, on reaching Sturgeon Bay, he found it lined with evergreens—pine, spruce, and cedar, and as he had heard that evergreens grew only on light soil, he refused to join them. This was a big mistake on the part of Iverson, because the land chosen was excellent in quality, and immediately north of it lies the township of Sevastopol, then without a single settler, and now one of the most productive townships in the state. These half–dozen Norwegians at the head of Sturgeon Bay became the first farmers on the Peninsula.

For a while, however, it looked as if the whole congregation would settle here in spite of Iverson's opposition. A wealthy Moravian in New York by the name of Clark heard of the hardships of the little congregation and offered to loan them money to buy land. With great anticipation they obtained the aid of the capable Oliver Perry Graham, the first settler at Sturgeon Bay, and with his help they selected 1200 acres. However, Mr. Clark suddenly withdrew his offer. The six families moved to Big

Creek, and for many years their relations with Iverson were very cool. The half dozen that remained in Green Bay (Fort Howard) picked up a very precarious living because there was little that they could do.

Finally, after more than a year of distress and disillusionment, Mr. Iverson had two items of good news to tell them. One was that Bishop Schultz in Bethlehem, Pennsylvania, had sent the congregation a loan of $500 to be used in buying land. The other was that a man named Ole Larsen had called on Iverson and told him about some good land that was open for purchase. Larsen lived on Eagle Island, seventy miles northeast of Green Bay, and made his living by supplying cordwood for the boilers of the Buffalo steamers on their way to and from Green Bay. Greatly cheered by this news, Iverson determined to go and inspect the land that Larsen had described. About the first day of March 1853, when the ice was safe for traveling, he with three companions set out afoot. After a march of three days on the ice of Green Bay they arrived at Eagle Island. Iverson describes his first impressions of the vicinity of the present village of Ephraim as follows:

> The next morning we felt a little stiff after our long walk on the ice, but soon I was out of Larsen's house and gazed to the southeast toward the land at the head of the deep bay. Soon I discovered that although the trees along the shore were evergreens, the timber behind was hardwood and quite different from the timber at Sturgeon Bay. With delight I looked for some time and ruminated. Perhaps our beloved little congregation should be planted here on this land by the romantic bay and with the high cliff opposite so grand in appearance. After morning worship and a good breakfast, we set out with Larsen in the lead over the smooth ice cross the beautiful bay, a distance of about two miles.

They climbed the hill where now stands the church, and the farther east they went the more beautiful was the forest, "the trees so high and straight, and so open it was between them that it seemed to us that, without clearing a road, one might drive through it with horses and wagon without hindrance." They were all well satisfied with the land, and when they returned to Green Bay, Iverson proceeded to the land office in Menasha, where he bought 425 acres at a cost of $478. He platted this tract into village lots about an acre and a half in size, with larger lots in the rear. In this he closely followed Tank's procedure at Green Bay. The congregation also adopted the name of Ephraim, which Tank had chosen for the new village. This was the beginning of the second permanent settlement in Door County, the first being the Norwegian Moravians at Big Creek near Sturgeon Bay.

One day in May 1853 a small vessel tied up to a little pier in Green Bay to take the colonists off to their future home. The day was radiant with the promise of spring, but it was the darkest day in Tank's life. Down to the vessel he saw the deluded emigrants hurry with their few earthly possessions. There were not many of them, only four small families. The children carried their simple homemade tools, the poor wives struggled with the heavy emigrant chests, and the men shouldered their sacks of potatoes and flour. Of livestock they had none except a few chickens. As Tank looked on their honest faces, pinched with poverty, and saw the heavy movements of their limbs which, stiffened by excessive labor, were now about to carry them off to greater privations and toil, they looked to him like wayward children, sulkily denying themselves a gentle father's care. And yet how his heart yearned for these people! How gladly he would have gathered them into his arms like a hen gathering her chickens under her wings, but they would not!

But he could not follow these people. They had spurned his gifts, and to urge further kindness upon them would but confirm them in their suspicions. Their paths and his had no future crossing. Nor would he return and take possession of the ancestral hall in Norway. His complacent relatives, smugly intrenched in Pharisaic conventionalism, who with pity had seen him give up the honors and pleasures of a brilliant career to become a missionary to the slaves of South America, would see little additional honor for him in being jilted by a lot of praying emigrants. Better a secluded life on the banks of the Fox, where there was time to ruminate on the futilities of life. And there Tank remained until his death, with the exception of a few trips abroad for the education of his daughter.

Disappointed in philanthropy, Tank now turned to business, chief of which was his share in building the Fox River canal. In those days, before the railroad had become a recognized success, water transportation was the great problem, and canal routes were everywhere surveyed, chief in importance of which was the

Fox River–Portage route, the old highways of the Indians and the voyageurs. Millions were spent on this enterprise in the expectation of reimbursement by state lands, but the legislature refused to recognize the claims of the company, and Tank, with others, suffered very heavy losses.

In the midst of the protracted annoyances incident upon the settlement of the canal affairs, Mr. Tank took a sudden illness and died in 1864.

The Tank library, numbering 5000 volumes, was presented to the Wisconsin State Historical Society in 1868. It was information gleaned from these books which settled the boundary dispute between England and Venezuela during Cleveland's administration and thus averted a threatening war. The Tank Cottage was purchased by the City of Green Bay and moved to Union Park, where it is now used as a museum of Tank relics. Only a very small part, however, of the furnishings of the Tank home are here. These were of such rare excellence that when Mrs. Tank died in 1891, an art expert from New York was sent for to manage their sale. He shipped the more valuable paintings, rugs, and furniture to Chicago, where they were sold at auction, attended by art dealers from all over the country. A large number of smaller articles including porcelain, bric-a-brac, linen, copper utensils, etc. were sold at auction in Green Bay for trivial sums. Thus this splendid collection of centuries was scattered everywhere. So much of the famous Wedgwood ware was acquired by the women of Green Bay at this auction, that the city is said to have more of these ceramics than any other city in America.

When Iverson and his little company moved to Eagle Island in May 1853, they put up some small shanties in which they lived until November. Meanwhile the men divided their time between fishing, clearing land, and house–building. Writing forty years later, Iverson describes the first day's work on the mainland as follows:

> I remember so distinctly the first morning when we began to clear land. There were eight of us who rowed over from the island. Arrived at my lot, I kneeled among the bushes and prayed earnestly to the Lord that he would bless the work and here plant and water His own congregation. When I for the first time swung my axe over my head, it was with a vivid realization of the Psalmist's words when he exclaims "Here has the sparrow found a home and the swallow a nest." Soon

the first tree crashed to the ground. I had two young men to assist me. We worked with rare energy, and soon our perspiration flowed like tears. In the afternoon heavy columns of smoke were seen to rise from four different places, in that we sought as much as possible to burn up the brush as fast as we made it.

About the middle of November the colonists moved across the bay to the new village of Ephraim, where by this time four houses were erected. Among these was Iverson's which is still standing in its original shape, size and place. It is now one of the two or three oldest houses on the Peninsula.

The next summer the little colony was augmented by a company of Norwegian immigrants who came directly to Eagle Island in response to letters written by Ole Larsen to his relatives in southern Norway. There were about fifteen families of them, and for a time they all lived in the shanties which the Moravians had erected on the island. Unfortunately they brought with them the germs of the dreadful Asiatic cholera, and an epidemic broke out. There was no physician on the peninsula and no remedies of any kind. One after another became sick, and many died. Seven cholera victims were laid away in the stony soil of the island without coffins or priestly rites. Eventually the survivors pre–empted lands in the vicinity of Ephraim, and resolutely began the toil of carving farms out of the tangled wilderness.

During the first years there was sometimes great want in the colony. The nearest place where supplies could be purchased was Green Bay, seventy-five miles distant. But there were no roads, not even a path through the primeval jungle. Sometimes it was necessary for men to walk that long distance, following the stony beach, and carrying a sack of flour home on their backs. But it was exceedingly toilsome to walk on the beach, and it took a week to make the trip. During this time it was necessary to camp out every night, and there was danger of getting the precious flour wet.

Late in the autumn the settlers used to send a committee to Green Bay to purchase what supplies were needed for the coming winter. A small vessel was then found to carry the supplies to Ephraim. One fall the vessel that had been engaged for this journey was delayed by other trips. Day after day the pioneers watched to see it come around Eagle Point. They were waiting for their flour, their coffee, their salt, and a score of other household necessities. Their clothing was worn out and their children were in need of shoes and underwear. But no sail was to be seen. Finally Christmas came, bleak and bare, with none of the common holiday extras. A committee was then sent off on the long tramp to Green Bay, along the frozen beach, to learn what had happened to their vessel. When they finally arrived, they found that the vessel had been frozen in, ten days before, just as it was ready to leave the harbor.

That winter many of the settlers had nothing on which to live but potatoes and fish. Fish for breakfast, fish for dinner, fish for supper. Occasionally the menu was varied when they were unable to catch the fish. And no salt. There was only one cow, and she went dry from lack of fodder. The ice was very rough that winter, but a couple of times some of the more hardy set out for Green Bay as if on a polar expedition, cut their way through the ice drifts, burrowed in the snow, and brought home a few of the most needed articles on a hand sled. But it was a bitter task.

It is strange what expedients people will use when in need. About this time was born Cornelius Goodletson, a later well-known, hale, and jovial citizen. After his birth, his mother had some ailment with her breasts, and was unable to nurse her baby. They had no cow. "Doctor" Jacobs was consulted. He could not relieve the mother, but he suggested that they mix some of the cheap black syrup, which was then in vogue under the name of "niggersweat," with water and give it to the child. The mother was extremely doubtful whether he would survive such an unnatural diet, but little Cornelius belied her fears. One day the father came triumphantly home with a cow which he had persuaded someone to give up. But by that time the baby had become so addicted to his diet of "niggersweat," that he indignantly refused to take the milk. He kept on growing and in time became six feet three inches tall and the father of a dozen children

By this time so many people had settled in and near Ephraim that Iverson's sitting room was insufficient to accommodate all who came to attend the regular religious services. But the people were very poor and could not provide the money to build a church. In the summer of 1857 a gift of money was received from Rev. H. A. Schultz, which he had collected in Bethlehem, Pennsylvania, to be used for a church building at Ephraim. This was such an encouragement to the people that with much self-denial they subscribed a considerable sum, and the building of the church was started. With their characteristic veneration for sacred things, it was agreed that their little temple of worship should not be built of the rough logs of the forest, such as they had used for their humble homes, but must be built of sawed and planed lumber of excellent quality, and in such a manner as would dignify the church for religious use for generations to come. Accordingly, Captain Clow of Chambers Island was sent for to go to Cedar River, Michigan, with his little flat–bottomed schooner, Pocahontas, after a cargo of lumber. Iverson writes: "He soon came, but was alone on board, so that on the trip I had to serve both as deckhand and cook, as well as supercargo, which was all very interesting." They managed to get the church enclosed and roofed that fall (1857), but were then obliged to drop the work for lack of funds.

The fact was that the little settlement that fall was very near starvation. The crops in 1857 were a complete failure, due to excessive heat and drought, and in dismay the colonists looked forward to the winter with nothing to eat. The banks at Green Bay would not lend a dollar on their real estate. The mills of Sturgeon Bay, Marinette, and Cedar River were shut down on account of the hard times. They were almost without clothing and shoes. There was not an overcoat in the settlement. Their summer garments, made largely of old grain bags, were now in tatters. They thought of the hardships of the winter two years before, when they were so near starvation. Now their potato bins and corncribs were empty. What were they to live on?

In this dire extremity, Iverson launched a little sailboat which he had made, and started for Green Bay. When he arrived he hunted up Mr. Gray, a good–natured Irish merchant who owned a large schooner. He told Mr. Gray of the colony's serious plight, and said that if the merchant would advance the most necessary provisions and clothing, the colonists would pay for it by getting out as many cedar posts as he wished. Mr. Gray could not accept this proposition because there was no way of insuring the payment of the goods, which would amount to several hundred dollars. Disconsolately, Mr. Iverson went off to seek lodgings for the night.

Quite by accident, Mr. Tank learned of this difficulty, and he told Mr. Gray that he would guarantee payment on condition that his name would not be mentioned. The next morning when Iverson returned to make a final desperate appeal to the merchant, he was overjoyed to learn that the colonists could have the goods requested, on condition that all the men in the colony would come personally to Green Bay and sign the required contract. With joy they heard of this plan and they all made the long trip to Green Bay to sign their names. Personally, Iverson undertook to deliver two thousand fence posts. For these posts, 7 1/2 feet long, with square ends and 4-inch top, all bark removed, Mr. Gray agreed to pay two cents apiece, to be delivered on his vessel the next spring. As there were neither horses nor oxen in the settlement, it was necessary to carry these heavy posts many hundred feet to the banking ground and later bring them abroad. The price on 8-foot railroad ties with double 6x6-inch face was eleven cents; but as these big timbers were very heavy to carry, only one man delivered any; but Gabriel Wathne, a short thickset man of enormous strength, took them two at a time and carried them down to the beach.

Finally came the great day, two years later, when their church was dedicated. It was the eighteenth day of December, 1859, and was probably the greatest day that Ephraim has seen. A large bell had been hung in the belfry, and Gabriel, the strong man, was appointed bell ringer. He put all that he had into his work, with the result that the bell soon cracked, but to Gabriel it was still heavenly music. He kept on until he was finally stopped by Mr. Iverson.

Meanwhile, the worshipers were coming. A heavy snow had fallen the night before, and now when the bell tolled for the first service in the trim little church, slowly moving oxen were seen to come from every direction, drawing crude sleighs packed with worshipers. They came, the Thorps, the Larsens, the Weborgs, the Hansons and others from the west; the Nortons and Jarmans from the south; the Dorns, the Hempels, and Langohrs, from the east; the Amundsens, the Andersons, the Knudsons, and others from the north; and last, but not least, the village congregation itself. When the bell ceased ringing, the church was filled to the last seat, a well-instructed choir was in the gallery, and the memorable service began. With more than his usual fervor their pastor preached, and the people, stirred partly by his ardent address and partly by their own feelings, were moved to tears. As they sat in their own well-built house of worship, it seemed to them such a great achievement that they could hardly believe it. They had suffered so long in toil and tribulation, in cold and sickness, in hunger and nakedness, that this dedication of their own church seemed to them to inaugurate a new era. For ten years the congregation had been buffeted about, moving from place to place in the wilderness, like the children of Israel, but suffering far greater hardships than they. No manna fell daily from heaven to feed them—they had to toil for it in the forest primeval. When their wives or their children were sick, there was no golden serpent hung on high, upon which they might look and be healed—they could only pray in anguish over their afflicted ones. Here no grand ceremonial cheered them on from day to day with impressive pomp and the sound of trumpets—they had to work out their own material and spiritual salvation in solitude and humility.

Poor, brave, self—denying, suffering pioneer fathers and mothers! Like the seed corn planted in the ground, perishing unseen to produce the luxuriant life that springs from it, so these pioneers buried themselves in the wilderness, and wore themselves out with hard work, that their children might have a better chance in life. But the children of this new land, how little they appreciate the sacrifices of their pioneer ancestors! They remember only with disdain their fathers' rags and bent backs, their mothers' wrinkles and rough hands, and forget that these are the price of their own prosperity.

This date marked an epoch in the history of Ephraim. For many long years it continued in its isolation, like an oasis in the desert, separated from other settlements by vast stretches of untracked forest, yet it prospered and grew. In 1864 the founder of the settlement was called to another field, and was succeeded by Rev. J. J. Groenfeldt, who did not suffer the light that had been lit on "Mount Ephraim" to grow dim. For a hundred years that church bell has tolled each Sunday morning, calling the people from far and near to worship. For a century a minister of the gospel has stood in its pulpit, calling upon the people to turn their thoughts from material to spiritual things. Such teachings make for steadfastness of character, for higher standards of living and thinking. The dance hall and its devotees have never found an opening in Ephraim. No saloon has ever poured out its foul stench and vulgar laughter upon this community. While the village and its people are not perfect, it is a clean, sweet place to dwell in, with high ideals and sterling honesty. As Coleridge says:

> "O sweeter than the marriage—feast,
> 'Tis sweeter far to me,
> To walk together to the Kirk
> With a goodly company!—

"To walk together to the Kirk,
And all together pray,
While each to his great Father bends,
Old men, and babes, and loving friend
And youths and maidens gay!"

In closing this account of the early history of Ephraim, a few words about Iverson's character are needed. Unlike Mr. Tank, he was by no means a great man. With a very limited education, he was opinionated and obstinate, as is shown in his opposition to the sensible suggestion of those members of his congregation who settled near Sturgeon Bay. He was intolerant of ministers of other sects, quarreled unceasingly with Baptists and Adventists, and repeated with relish a silly story that a visiting Lutheran minister demanded pay at the rate of ten cents a word. Most unfortunate was his gullibility, which led him to believe that Tank was a ruthless, scheming land agent. This false suspicion wrecked the congregation and reduced it from forty families to four.

But these very serious faults were involuntary reactions toward outside influences. When he was undisturbed in his own work with the congregation, he was all tenderness and energy. He was not only its founder; he was also its nurse and teacher. Like a mother watching over her child, so Iverson worked for Ephraim with unceasing diligence and love. This comes out clearly in his narrative of his fourteen years' labor as pastor of the Ephraim congregation, written about forty years later when he was an old man. The reader gets a vivid impression of a consecrated and a faithful flock, living together in primitive conditions, but rich in Pentecostal blessings.

Sequestered as this northern part of the Peninsula is by large bodies of water and far from the main lines of travel, its people for a long time retained an original freshness and simplicity, not often met with in this land of sophisticates. They went about their somewhat unusual daily occupations unembarrassed by a knowledge of outside standards and thus developed marked individual characteristics of their own. Professor C. M. Moss of Urbana, Illinois, who was one of the first to discover the beauty of Door County and who spent forty summers here, once wrote this letter in which he aptly describes the charm of Ephraim. He wrote:

I cannot picture it as much less than a bit of the
outer rim of paradise. What with the rugged newness of
the surroundings, its peaceful quiet so full of the very
breath of serene life to one who could appreciate its
soul-invigorating influence, the simple, genuine
kindness of the people, their calm and hopeful religious
life, it resembled the sleep of a young child, trustful and
undisturbed by the clamor and disquiet of the day, yet
throbbing with a fresh life animating its being.

This Ephraim community became the mother settlement of all
the Peninsula lying north of it. It was the first place on the
Peninsula where public religious services were held for many
years, and many pioneers settled here for that reason. Later they
found better land farther north, and eventually a dozen
Scandinavian congregations were organized which are now going
strong.

While much has been told about Iverson, the real founder of the
settlement was Ole Larsen. He built a large log house on Eagle
Island in 1851 and supplied the Buffalo steamers with cordwood
for their boilers. By the summer of 1853 the timber was all cut and
sold. Larsen then dismantled his log house, made a raft of it and
towed it to Nicolet Bay a mile away where he rebuilt it. In 1957
this oldest house on the Peninsula was torn down by order of the
Wisconsin Conservation Commission.

chapter thirteen

THE LIFE AND DEATH OF
TWO EPHRAIM OLDTIMERS

I know it is a sin
For me to sit and grin
At him here.
But the old three–cornered hat
And the breeches and all that
Are so queer.

OLIVER WENDELL HOLMES

THE finest farm on the Peninsula, and perhaps in all Wisconsin, was the old Hanson farm, across the harbor from Ephraim. It had rich, deep soil, well drained, and was protected from strong winds by high, wooded hills on the north, west, and south sides. There was never a crop failure on this farm. In addition, it had an unsurpassed scenic location. It is now no longer a farm but a first class golf course in Peninsula State Park.

Here, in 1854, settled Henry Hanson with his father, Soren, and his family. They came directly from Norway and were members of that group of immigrants who were so severely ravaged by cholera upon arriving at Eagle Island as told on pages 108-109 herein. However, Henry and his family survived and were able to start clearing the timber at once. Thus this farm became the first profitable farm in Door County. As a comparison may be mentioned that the Town of Sevastopol, which is the best farming area in the county and lies immediately north of Sturgeon Bay, had no settlers until 1856 when George Bassford settled five miles north of the city.

Henry Hanson was also interested in fruit growing and planted many apple trees which were doing well until they were cut down some years ago. Among these oldtimers is the largest apricot tree in Wisconsin which fortunately escaped destruction. Its trunk is thirty inches in diameter, and its bushy top is forty feet in diameter. It is still in good condition and stands a couple of

hundred feet north of the Totem Pole, a glorious bouquet of
countless thousands of blossoms. Nearby is also the well-marked
grave of Chief Simon Kaquados, the last descendant of the great
Chief Onanguissé.

One would think that a man who possessed such a fine farm in
such beautiful surroundings would be very happy and sing like a
lark. But neither Henry nor his son Olaf were ever heard to sing.
As Olaf was my nearest neighbor, I knew him well, and I never
saw him reflect a pleasant mood. There were his brothers, more or
less fretful like himself, and there was no peace between them.
There was also the local church which, according to Olaf, was a
band of stupid troublemakers, and the town board was a group of
helpless nitwits. He found fault with everything and everybody
except himself; but no doubt he was sorely punished for it, because
it must be most depressing to go around in such a petulant mood.
But these bald statements do not do Olaf justice. He was not as
bad as it sounds. He was honest and progressive, and people
seemed to understand that his grouch was more a burdensome
inheritance from a cross-grained ancestry than an expression of
his own personality.

Sometimes Olaf had reason to feel chagrined. There was for
instance the time when the State was buying the lands to create
the future Peninsula State Park. His farm of 303 acres, of which a
couple of dozen lots had been surveyed for sale to summer visitors,
was even at that time easily worth $30,000, but the State Park
man in Madison had other ideas. He was a well meaning man, but
he had a grotesque idea that lands so far from Madison could not
be worth more than five or ten dollars per acre. Olaf therefore
hired a lawyer to protect his interest. Unfortunately, Olaf had no
faith in the lawyers of Sturgeon Bay, but entrusted his case to a
lawyer in Green Bay. The lawyer was busy and did nothing.
Finally the State made an offer of $8,000. This was accepted by
the lawyer, who kept $1,005 for his 'work'. Could anyone blame
Olaf for being sore?

But Olaf's worst gripe was the condition of the roads. He was
one of the early auto buyers, and his adventures were most
distressful. The present generation has no conception of the
old–time roads or the old-time automobiles. The tires of the latter
cost forty dollars apiece and were not good for more than a
thousand miles; and that mileage represented numerous engine
troubles, broken springs, blowouts, and punctures without
number. It was always necessary to carry a vulcanizing outfit. The
roads were either a cloud of dust or a lane of mud; in winter they

were usually impassable here on the Peninsula where we have considerable snow. Our highway supervisors at that time had neither the knowledge nor the equipment necessary to keep the highways clear. In many places the roads in winter were only a one–way passage through a deep tunnel without a roof.

Well, finally Olaf died, and he no longer had to get down on his hands and knees and struggle with bitter imprecations to wrest the tire off the rim of a Model T. But that was not the end of his troubles. Poor man! He had lived a life of vexation, particularly with his own family; he had died a most painful death; and for a while it looked very dubious about the funeral.

As he was a member of the church, the funeral service was announced to be held in the church on Sunday, March 2nd, 1928, at 2 P.M. But he died in the hospital in Sturgeon Bay, and on Saturday we had a howling blizzard. The snow did not come down gently, peacefully, as was fitting for a funeral in the country, but flung itself upon us in piercing, blinding violence, and all roads became impassable. Only an aeroplane could bring the body to Ephraim, but no aeroplane could start or land because of the snowdrifts. Saturday passed and also Sunday, and nothing was heard from nowhere. The world was apparently dead.

Monday came, and the roads were still unbroken. But after some hours it was learned by telephone that one of Olaf's sons-in-law had hired the big county snowplow and expected to reach Ephraim at 2 P.M. The hearse and the mourners would closely follow the snowplow.

At 1:30 we were in the church and took our seats reverently. We thought we could hear the huge snowplow cough and sputter over in the hills toward Fish Creek. But after we had sat there an hour, we heard that the plow had not yet reached Egg Harbor. We mentally anointed ourselves with patience and remained seated.

After we had sat there for two hours more, we heard that the snowplow was four miles south of Egg Harbor, but nothing was known of the hearse and the mourners. We sat down again, but it was difficult to maintain a solemn contemplation of death and the hereafter so long. The benches in that church were indescribably hard.

After we had sat there for another hour we decided it was best to get home, eat supper and go to bed. You know how it is: The spirit is willing, but the flesh is weak.

We put on our overcoats, wrapped the scarfs around our necks and ambled out. Then suddenly we saw a sleigh coming down the hill from the north with six tall men in long overcoats standing upright and a coffin behind. All six raised their arms up and down repeatedly. The signal was plain: we were to toll the church bell. But for a moment we stared at them openmouthed and wondered how a dead man who was expected from the southwest could arrive from the northeast? But as the signal was to ring the bell, we finally got it tolling. We concluded that perhaps it was as it should be. Olaf was rather twisty in his mortal life, so perhaps it was not strange if he arrived from the wrong direction now that he was dead.

The bell was tolled until it almost burst, and finally the Ephraimites managed to wade to the church. Here we were repaid for our long vigil, because we got two funeral sermons, one from Austad in Sawyer and one from Belsos in Ellison Bay.

After the service we placed the coffin on the sleigh again, and some of the principal mourners sat on top of it. We common people and the pallbearers and the two ministers plodded along behind the sleigh. The snowplow had not yet reached Egg Harbor.

We now learned that the hearse and pallbearers had followed the snowplow almost up to Egg Harbor. Here the latter was stuck, so the autos were turned around by hand power and the party returned to Sturgeon Bay. Then they drove up Highway 57 to Oscar Smith, two miles east of Ephraim. Here a sleigh was hired and thus they reached Ephraim.

Finally the funeral was complete, partly by moonlight. We went home to bed; funerals are exhausting. A little after ten the hills reverberated with the groaning of the county snowplow. Thus ended the life of Olaf Hanson.

The Old Goldsmith

Once upon a time there was a goldsmith in Ephraim. He was a wrinkled old Swede, past eighty years in age, and he was only a little more than four feet in height. Of hair and whiskers he had an abundance, and he mumbled his words, so it was difficult to understand him, even for a Swede. He repaired old clocks and jewelry ornaments as well as tin pans and coffee pots, and he sometimes even made brooches and earrings. His home was on the upper side of Moravian Street, half house, half cave, in under the vertical cliff behind the house. Here he had a fine view across the harbor to Eagle Cliff and Eagle Island.

He had a daughter nearby with whom he stayed part of the

time, especially in winter. But their relations were not happy. She was a poor, middle-aged widow with many children and many troubles of her own, and he was not a considerate visitor. On the first sunny day in March he was always back in his little one-room hut up in under the cliff.

The goldsmith's nearest neighbor was Professor Moss whose house was on top of the cliff immediately above the goldsmith. As the latter had very little goldsmithing to do, he spent most of his time with a crowbar, twisting and moving large rocks about. I asked him what he was planning to do with the rocks, but his speech was so slurred I could not understand much of what he said. All I understood was that he was trying to create a memento of a place in Sweden.

The old man was very valiant with his crowbar and attacked even the cliff itself. Professor Moss believed that he owned the cliff and became much annoyed when he saw the old man attempting to change the weathered and mossgrown cliff into a stone quarry. He therefore went down to the goldsmith and in plain unvarnished English he attempted to explain to the goldsmith that the latter was trespassing. The old man did not understand a word of this and made a long reply which was equally unintelligible to the Professor. Mr. Moss then took his deed to the town board and asked for a clarification. We studied the description, but as it followed only straight lines from point to point, it left the ownership of projecting points uncertain.

The Professor then decided to offer the goldsmith a compromise. He went down to the little cabin, but as he looked at the shabby old man, he realized that it was impossible to make himself understood. And he also felt that it was beneath his dignity to quarrel with this poor, poverty-stricken old man. In a burst of sympathy he took the right hand of the goldsmith in both of his. Like a dog somewhat uncertain of the friendly pat of a stranger, the goldsmith looked up at the kind face of his visitor. Upon reading the message of brotherly love in the Professor's eyes, the old man placed his wizened hand on the Professor's and thereafter peace reigned between the two.

And peace was what the old man needed, because he was a poet. As a goldsmith he was not much, and as a stonebreaker he was nothing, but as a poet he spoke with words that touched the heart. They were all about the beauty of Sweden. He wrote about Sweden's great pine woods, of its beautiful lakes and its roaring waterfalls. He and I became fast friends because I appreciated his poetry. It was by no means perfect in rhyme and rhythm, but he had a surprising depth of feeling. I pleased him highly because I asked him to read some of his poems. First, however, I read them to myself, because his enunciation was too difficult to follow.

His relations with his daughter became worse and worse. Finally came the time when he decided to end it all. In the gloomy pre-dawn hour of a certain day he got up, cooked himself a cup of strong coffee, ate a breakfast of bread and sausage, and then took a heavy dose of poison. But no sooner had he swallowed than he regretted the action. He looked around the little room which had been his home so long, thought of his book of manuscript poems, and wished he had not done it. In panic he rushed out to seek aid from his daughter. Then in his hurry he stumbled over an obstacle and fell headlong on the hard ground. This violent shock was enough to make him vomit his poison as well as his breakfast. Greatly relieved and full of new energy, he continued down to his daughter and bawled her out for not being up by five o'clock in the morning.

After this the situation improved for a couple of years, and the goldsmith passed his ninetieth birthday. His daughter was not without some affection and respect for her father, but he was a troublesome guest. It bored him beyond description to sit all winter in her stuffy little kitchen and he seemed unable to ease her burdens. When the next winter approached, she told the town board that she could not take him, she refused absolutely.

Efforts were now made to find someone else to take him as a paid boarder, but in vain. No one in the village would take him at any price. As he had to be fed and housed somewhere, we made arrangements for him at the old people's home in Peshtigo. The goldsmith at first was unwilling to go, but he was induced to go for a ride. We took him to Peshtigo and showed him the sunny rooms, the modern plumbing, the good food and the friendly management. He was favorably impressed and consented to stay. We were happy that he now had a comfortable home in which to spend his last years.

We heard nothing from Peshtigo all winter, and the old man was almost forgotten in the rush which comes with spring. Then one day in June we received a telephone message that the goldsmith had hanged himself the night before.

This was bad news, and we rushed over there without delay. We learned that he had been apparently well satisfied all winter, but said he was going back to Ephraim in spring. All through the month of May he had inquired about people from Ephraim who were coming to get him. Then when June came he lost hope. He found a rope somewhere, looped it over a door, put the noose around his neck and kicked away the chair.

We took the body with us back to Ephraim and felt very gloomy. Evidently his dreams of Sweden as a fairyland had been succeeded by fond thoughts of Ephraim. He wanted to get back to his little hut under the cliff where he could see the sun set in the waters of Green Bay. If he could not live in Ephraim, he did not want to live at all.

chapter fourteen

FISH CREEK

A funny lot of folks there be
A–living in our alley,
From battle–scarred old roustabouts
To charming, sparkling Sally.
And some are crude, and some are shrewd,
And some just full of tattle.
But some are true as tempered steel,—
Fit men to fight Life's battle.

ONCE upon a time there was a New York Yankee by the name of Asa Thorp. He assisted his father in tending the locks of the Erie Canal at Lockport. At that time (in the Forties) a very large part of the traffic on the canal consisted of immigrant passengers bound for the West. They were carried in huge, flat–bottomed scows, much the same as those now used in freighting stone on the Great Lakes. These scows were pulled along at a very slow speed by a mule walking on the bank of the canal on either side. Every day there passed one or more of these scows, loaded with stocky Germans, tall, blue-eyed Norwegians, or hopeful Irish, and piled high with all manner of painted chests, carpet bags and bundles. It seemed to young Asa, judging by their numbers and by the variety of their strange and outlandish garb, that all the world was heading for the West. Day after day they passed by, a mighty army of toilers, mostly young people, determined though weary, hopeful though ragged.

What strange attractions that mighty, mysterious West had to draw so many people from the ends of the earth! Asa began to wonder if it had any for him. Tending the locks of the canal was a job for a machine and not for a man. He began to feel the call of the wild. So, being of an adventurous disposition, one day in 1844 he stepped into one of the passing scows and joined the caravan of fortune hunters bound for the distant West.

Little by little the passengers scattered, but most of them were

bound for Chicago and Milwaukee. They stayed in the scows until
they reached Buffalo. Here energetic agents herded them into lake
steamers on which they passed up Lakes Erie and Huron and
down Lake Michigan to Milwaukee. Here in a crude little town of
unpainted shanties and mud, filth and riot, they were routed out
and left to their own resources.

Back in Lockport Asa Thorp had learned the trade of making
butter firkins, tubs, and similar woodenware. Being desirous of
seeing the country, he started out on a pioneer road that led into
the wilderness, paying his way by making butter firkins. The road
soon dwindled into a path, and after a while was nothing but a
blazed trail through the timber. But along this blazed trail he
would every little while come to the cabin of a new settler, and
everywhere the butter-firkin man was welcome. He would stop for
a few days with each settler, make up his needed stock of
woodenware, inquire into the conditions of the land round about,
and then push on to the next settlement.

Finally he came to the last little settlement in Dodge County
called Rubicon, a few miles west of the present city of Hartford.
Here the blazed trail ended and what lay beyond was a sealed
book to all. However, the soil here was so fertile, the timber so tall,
the conditions so promising, that Asa Thorp was well satisfied to
go no further. He selected forty acres of land that suited him best.
Then he hurried back to Oswego, for there was a young woman by
the name of Eliza Atkinson who took the keenest interest in the
outcome of Asa's journey of discovery.

Back in Oswego Thorp waxed eloquent about the wonders of
the distant territory of Wisconsin. He told of the fat soil, the gently
rolling land covered with huge oaks and maples, and described his
own selection of a home for Eliza and himself. The result was a
rousing wedding participated in by all the members of the clans of
Thorp and Atkinson. This was followed by a general exodus from
Oswego of nearly all the members of the two families. To Rubicon
they went and raised their own cabins in the wilderness.

The land office at that time was in Menasha. Asa Thorp, being
the most experienced in western ways, was delegated to go there
and make formal entry of the lands. He started out and again
became a maker of butter firkins. When he came to Menasha he
found it was a small village on the banks of the large river flowing
northward. He was told that there were many settlers on this
river and that there was quite a city about thirty miles north at
the head of Green Bay. Being in need of cash, Asa decided to visit

these new settlements and earn some money by his trade before returning to Rubicon. He followed the river down and met with success.

One day he was sitting in front of a store in De Pere repairing butter firkins, when a tall stranger accosted him. "Say," he said, "you ought to quit that puttering with butter firkins and come with me to Rock Island and make fish barrels. There you'll find the boys that have the cash."

"Rock Island!" said Asa, "what county is that in?"

"Dunno," said the stranger, "we ain't got no county down there."

"What state or territory is it in?"

"Dunno that," replied the stranger, "and what's more, don't care. We have no state, county or town organization, we pay no taxes, we have neither lawyers nor preachers, but we have fish and we have money. It will keep you busy twenty-four hours a day to make fish barrels at your own price. If you want to make money come along with me. It is about a hundred miles down the bay and I have my own boat."

This sounded pretty good to Asa. Big earnings and no taxes. The result was that he went with the stranger whose name was Oliver Perry Graham, to Rock Island.

He found the conditions on the island as Graham had described them. There was a large community of prosperous fishermen and they hailed the coming of the cooper with joy. While they all could make fish barrels at a pinch, it was beneath their dignity when money was plentiful to handle tools other than their fishing outfit. Asa would have settled there for good if it had not been for Eliza back in the woods at Rubicon.

Late in the fall of 1845 when most of the fishermen left the island to spend the earnings of the summer in Milwaukee and Chicago, Thorp also pulled out. He obtained a passage on one of the Buffalo steamers that made occasional trips to Green Bay. On the passage he got acquainted with the captain who told him of the difficulty of running the boats because of the lack of fuel. Wood was used for fuel and while the entire Door County peninsula which they were passing was one vast forest, there was not a pier from Washington Harbor to the head of the bay where they could take on a dry stick. Sometimes steam failed and much time was lost sending the crew along the beach picking up snags and driftwood whereon to limp along until they could make port.

As the captain was telling his troubles, they were just passing the place where the smoke from Increase Claflin's newly built cabin could be seen rising above the tree tops. This was the only cabin on the entire peninsula north of Little Sturgeon Bay and stood on the point of land opposite the cliff beneath which the village of Fish Creek was later built. "Now, there," said the captain, "is just where a man could build a pier and earn lots of money by supplying the steamers with wood."

This suggestion at once took root in Thorp's shrewd Yankee mind. He made a sketch of the indentations of the shore line, and when he reached Menasha compared his sketch with the government maps and recognized the harbor which the captain had pointed out. This done, he filed preemption claims on all of the land south and east of this harbor for a considerable distance back.

He was much elated when he reached Rubicon and told of the coup he had made. It was his intention to return to his harbor in the spring and build his pier. But hard luck and unexpected difficulties developed and he was obliged to remain in Rubicon for many years. Meanwhile his dream of riches in the vast timber resources of the peninsula floated before his vision like the thoughts of an unattainable paradise. At last, in 1854, he was able to move and build his pier, the first between Sturgeon Bay and Washington Harbor. He acquired seven hundred acres around Fish Creek and gave employment to many men cutting cordwood for the passing steamboats. Soon Fish Creek became an important business center.

Asa Thorp was a gentle-minded, capable man, always doing the right thing without ostentation. As he had lived an upright, dignified life, he looked with calmness to the end so dreaded by all. Long before his death he caused his own grave to be dug, building up its sides with slabs of slate and covering it with a slab of rock. Here he was prepared to go

"not like the quarry-slave at night
Scourged to his dungeon, but sustained and soothed
By an unfaltering trust . . ."

This detail attended to, he went about his work of being a useful citizen in his quiet, unobtrusive way.

The Fish Creek community is not the product of a concerted purpose, such as in the case with Ephraim. It was the accidental meeting place of a number of individuals, who were driven thither by fortuitous circumstances. One thing they had in common, however, and that was the bitter struggle of finding their way through the world and battling with a merciless wilderness. With illusionary optimism they moved hither and thither, ever hoping that at the next turn they would find the pot of gold at the end of the rainbow. As an example may be mentioned Stephen Mapes. From Sheboygan he came full of hope, moving all his earthly possessions, including fourteen children, for two hundred miles through the timber on a two-wheeled cart drawn by two oxen. When he came to Sturgeon Bay there was neither bridge nor ferry. But he made a raft and managed to get the oxen and all on board. With his wife standing in front of the oxen feeding them corn to keep them quiet so that none of the fourteen children would be spilled out, he paddled them across to the promised land where riches and happiness were soon expected, but which, alas, were never realized.

In time this miscellaneous gathering learned to pull together and established a school and a church. This last was the work principally of two estimable women, Mrs. Griswold and Mrs. Jeffcutt, of Episcopalian persuasion. With the help of friends from the East they purchased the unfinished dwelling of a fisherman and had it remodeled. They built better than they knew, for this little chapel has a suggestion of peaceful sanctity about it which many a costly temple has failed to acquire. For a time a resident rector held regular services there. The Episcopalian form of worship seemed, however, to lack that element of dogmatism which a hard–fisted pioneer community seems to crave. This was found a few years later when a zealous Seventh Day Adventist arrived and held stirring revival meetings, centering on the saving grace of Saturday as Sabbath. His labors were amply rewarded and in the early spring of 1876 thirty-four grown persons were baptized by immersion amid the bobbing ice cakes.

Fish Creek has always been a well behaved village and, until Prohibition created temptation, it was many years since any saloon had been permitted in the village or town. In the early days a saloon was in operation where the villagers would meet to swap fish stories over a glass of stale beer. This public forum came to an abrupt and dramatic end through the energy of a resolute lady of the village, the forerunner of the famous Carrie Nation. One Sunday evening as some of the village notables were dozing over a quiet game of penny-ante, the door suddenly flew open revealing a woman with a basket full of cobblestones. She wasted no time in words but let fly a cobblestone at the barkeeper. Being a woman she missed her mark but struck and shattered the smoky lamp. Thereafter darkness and pandemonium ruled the room. The lords of the card table forgot their dignity and dived head first under the billiard table while stones and curses flew through the air. A door finally opened to the barkeeper's kitchen, when, seeing this avenue of escape, the men stood not upon the order of their going, but flung themselves out all in a heap, leaving the doughty woman a defiant victor.

This energetic woman, whom we may call Mrs. Squeak, had a husband. To all observers he seemed a meek and estimable man and his memory is respected. But to Mrs. Squeak's penetrating eye he seemed to reveal a heart full of incipient wickedness, and she was greatly concerned to eradicate this latent unrighteousness. Once, for instance, he and a few others were having an innocent celebration in a fish shanty. Someone was caressing a fiddle, another was demonstrating what he did not know about a jig, and Mr. Squeak, utterly forgetting his domestic experience, was singing with a woeful voice, "Oh, I'm a ti-ger! Oh, I'm a ti-ger"!! It was a scene of blissful contentment.

Then the door opened, revealing Mrs. Squeak with a whip in her hand. For an instant she viewed the paralyzed inmates with a baleful glare. Then she snarled: "Well, if you are a tiger I'll put the stripes on you!" Whereupon she unmercifully lashed the cowed tiger to his cage.

Who could stand before such defiant zeal? One withering look from her keen eyes was enough to blast the sunshine out of any ordinary man, dry up his laughter, and shrivel him into a speechless nonentity. And when she opened the floodgates of her wrath, the stoutest hearts in the village forgot dignity and forthwith sought refuge in flight. Once, however, she met a disastrous defeat.

There was a middle-aged woman in the village who, for a time, was dock agent. It was therefore necessary for Mr. Squeak, who was a businessman, to have some conversation with her. Mrs. Squeak felt convinced that these conversations were filled with evil and she longed to annihilate this temptress. One Sabbath morning, attired in all her finery, she encountered this woman's husband. Being a lazy man he had just milked and was crossing the road with a pail of milk in his hand. She stopped him and gave him a piece, a long piece, of her mind. She told him what she thought of his own low-down self, his unspeakable wife, his worthless children, and his despicable ancestors as far back as she had ever heard of them. He received this cloudburst meekly, with a bowed head realizing abjectly that his sins had overtaken him.

But when she stooped down in frenzied indignation, picked up a handful of mud and threw it into his milk, the worm turned. He looked into his grimy milk pail a moment and then said: "Well, if you want mush and milk you can have it right on the spot!" With that he doused the whole milk pail over her.

She gasped and choked. "You—you—you—!" she spluttered, but speech for once failed her. She turned on her heel, trailing milk, misery, and mortification to her home.

Ezra Graham was his name. Ezra Graham. It is only meet that the conscientious chronicler give all proper credit to such heroism, no matter how misguided.

There are here and there people who by their disregard of accepted standards of conduct become public character. Gossip does not create their reputations. They have, as it were, shouted them from the housetops, and their record becomes a part of the traditions of their community.

There are also people whose quaint and usually harmless eccentricities add a smile to the recollections of their neighbors. Fish Creek had many of these.

Well remembered among them is old Myron Stevens. He had a slant for law which, coupled with his wit, made him a famous pettifogger. A good time was always expected when Myron Stevens took a case. His wit usually won him the goodwill of the jury, and his strange lines of defense always mystified and perplexed the opposing pettifogger. Sometimes, prompted by mischief, he would read a paragraph from the statutes, modifying the phraseology and interlarding it with clauses of his own invention. On hearing this strange reading of Wisconsin law the opposing pettifogger would jump up and shout "Say! Hey there! Let me see that! Where do you find that paragraph?" But old Myron would solemnly snap the book shut and haughtily reply: "I am here to defend my client; not to teach law to greenhorns."

When old Myron had anything, he was very generous and when he did not, he expected others to be so. One day he came into a neighbor's house and said: "Say, John, can you let me borrow a piece of bacon? I'll bring it back when I have cooked my beans." Another time in winter he was riding along behind a slow horse, blue with cold, his teeth visibly chattering. A passerby called to him, "Say, Myron, why don't you get out and walk and get warm?" "N–no," replied Stevens in frozen dignity, "I would rather sit and freeze like a man than run behind like a dog."

The boss of the town for a long time was Alexander Noble, who had a disposition as haughty as that of a traditional English lord. He was an expert blacksmith and knew it well. When anyone wanted Alexander Noble to do anything it was necessary to use much circumspection of speech. Once a farmer came in and said, "Say, Mr. Noble, can you shoe my horses?" Haughtily the blacksmith turned and said: "Do you mean to insinuate that I who have been shoeing horses for thirty years can't shoe your worthless plugs?"

"I meant to say, will you shoe my horses?" faltered the farmer.

"Why don't you say what you mean then? Now get out of here till you learn to speak intelligently."

Among the queer characters who helped to make things lively in the village was a "Doctor" Hale. He and his wife had been traveling members of the Kickapoo Indian Remedy Co., which was a cross between a circus and a patent medicine agency. His wife had been a performer on bare-back horses and profoundly impressed the populace and shocked Mrs. Squeak by dashing about on horseback in all manner of perilous postures. No less were they impressed by "Doctor" Hale, who carried in his pocket a $1,000 bill. It is still a matter of debate whether it was bogus or genuine, but it was remarkably efficacious in winning respect or securing credit.

About this time E. S. Minor, another old settler, opened his campaign for congressman. "Doctor" Hale let it be known that he had been Senator Gallinger's private secretary and had practically "made" the Senator. He offered to give Mr. Minor the accumulated wealth of his vast experience, and guaranteed his election if he were given free hand as campaign manager. Mr. Minor's friends now felt that the election entirely hinged on Hale's cooperation and besought Mr. Minor not to commit political suicide by refusing to engage Mr. Hale. Mr. Minor, however, stolidly refused the potent aid of the $1,000 bill and went ahead and was elected just the same. It later developed that while "Dr." Hale was from the same state as Senator Gallinger, he had had no connections with him whatever.

Fish Creek was for a long time the principal fishing center of the Peninsula. Nearly every man in the village was a fisherman, and north and south of the village the shore was lined with fishermen's homes and nets.

The first fishermen in this region (after Increase Claflin) were two stalwart Norwegians named Peder Weborg and Even Nelson, who built their homes side by side three miles north of Fish Creek in 1852. For many years the twin lights from their evening lamps served as a lighthouse to the many schooners which passed up and down the bay. Behind them, on top of the cliff still stands the house of Sven Anderson, another fisherman and a gentle–minded old bachelor who settled here because of the transcendent beauty of the scenery. He built his home on top of Sunset Cliff, also known as "Sven's Bluff," where he could enjoy one of the finest views in America. This made it necessary for him to tote his water and other supplies two hundred feet up the steep hill, but he considered this a slight inconvenience in comparison with the panoramic feast which he enjoyed up there. His house was a Mecca for all the children of the neighborhood, because he always treated them so kindly and generously. Older people also liked to visit him because of his dignified courtesy and sage interpretations of the vicissitudes of life.

To be a fisherman in those days required much resourcefulness and efficiency. In addition to their regular work of fishing they also had to build their homes, fish huts, piers and often their boats. They also made their own nets, or had them made by some of the women of the neighborhood. For weaving a gill net, six feet wide and one hundred and sixty feet long, two dollars was paid. A beginner at this trade would work for weeks to make a net.

chapter fifteen

EGG HARBOR

O Willie brewed a peck o' maut,
　And Rob and Allan came to see;
Three blyther hearts that lee–lang night
　Ye wadna found in Christendie.

BURNS

BACK about two hundred years ago, Egg Harbor was a cherished spot, better known than Milwaukee or Chicago.

In those days—from about 1650 to 1825— the main line of traffic did not go across the middle of the western states from the Atlantic to the Pacific because its big cities—Chicago, Omaha and Denver—were still not even conceived of. Instead, it poked its crooked way from the Lower St. Lawrence up the Ottawa and westward to Mackinac. Here was the first big junction—one branch turned northwest to Lake Superior and its western end. The main line, however, continued westward to Washington Island and then followed the Door Peninsula shore to Fort Howard—now Green Bay—and then across the state by way of the little Fox River to Prairie du Chien. Here was a big junction point because there were numerous fur traders up and down the Mississippi and also across the western plains. All these knights of the wilderness made a trip each summer back to Mackinac to deliver their furs and get a new supply of trade goods and food supplies for the next winter.

The main line of this traffic line was therefore the section between Mackinac and Fort Howard. For most of its length there were numerous sheltered spots well fitted for camping, the best of which was Eagle Island near Ephraim, but between Fish Creek and Little Sturgeon was a stretch of rocky exposed shore unsuitable for camping, except for one little harbor. This was Egg Harbor. Here was a small sheltered sand beach where the bark canoes could be pulled up. Being the only suitable camp site for a distance of almost thirty miles, it was much in use.

It is not known what name it had, if any, in the early years, but the Hon. Henry S. Baird of Green Bay has told how it got its present name. He writes:[1]

"In the summer of 1825, Mr. Rolette, a prominent fur–trader, arrived at Green Bay from the Mississippi with three of four large boats, on his annual voyage to Mackinac, with the returns from his year's trade. Since there was no vessel at Green Bay, he kindly offered passage on his own boat to Mr. and Mrs. Baird, then 'young folks' who resided in Green Bay and were anxious to visit Mackinac. On a fine morning in June the fleet left the Fox River and proceeded along the east shore of Green Bay, well supplied with good tents, large and well filled mess baskets, especially a large quantity of eggs. On the second day at noon the order was given by the 'Commodore' (Mr. Rolette) to go ashore for dinner. The boats were then abreast of Egg Harbor, until then without a name. On board the Commodore's boat, there were besides himself, Mr. and Mr. Baird, and nine Canadian boatmen or voyageurs, as they were called. On another of the boats were two young men, clercs in the employ of Mr. Rolette, one of whom was John Kinzie, and a like number of boatmen.[2]

"It was the etiquette on those voyages, where several boats were in company, that the principal person or owner took the lead. Sometimes, however, a good–natured strife would arise between the several crews, when etiquette was lost sight of in the endeavor to outstrip each other and arrive first at the land. . . . At the entrance to the harbor, Mr. Kinzie's boat came alongside the Commodore, with the evident intention of running ahead of him. Mr. Rolette ordered it back; but instead of obeying, the crew in the boat, urged on by Mr. Kinzie, redoubled their efforts to pass the Commodore, and, as a kind of bravado, the clerks held up an old broom. The Commodore and his crew could not brook this. The mess baskets were opened and a brisk discharge, not of balls, but of eggs, was made upon the offenders. The attack was soon returned in kind. It became necessary to protect the only lady on board from injury, which was accomplished by covering her with a tarpaulin. The battle kept up for some time, but at length the Commodore triumphed and the refractory boats were obliged to fall back. Whether this was the result of superior skill of the marksmen on board the Commodore's boat, or the failure of ammunition on the other, is not now remembered.

"The boats and the men presented a rather unusual appearance, and the inconvenience was increased by the fact that some of the missiles used by the belligerents were not of a very agreeable odor. The fun ended in Mr. Kinzie having to wash his outer garments, and while so employed, some mischievous party threw his hat and coat into the lake. All enjoyed the sport, and none more so than the merry and jovial Canadian boatmen. And thus ended the sham battle at 'Egg Harbor.'"

In 1853 the first permanent pioneer in Egg Harbor came and settled on practically the same spot where the battle with the eggs was fought. His name was Milton E. Lyman, and he became a famous man in Door County. There was much speculation on how it happened that a man of such education and dignity sought a home so far away in the wilderness, but being the first settler, he was not called upon for his antecedents. That obligation devolved upon later arrivals. Moreover, while he was admired for his wit, he was feared for his sarcasm. He became the first County Judge and was also at the same time Clerk of Court and County Superintendent of Schools. Later he was Justice of the Peace, and as such united no less than seventy-three couples in marriage. He was assisted by a small following of constables and pettifoggers who were experts in drumming up business. Down to his little house on 'The Point' a well beaten track was worn, on which was often seen a procession of pettifoggers, plaintiffs, defendants, witnesses, constables and spectators. Heated trials were held and the 'Judge' would gravely announce his decision. No matter who won, a celebration at the nearest barroom followed, where the Judge was not permitted to buy any drinks.

When business permitted, Judge Lyman was always in demand as pettifogger in other justice courts, and as such had many sharp encounters with the valiant champion of Fish Creek, Myron Stevens. In those days each little community was as vain of its principal pettifogger as a present day college is of its principal football star. There was therefore much scoffing between the rival clans. Once a native of Egg Harbor was arrested for stealing a pig. He had chanced upon a plump suckling asleep in the corner of a rail fence. Temptation overcame him and he slipped the little animal into the folds of a coat that he was carrying. Unfortunately for him, the little captive wriggled out just as he was passing through the village. Here no pettifogging could obscure the facts in the case, and the prisoner pleaded guilty. In pronouncing sentence Judge Lyman said: "I will give you the choice of thirty days in the county jail—or three days in Fish Creek."

The prisoner groaned in dismay at the dismal alternative, but he was loyal to the core, though otherwise a reprobate.

"Gimme the county jail!" he exclaimed.

The Judge stroked his beard of dignity, paused a moment and said: "Such unselfish loyalty to local standards deserves a reward: the sentence is remitted."

It developed later that Judge Lyman was far from being as circumspect in his own conduct as was expected of a dispenser of justice. There were incidents in his private life which are unmentionable. His public delinquencies were also numerous. His last public office was that of town treasurer, during which he embezzled a thousand dollars. When confronted with the evidence of his crime, he brazenly gave the town board the choice of sending him to jail and losing everything, or letting him go free and taking his note which "would soon be paid." The second alternative was accepted, and the note was handed down from one set of officials to another as a doubtful asset. Finally it was worn out. The signer also in time wore out and died as a town pauper.

Asa Thorp, the founder of Fish Creek, appears to have been the first man on the Peninsula to realize that the most promising way to make money was to ship cordwood. With this in view he bought several hundred acres of government land when he in the late 1840's returned from his cooperage job on Rock Island. But a pier was the first requirement and it was necessary to sell his farm in Rubicon in Dodge County. This was not accomplished until in 1854.

In the meantime his brother Jacob had gone to Fish Creek to make fish kegs for Increase Claflin. He stayed there for five years and married one of Claflin's daughters. Finding that the next best place for a pier was at Egg Harbor, Jacob moved there and became its second settler. This was in 1855. Here the first child in Egg Harbor, and perhaps in Door county, Roy Thorp, was born in Oct. 29, 1856. He was the grandfather of Duncan Thorp, the novelist.

There was another brother of Asa named Levi. In 1849 when report came about the discovery of gold in California, he set out to try his luck. He did not try the overland route, but went to New York where he got a job as seaman on a schooner. This took him down to Cape Horn. Then followed a northward voyage of about

10,000 miles to San Francisco. He was among the lucky ones, and when he returned to Rubicon by way of Panama, he found he was 6000 dollars ahead of his expenses, which was a respectable fortune a hundred years ago. This money was used up in building a pier and buying many hundred acres of land at Egg Harbor. He prospered from the start and soon he became the leading business-man north of Sturgeon Bay. In the 1870's he built a large residence in the center of the village, then by far the best built and largest home in the county. It is still standing, a fine piece of construction.

This was the sunny side of pioneer life and does not reflect the conditions among the pioneers generally. In the Fifties and Sixties there were very few settlers, and Levi Thorpe got most of his wood cut by Indians and Belgians. But after the Civil War there was a large and steady flow of home seekers. Egg Harbor was then a wilderness of swamps and stony hillsides, with very little promise of homes and cultivable land, but there was the chance of earning a little by cutting cordwood. Nowhere was it more laborious to subdue the land to the needs of man than in the region around Egg Harbor. Into this jungle without roads or paths, far from the comforts of civilization, the pioneers penetrated, often carrying their cookstoves on their backs. When they had built their little 12 x 12 log cabins with one small window for light, they felt they had made good progress. With the daily pea soup simmering on the stove, the pioneers worked in pairs felling huge maples to be made into cordwood. For this they might get as high as two dollars per cord, after they had transported the wood a half dozen miles to the nearest pier. One is prompted to ask, what inducements were there to take up such laborious toil? The answer is, only the wish to be independent landowners. They were men who had the lust of conquest in their hearts, and they laughed at hardships because it was to them only a challenge of endurance. These pioneers were therefore a select lot of men of superior quality. They had marvelous appetites, and at times were hard drinkers, but their chief pleasure was the battle with the wilderness, and the smoke from the smouldering brush piles at dusk was incense to their nostrils.

About four scant miles south of Egg Harbor is a small indentation in the shore, and an enterprising Norwegian named Andrew Anderson hopefully named it Horseshoe Bay. He built a pier there, bought and shipped cordwood and kept a store. A mill was built and a cooper shop. This was followed by a blacksmith shop, a general store, a half dozen dwellings, and a school. All roads led to Horseshoe Bay and vessels daily came and went. In 1890 an ice company made up of Sturgeon Bay people was organized, employing about sixty men at Horseshoe Bay. Henry Fetzer, the later president of the Bank of Sturgeon Bay, was bookkeeper. The ice harvest farther south was poor, and the Horseshoe Bay Company was confident that the price would go high up and all would make much money. They therefore held the ice, but too long. When they finally decided to sell, the ice had turned to water and returned to the bay.

This was the last exploit in the village of Horseshoe Bay. The mill closed, the schoolhouse was moved away, and the buildings fell into decay. After some years it was almost forgotten that it had ever existed.

But Horseshoe Bay still had some charm. It had a sandy beach about 1700 feet long, and there was a nice growth of cedar. The County Park Committee cast longing eyes upon this tract, so suitable for a county park, and Robert Murphy, a retired business man in Green Bay, finally gave it to the county on condition that it be enclosed by a stone wall. This was built and also a ponderous gateway of stone, and the people of the Egg Harbor area have a fine picnic place.

Up at the corner of the park where stood the offices of the Horseshoe Bay industries, stands the wooden statue of a Menominee Indian chief. It is doubtful if Dr. Cowles who owns the land is old enough to remember the wooden Indians, one of which stood before the door of every respectable tobacco store in all our cities (alas, where are they now?) But if he did not see them, he is so much more to be thanked for having restored to us a sample of the art that was really appreciated by the younger generation of the previous century. The sculptor is Ernst E. Dombrowe, and he had Chief Oshkosh of the Menominee Indians (who lives in Egg Harbor) as a model.

The cordwood days of Egg Harbor are long since past, and it is no longer a land of swamps and stony hillsides. Instead, it is one of the leading townships of the State in the production of fine foods—cherries and apples.

---

[1] From the Door County Advocate, April 1862.

[2] The latter was the son of John Kinzie, the first trader and settler at Chicago.

chapter sixteen

THE LAST MATCH

Three fishers went sailing out into the West,
Out into the West as the sun went down;
Each thought on the woman who loved him the best;
For men must work, and women must weep,
And there's little to earn, and many to keep
Though the harbor bar be moaning.

CHARLES KINGSLEY

BILL Stahl was the best boatbuilder on Green Bay. His boats had a cunning curve to them which permitted a little more sail and a smoother cleaving of the water than was to be found in any other boat suitable for commercial fishing. But this excellence often proved a snare. Delighted with the graceful lines of the boat, the reckless purchaser would crowd it to the utmost, until finally he would have her keel in the air. The Stahl boats therefore got a bad reputation for killing fishermen. However, the true cause of the trouble was charitably not mentioned, for the worst or almost the worst thing that could be said of a fisherman was that he was a poor sailor. The blame was therefore laid on the whiskey which, no doubt, was often a contributing cause. A Stahl boat and a bottle of whiskey came to be looked upon as a combination that meant a sure end to the owner.

But in fall and early spring Bill Stahl put his tools away, for then was the time to go after the trout and whitefish.

These fish are more than ordinarily migratory. One season they are in the north end of the lake, the next in the south or somewhere else. He is the successful fisherman who can foretell their wanderings.

One fall about 1860 three men on Washington Island compared notes on where to find the whitefish. They were Bill Stahl, Ingham Kinsey and Allen Bradley. After much deliberation they came to the conclusion that the most promising fishing grounds

were on the west shore north of Menominee, and thither they
went each in his boat, Bradley being accompanied by his young
son. They were highly gratified to find that their prognostications
were correct, for the whitefish were so numerous that they had all
they could do to empty the nets. Two hundred whitefish, weighing
from three to six pounds each, were frequently taken from a net at
each lift.

Pleased with their success, they kept on with their fishing until
rather late in December. Finally the day came when they decided
to pull up and return home. They loaded their nets and winter
supplies into their boats and set sail.

The day was a cold and cloudy one, with a rather steady wind
from the southeast which promised to land them on Washington
Island in reasonable time. It was their plan to keep the boats
together, for Kinsey and Stahl were alone in their respective boats,
which fact rendered their journey somewhat difficult. For a
considerable time they got along very well. Finally it began to
grow dark, and the wind began to swing around to the northeast,
blowing briskly dead ahead. It soon veered to the north, and blew
furiously, while the weather became intensely cold, the mercury
falling almost to zero. By this time the boats had become
separated and lost to the sight of each other, and each man
struggled as best he could.

But it was a desperate and apparently useless struggle. The
flying spray had saturated their clothing, and every outer garment
became frozen. Their sails also became stiff and unmanageable,
and their ropes like rods of steel. Meanwhile the wind was
howling, the waves roaring, while the storm tossed the ice–laden
craft as it would. They felt the numbness of intense cold and
despair coming over them. Through the darkness of the night they
were driven helplessly to their doom.

Allen Bradley's boat had outdistanced the others, since it had
two men to navigate it. Bradley, moreover, was a very strong man
with the endurance of a wild animal. In the coldest weather he
was never known to wear coat, overcoat, or mittens. As he sat in
his ice-encased garments, gradually feeling his limbs turn to the
numbness of death, his ear suddenly detected a sound different
from the roar of the storm. It was the booming of the sea on the
rock-bound shore of Door County. With sudden life, he jumped to
the mast and with a tremendous wrench tore it out of the socket.
Another jerk or two and the spar and the foresail were also
thrown overboard. He then seized the oars, and, seconded by the

feeble but earnest efforts of his son, got the heavy-laden, ice-encrusted boat under control. Tugging incessantly at the oars, he managed to keep it clear of the shore. After two hours of this work he was finally rewarded by turning the point of a little cove and finding himself safe in Fish Creek.

There was great surprise in the little village the next morning when it was learned that Allen Bradley had arrived during the night. The cold had been so intense and the gale so terrific that it seemed incredible that anyone could have survived it in an open boat. It was generally agreed that the other two fishermen must have perished, but some efforts were made along the shore to discover their bodies. A heavy fall of snow, however, covered everything with a cloak of white.

Toward evening a searching party from Fish Creek saw a slowly moving body about a mile away. At first they thought it was a bear because it was moving on four legs. They approached nearer and, to their surprise, saw that it was a man moving painfully through the snow on his hands and knees. It was Ingham Kinsey. During the preceding night he had been hurled almost insensible with cold on the beach four miles south of the village. His boat had been smashed on the rocks. During the night and the next day he had staggered along the beach, first north and then south, vainly looking for a human habitation in the unsettled wilderness. Finally his limbs refused to support him and with the last fragment of endurance, he was crawling along, his hands and feet frozen, when he was discovered and saved.

Meanwhile, where was Bill Stahl?

William Stahl was a famous water dog who had survived so many adventures that he believed himself immune from death in the water. He had built both his own boat and the one that Kinsey had, and had unbounded faith in them. Yet he recalled now that his boats had a bad reputation. His thoughts went back to the long list of fishermen who had lost their lives in boats built by him. There was old Peter Bridegroom who went down the first time he had sailed his boat. Then there were Robert Kennedy, James Love, and Frank Wolf, splendid fellows all, but a little too fond of whiskey. Were there more? Yes, to be sure. There was Ed Weaver and that fellow Casper, both of whom still owed for their boats. A Bill Stahl boat and a bottle of whiskey had sealed their fate. Was the combination going to prove true with him also?

As he felt his boat settling deeper and deeper with its load of ice, and becoming quite unmanageable, he gave up all attempts at navigating her, and devoted his energies to keeping his hands and feet from freezing. But it was a practically useless effort. He was soaked with water and frozen with ice and more ice was forming around him.

As he listened to the howling of the wind, the swish of the whitecaps, and the heavy thud of a wave striking his bow in the trough of the sea, it seemed as if the resistless cavalry of hell were hitched to his boat, dragging it onward to that brink where he would tumble over into the next world.

Sitting thus, with distressing fancies flitting through his mind, his boat suddenly struck hard on a rock. Before he realized what had happened, another wave followed, smashing the boat upon a rocky beach, while he was thrown into the water.

He scrambled out and looked around him, but nothing could be seen in the darkness. But, now that he was on firm ground he felt new hope within him. He would strike out at once following the shore till he came to a boathouse or human habitation. He stumbled over the driftwood that littered the shore, slipped on the stones, but struggled on. He felt that his limbs were not yet frozen and with good luck he would soon reach a shelter. Then he stopped in amazement.

There in front of him was another overturned boat lying in exactly the same position as his.

He reached into the bow of the boat and pulled out an oblong box. It was his boat! Here was his tool box.

He stared vacantly at the boat. How could it be his boat? He must have turned in his tracks and retraced his steps. Was he losing his mind?

He started along the shore once more, keeping the water on his left, the land on his right. He walked carefully to avoid confusion. At the end of a half hour he was again in front of the boat!

Suddenly he realized the situation. He was on an island, and the reason that he had come twice upon the boat was that he had twice walked around the island.

By this time it was beginning to grow light in the east. By looking in that direction he could now distinguish the high cliffs of Door County. Straining his eyes northward he could also discern a long low shore which must be Chambers Island. He now recognized where he was. He was cast ashore on Hat Island, a barren little rock supporting a few stunted trees about five miles southwest of Fish Creek.

The dejection that followed upon this discovery struck him like a blow. He had toiled and struggled and suffered all through the day and night before, his clothing was frozen stiff, he felt numb with the cold. He sank down, overcome with weariness.

He did not know how long he had lingered hopelessly when suddenly he started up—in his pocket was a match box. There were birch trees on the island. He required only a little of this bark, and in a few moments he would have a fire.

He stripped some bark from the birches, broke some dry twigs from the trees and struck a match. It refused to ignite. He struck another and another till the box was half empty. Still no success. Then he examined the matches, and found that they were all water soaked. Still clinging to hope, he struck the matches with greater care than before till the last was tried in vain.

Almost stunned by this experience, he went through his pockets one after another. Some were so frozen that he had to tear them apart with main force. What chance had he unless he could make a fire? In his exhausted condition he could not endure it another hour. In his hip pocket was his can to tobacco. It had a tight fitting cover. He opened it and found it almost empty of tobacco. But down there among the crumbs lay a match. He could see no sign of moisture inside the can. He poured out a little tobacco in his hand and examined it. It seemed as dry as ever. If the tobacco was dry, it was likely that the match was also. He carefully refrained from touching it, however, lest his clumsy fingers might drop it in the snow.

One humble, forgotten match. Yet it might mean another lifetime for him.

With this thought in mind he once more made his preparations for a fire. This time, however, he proceeded with much greater care than before. First he picked out the spot on the island which seemed most sheltered from the wind. Then he made a windbreak of his frozen sail which he propped up with a number of supports. Then he gathered a good sized pile of dry twigs and birch bark. Finally he carefully gathered up some dry leaves which he found inside a hollow log. These he tested for dryness, one by one, before he put them in their place. Finally he selected a flat, dry stone, not too rough, under the same log. This was to strike his match on.

He took out the match, but hesitated to strike. What if it were defective? What if it broke and fell into the snow? What if the tinder refused to ignite? No more boats would sail the bay till next spring. No travelers would pass on the ice for at least a month. He knew that within an hour or two his stiff limbs would be frozen. On the outcome of that match hung life or death.

Lifting the match in silent supplication to heaven, he scratched the stone gently. It failed to spark. He felt sweat break out beneath his sodden garments. Then he pulled himself together with a jerk, muttered an oath and struck the match with greater force. The flame burst out and he thrust it down among the dry leaves. Then followed an interminable interval. Finally the thin veil of white smoke was succeeded by a leaping flame. Carefully he fed the fire with birch bark, twigs and sticks until he soon had a large fire blazing. He was saved!

Toward evening it occurred to him that he ought to have his fire out on the beach where it might attract attention from the mainland. He made a roaring bonfire, fed with stumps and logs, snatching a nap intermittently.

This fire was seen from Fish Creek. When the good people of the village found Kinsey that evening, they appointed a lookout to patrol the beach and keep a watch for Stahl. About midnight the village was electrified into life by hearing this lookout shout in the street:

"Bill Stahl on Hat Island! Bonfire blazing!"

Quickly a willing crowd gathered at the pier to lend a hand in the rescue. But how were they to launch a boat? The heavy gale had packed a sheet of anchor ice into the harbor a half mile deep. This had frozen together into a solid mass in some places a foot thick. Meanwhile the storm was still roaring and it needed a good vessel to weather the seas. Saws, picks and axes were found and the whole village went to work to cut a channel. By nine o'clock the next morning a channel was cut a mile long and the best vessel in port was towed out. Sails were bent and before noon Bill Stahl saw it sweeping down on him a white-winged barge of life.

chapter seventeen

ADVENTURE ISLAND

She couldn't row and didn't know which end was bow or stern
Of any boat, and what was worse, she couldn't even learn.
But how she loved the water, crystal–clear on colored stones;
Calm and green, or ridged with white caps and the breakers
    rolling in;
Beach suppers after sunset, with red fires in the darkness,
And the lighted laughing faces, and the merry hungry din.

NORA CUNNINGHAM

BETWEEN Fish Creek and Chambers Island lie three small islands, formerly known as the Strawberries. But Bishop Kemper in his journal describing his trip from Buffalo to Green Bay in 1834, who got his information from the sailing charts of that time, calls them the Grape Islands.[1]

The two smaller islands to the North are known as Middle Island and Jack Island, but should be called Gull Islands because they are the mating place for all the gulls in the waters of Green Bay and part of Lake Michigan. In the months of March and April tens of thousands can be seen high up in the air above the islands squawking and fighting for mates while every square foot of land on these two islands seems to be occupied by female gulls sitting on the nests. In May and June the eggs hatch, and it is almost impossible to take a step without crushing an egg or molesting the brown fuzzy-feathered baby gulls that can barely stagger around.

The gulls are so numerous on these two islands that they have resisted all attempts at settlement by summer resorters. The latter have come and built expensive homes, happy in the ownership of such beauty spots. But when they came back the next year they found their buildings plastered with excrement of gulls. Undaunted the tourists scraped and scrubbed and devised cunning plots to exterminate the gulls. But when they returned the next year the gulls had plastered their objection everywhere. What mere son of man can successfully withstand such an avalanche of dung?

On the south island the situation is different. It is much larger—more than 43 acres—and the gulls are not interested in it.

In 1867 the island was bought from Door County by a dentist named E. M. Thorp. It was then a noble forest of primeval growth, and he was delighted with it. He built a two–story house on it with verandas both above and below and became the first tourist in Door County. He cleared the island of timber with the exception of a fringe around the shore. He also built a well constructed pier and a smooth driveway around the island more than a mile long. He planted a large vineyard, set out thousands of strawberry plants, and started a poultry farm with 600 hens.

But within ten years of his first appearance the story of Dr. Thorp came to an end. Apparently his resources were inadequate because his mortgage on the island was foreclosed, and he is not again heard of. But his improvements were so well constructed that they withstood the wear and tear of the weather and the ice, and for twenty years thereafter this island was considered the most beautiful place in the county.

The island now came into the possession of a lawyer in Sturgeon Bay named Dreutzer. During this time, Dr. Thorp's house burned down, his vineyard failed, the brush grew into big trees, but the strawberries survived. Miss Ella Weborg, now (1956) eighty–six years old, remembers how she and her sisters when young girls used to pick big strawberries on the island. Naturally, its name became Strawberry Island.

About 1885 the island was bought by Henry W. Leman, a lawyer in Chicago. He did not see the island when he bought it, nor did he see it for fifteen years thereafter. Then, in 1900 he decided to take a look at his island. He found it delightful and determined to organize a community club among his wealthy friends who would each have an acre for a house with waterfront. He planned to build a central kitchen and dining hall and hire a chef and assistant so that all the club members could eat together without the bother of housekeeping. Mr. Leman's wife accompanied him on this trip; the water was a little rough while crossing over to the island, and she got seasick. She mentioned this to a reporter on a Chicago paper and declared she would never again put her foot on the island. As this was printed in the paper, it was hardly calculated to promote investment in the proposed club. Mr. Leman clung to his idea and had elaborate architectural and landscape plans drawn up to create a high class club resort on the island, but owing to his absorption in legal matters he failed to make a reality of it. Finally, in 1924 Charles A. Kinney of Winnetka, Illinois, came to him with another plan for the island which appealed to him and he sold the island to Mr. Kinney.

When Mr. Kinney started his camp for boys, he was animated by a desire to give expression to that spirit of adventure which is inherent in practically every boy, and at the same time direct that powerful force toward socially desirable activities. That meant any activity which increased the freedom of an individual so long as that freedom was not at the expense of another's, the assumption being that a democratic life provides the only sound basis for the goal of individual freedom.

The first step toward the creation of his camp was the building of a ship. Mr. Kinney had sailed all over the Great Lakes in various kinds of boats. Now he planned to make a copy of a model eleven hundred years old, in which he and the boys he had gathered would sail to their Island of Adventure. He put up a large tent on the lake front in or near Winnetka, Illinois, and in the spring of 1925 he, with the help of nineteen boys, built the Serpent of the Sea. This is a somewhat smaller copy of the Gokstad vessels, built in the Ninth Century which was exhumed in Norway about fifty years ago. This is perhaps the only Viking vessel built in America.

Early in July he and the boys launched their vessel and sailed northward. It took them several days to reach their destination, but finally they arrived and took formal possession of it under the name Adventure Island.[2]

The camp's first years on the island were similar in emphasis to any pioneer's in any virgin territory. The aim of the founder was to establish the physical basis for a boys' world. The first year the only structure on the island was a partially built log lodge. The boys lived in tents. The drinking water came from the bay, carried in buckets. The second summer a hand pump was used. Then a junk car was bought for five dollars, and connected to the pump and wood saw. This released much time and energy for other jobs and to that extent raised the island standard of living.

The difference between this and most other camps for boys was that on Adventure Island all the maintenance, construction and routine work was done by the boys and not by hired help. This developed in the youngsters a sense of responsibility which was of great importance in their later adult life.

Each summer, as less time was needed on buildings and

fighting poison ivy, there was more time for cultural activities. Each proposal for a new project or activity was discussed in the daily morning assembly: Was the project essential? Was it desirable but not essential? Was it pure luxury? This invariably caused much examination of the community needs, with plenty of discussion.

Mr. Kinney was a capable director. Of commands and prohibition he had almost none: he found other ways to get the work done. For instance, the boy has not yet been born who loves to wash dishes. On Adventure Island he was under no obligation to do so. Instead, he was given the choice of (1) using his dishes unwashed, (2) washing them himself after each meal or (3) serving one day each week in a group. This simplified the problem and the burden greatly. No boy would of course use unclean dishes, and if he were to wash his own, he would become too conspicuous. The third choice, which required the least time and effort, would therefore be adopted without friction. It taught them the advantage of community effort.

One of the early difficulties was to get the boys to write home. Letter writing was an ordeal, and the boys were too busy. However, that problem was resolved without any nagging. The Sunday dinner was the high point of the week, and the order was issued that only those having the proper ticket of identity would be admitted. This ticket was a letter to Ma and Pa properly sealed and stamped. Thereafter Mother was highly gratified to find that Johnnie regularly sent her a letter once a week.

Another problem which had little attraction for the boys was to keep the camp free from rubbish. After the first year of the camp, it looked like a city park on a Sunday afternoon in midsummer. Candy wrappers lay everywhere and there seemed no way to keep the camp clean except by stern orders which would be ineffectual unless every boy was under constant observation. But Mr. Kinney thought of a better way. On the theory that the desire of one boy to keep his candy bar would be as powerful as the desire of another boy to get it, the rule was adopted that any boy who picked up a wrapper dropped by another, could claim half the bar. That simple rule gave every boy a vested interest in keeping the camp grounds free of candy wrappers. So effective was this rule in practice that when a wrapper was absentmindedly dropped, the effect upon the careless boy was as automatic as would be the result if he had thoughtlessly touched a hot stove. He seizes his candy wrapper as if it were his most precious possession. There was no coercion, no resentment, the grounds were kept clean, and the boys learned a lesson in neatness.

Another way of getting the boys to do what they at home would consider sheer drudgery, was by appealing to their imagination. Boys from nine to fourteen years of age live largely in a world of make–believe. They are always ready to play any imaginary game and love to impersonate being pirates or Indians, or soldiers or Vikings. Mr. Kinney tells of how he got the boys to enjoy weed pulling:

> When camp opened in June, yarrow or 'nose–bleed' had got such a start it threatened to completely overrun our clearing. All of us were so busy with necessary camp jobs, we couldn't do much about it. Besides, as you may guess, pulling weeds as large as yarrow is one of those tasks we always found reasons for dodging. It was only after our youngsters had produced huge quantities of weapons of war (wooden sticks for guns and swords), without an enemy to use them on that the solution of our yarrow problem began to take shape. Probably you know the molecules which make up what we call dynamite go on living together peacefully year after year unless set against each other by a detonator—a simple cap which sets free the forces which we call the explosion. Here at the camp we had youngsters literally bursting with stored up energy, armed to the teeth with weapons of destruction, and needing only an objective which would release that energy and give meaning to those weapons. In our midst we had all the elements of human dynamite that could wipe the yarrow from the face of our clearing. All we needed was a detonator. We found it in a single word. One magic word transformed the large masses of yarrow into enemy infantry, small clusters into machine gun nests, single stalks into deadly snipers. For two days the military maneuvers and strategies effected on the island would have intrigued General Eisenhower. There were frontal assaults, pincer movements, infiltration tactics and flanking movements galore, the success of each being measured solely by the number of yarrow uprooted. Hand grenade throws were counted misses unless ten of the enemy were destroyed. Older boys and counselors watching the progress of the campaign were seized with patriotic fervor. Soon many enlisted, devoting themselves mainly

to mopping up operations and carting off the dead for cremation, pausing at times long enough to wipe out a machine gun nest with a single sweep of the hand.

That single magic word that loosed the forces of destruction upon the hapless yarrow was the word *Jap*! When the campaign was over the yarrow had disappeared. With it went practically all of the war spirit. The island was again quite peaceful.

For the boys, "life on Adventure Island was like a bountiful feast." It came in courses, each leading up to the final dessert. There was no sailing until they had done their share in scraping, painting, rigging and launching the sloop. Then came the sailing and instruction in rope work and seamanship, and so on like a huge chocolate layer cake.

The menu had many things to offer. There were water sports with swimming and diving contests, water games, sailing and rowing. There were also the land sports, with games, treasure hunts, greased pole contests, overnight camping, and going on exploration trips. There was Chambers Island on the west, a land of mystery which required many days of exploration. It had a lake with two islands in it, both of which no doubt had their history. There was also another lake called Lost Lake, because it was forever getting lost in the woods and much exploration was required each summer to rediscover it. Over on the west side the wreck of a schooner was discovered and nearby was found an opening in the steep bank which suggested the remains of a moonshiner's still. The boys spent much time digging for copper kettles, bottles, and other requirements of a distiller. It did not require much imagination to picture that wreck as a schooner under full sail with a full cargo of moonshine whiskey.

Over on the east lay Peninsula Park, a vast area of public land, with eight miles of waterfront where anyone could camp. There were also countless caves which called for examination, and fine little springs which cascaded out of the limestone cliffs. To those who wanted still more of what was new and strange, there were also long cruises in their Viking boat. There was also the Dream Queen, a sturdy motor launch. These two boats made many trips along the shore of the Peninsula with camping and cooking in the wilds.

The building of a row boat or a kyack was a long continued feast. There was so much that was new and exciting about the process, but with the help of a counselor (one counselor for each group of five boys) it was finally and triumphantly accomplished.

This incomplete narrative of the boys' camp on Adventure Island gives a brief account of an important part of the history of the Peninsula. During its twenty-seven years of active existence more than 1200 boys from 36 states spent some of their most formative years here. They not only had a most pleasant time and learned handicraft and swimming, three very desirable attainments. More important was the fact that through Mr. Kinney's excellent leadership they gained a new self-reliance, and fairness in dealing with their associates. Round about in these many states they are now occupying positions of trust and usefulness as doctors, lawyers, teachers and businessmen, and it is probable that practically all of them look back upon their camp life on this island as one of the best experiences they ever had.

The woods and clearings on Adventure Island are now silent. No longer is heard the joyous shouts of young boys vying with the birds of the air in expressing their joy in life. In 1952 a violent gale at a time of very high water wrecked the pier, and the expense of building a new one was too much for Mr. Kinney. He was obliged to give up the leadership of a large group of boys. Probably another boys' camp will take over the island, because nowhere can be found a spot better suited for such a purpose, but to those who enjoyed his leadership on the island he will always be remembered for his tactful, kindly administration. He showed them that obstacles were mere challenges to their persistence. He helped them conquer their difficulties, and the resultant glow of victory gave them confidence in new and greater struggles.

-----

[1] *Wisconsin Historical Collections*, Vol. 14, pp. 394-449.

[2] Application was later made to the proper federal government bureau that the name of the island be changed from Strawberry Island to Adventure Island. On January 6, 1938, this change was made by the U.S. Geographic Board.

chapter eighteen

A STERN JUSTICE OF THE PEACE

*The Law is a sort of hocus–pocus science, that
smiles in your face while it picks yer pocket; and
the glorious uncertainty of it is of mair use to the
professors than the justice of it.*

CHARLES MACKLIN

THE American people recall with veneration the early pioneers who settled in New England more than three hundred years ago. They were courageous men and women, who will always be honored in history.

But it is doubtful if we would have enjoyed life with them because they appear to have been a morose lot of people. It was customary in those days to have quarterly town meetings. Many records of these meetings have been preserved, and they reflect a quarrelsome attitude. They abound in legal squabbles, especially trespass. One gets the impression that a man felt personally insulted to see a neighbor cross his pasture. It was the temper of the times. They had many ordinances against trivial things such as sleeping during the sermon, and smoking in public. Every town had its jail, and some poor wretch was frequently seen, his feet in the stocks, while a lot of small boys were jeering at him. Life was stern and gloomy.

Two hundred years later, similar groups of pioneers settled on this Peninsula. They experienced much the same stern experiences as their predecessors in New England, but they met their problems with greater cheerfulness, and they were not at all quarrelsome. They needed no jails until their communities had grown into cities, and even then they did not humiliate a culprit by putting him in the stocks.

However, long ago when Ephraim was the only post office in all that part of the Peninsula lying north of Fish Creek, there was in that large area a Justice of the Peace who seemed to be a reincarnation of some stern Boston ancestor. His name was Jasper

Morefield, and he has already been mentioned in the chapter on Chambers Island. He produced the first preserved record of a pioneer court trial on the Peninsula.

It happened that a man somewhere back in the woods, unknown to the Justice, was accused of assault and battery upon his wife. He was summoned before the Justice of the Peace, who hated sinners of all descriptions. This was a new kind of entertainment, and a large crowd of people was present.

The Justice called the Court to order. Then he addressed the accused:

"You are charged with having assaulted and battered your wife, Mabel. Do you plead guilty or not guilty?"

The defendant, a good-looking man with a twinkle in his eyes replied:

"Not guilty; I have made no assault on my wife, and her name is not Mabel."

Suspiciously the Justice pondered this answer. (The culprit denies that he assaulted his wife, but does not deny that he had assaulted Mabel, the woman named in the complaint. Evidently this smooth talking fellow is a cunning rascal). Sternly the Justice demanded:

"Do you mean to say that, in open defiance of the laws of God and man, you are also living with a female who is not your wife?"

"I said nothing of the kind. I denied that I had beaten my wife, and her name is not Mabel but Anna Marie. I would no more think of striking her than to strike my old mother. You can ask her yourself. She is right here."

The Justice, confident that he had discovered a shameless reprobate, called the wife to the witness chair. He asked:

"How long has this been going on?"

"I don't understand what you mean."

"What do you know about this woman, Mabel?"

The young woman, highly indignant, replied:

"I know nothing about any woman named Mabel. And I think it's real mean of you to insinuate that my husband—that my husband—" Here she broke down and cried.

"Now, now," said the Justice pompously. "Take it easy. Nobody is going to hurt you. But watch your tongue or you will be fined $5.00 for contempt of court. Now tell me: has your husband ever beaten you?"

"He has never beaten me! And he is a much better man than you who sit there and publicly insult decent people." She was trembling with excitement.

The Justice banged his gavel on the kitchen table which served as desk. "Five dollars fine for contempt of court! Take your seat!" Then he turned to the defendant: "Who is this woman Mabel, whom you are accused of battering?"

"I know of no woman by the name of Mabel. The only Mabel I know is my cow by that name."

There was a loud laugh, which the Justice took as a personal insult. He banged his gavel fiercely on the table and shouted: "I'll have no more of this or the constable will clear the courtroom."

Then he turned to the defendant: "Is this cow the woman, I mean the Mabel, whom you are accused of having assaulted?"

"You got that all wrong, Judge. Mabel assaulted me. She is the worst cow on the Peninsula to kick over the milk pail. So when she kicks the milk pail, I give her a crack on the shin. That's the only kind of reasoning a cow can understand."

The Justice looked satisfied: "At last the defendant has admitted that he is guilty of cruelty to animals. The court will stand adjourned for fifteen minutes while I prepare my verdict. Adjourn!"

The Justice was left alone in the room. He felt that he had not shown the keen discernment which he prided himself on possessing. These farmers had actually laughed at him, and as for that young woman—but why get tangled up in a discussion with a woman? But he would write a decision which would show these simpletons that they cannot take liberties with a dispenser of justice. So he wrote the following verdict and commitment, called the court to order and read it to the constable:

"A. B. having made complaint that C. D. did assault and beat his wife Mabel, and the testimony presented at the trial proved clearly that the prisoner is guilty of cruelty to animals which covers both offenses:

"Therefore it is the judgment of this court that the prisoner be committed to the county jail for the term of sixty days, and the jailer is directed to feed the said C. D. on bread and water, and may the Lord have mercy on your poor soul!"

The Justice read this verdict with audible satisfaction. He felt that it was proper punishment of an unrepentant evildoer, but it ended with a benignant hope that the sinner would not suffer everlasting punishment. Then he turned to the constable:

"You will take this judgment and the prisoner and deliver both to the sheriff in Green Bay."

The constable, a scrubby little man, looked at the defendant who was almost twice as big as he. Then he shook his head and said: "I aint got time. I gotta go home and milk my cow." More laughter.

The angry Justice looked aghast: "What! You refuse to do your duty? Five dollars fine for contempt of court!"

The defendant yawned: "I guess the constable has the right idea." Then he turned to the Justice:

"By the way, Judge, when you get those five-dollar bills collected for contempt of court, bring them to me and I will give you Mabel. Then you can see what you can do with a kicking cow. Come on, Anna Marie, you Norskie girl! We'll go home to Mabel."

Someone outside started clapping, and the other followed suit. Soon everybody was roaring with laughter. To them it was a screaming comedy, but to the mortified Justice it was a tragedy. To be made the object of public derisive laughter in his own house and courtroom was more than he could bear. He would have liked to send every man in the crowd to jail for at least a year, but as this was impossible, he drove everyone out of his house.

An Obstinate Man

There was another legal case (not in Ephraim) which is also famous in the annals of Door County.

There was a German immigrant named Didrik M. He could speak no English, but he bought a tract of woodland and cleared some acres. Being a hard worker, he and his wife prospered and eventually built a new frame house. When he paid the carpenter, they had an argument concerning an item of seven dollars, which Didrik refused to pay, and the carpenter threatened to go to the law about it.

Before long a legal notice was served on Didrik that the carpenter's claim would be heard by the County Judge on a certain day and hour. But Didrik was not worried. He assured his neighbors that the carpenter was a liar, and the Judge would soon find it out. You can't fool a sharp judge. Having complete confidence in the keenness of the Judge, he did not go near the courtroom.

When the case was called, the Judge looked for the defendant. He was not there. As the claim was not contested, Didrik was informed that he was to pay the Judge sixteen dollars to cover claim and costs.

When Didrik heard this he was amazed and highly indignant. He told his friends that it was plain that the Judge was a nitwit, or, more likely, he had been bribed by that crooked carpenter. He would not pay it! No, not a cent! Then he learned that he could appeal to the Circuit Court. Didrik was mollified; he made the appeal. Now that the case would be heard by a judge who knew the law from A to Z, he felt confident that he would win.

But when the case eventually came up, Didrik was not present. This was partly because of his inability to speak or understand English, and partly because of his confidence in the Judge. Nor would he hire a lawyer. Why should an innocent man need a lawyer? Instead, he with his wife and some friends sat on the sidewalk, drinking beer out of a pail, happy in the thought that he would be vindicated, and that rascally carpenter would be sentenced to a year of hard labor in a stone quarry.

However, Didrik was born on an evil day. Judgment was entered against him by default, and the debt and costs now amounted to about a hundred dollars. Didrik swore he would not pay a cent, whereupon the sheriff was ordered to evict Didrik and his family out of the house until the court's claim was paid. Didrik learned of this and thinking his livestock would be seized, he secreted the animals in a swamp, where he also took refuge.

When the sheriff arrived with several assistants, he found Didrik's wife standing by a huge kettle of boiling water, and she and the children began shouting and howling like lunatics in the belief that if the sheriff was unable to make himself heard, the document would be void and of no effect. As the sheriff approached, Didrik's wife plunged her dipper into the boiling water, prepared to give him a scalding welcome, but the sheriff was too quick for her. He held her while the order was read and then his assistants emptied the house of all its furnishings. No sooner was that done when it began to rain, and the household goods, bedding, furniture, etc. were thoroughly soaked, as were also the minions of law.

Debarred from their home, Didrik and his family now took refuge in the barn. Didrik was as obstinate as ever, although he found it was an expensive indulgence. After pondering the problem from every angle, he decided that justice was unobtainable in Door County. His only hope was to complain to the governor of the State. He would go in person, for the Governor was no doubt a man of education who could speak the great German language as well as he himself could.

But there was the problem of transportation. It cost a lot of money to go to Madison, and Didrik had very little. Moreover it was unwise to go by train because, if it was noised abroad that he had taken a train, those evil-minded men in Sturgeon Bay would guess his intention, and they would not doubt poison the mind of the Governor by telegraph before Didrik could get there. No, he would take an ox, as if he were going to the market with a surplus piece of livestock. Thus he would fool them.

Well satisfied that he was as crafty as any of them, he set out with his ox. They were good company because, having much the same intelligence, they understood each other. The ox was honest and hardworking like himself and did not object to carrying his master part of the time. At night they laid down side by side and thus saved the cost of lodgings. Didrik regretted that he could not eat the grass of the wayside like his companion and thus save his money, but then, he could eat the ox if necessary. The ox was therefore good insurance. Who knew but he might be robbed by some rogue among the people that buzzed along on every highway. In such case he could sell the ox and keep out of jail. Musing thus, he and his ox traveled along, day after day and week after week for two hundred miles, until he saw the lofty walls of the State Capitol.

Unfortunately, no record has been preserved of his interview with the Governor. But there is reason to believe that his Excellency, upon hearing about the gang of ruthless thieves up in Sturgeon Bay, was greatly shocked, and promised to clap the entire lot in jail. Nothing less could have induced Didrik to make him a present of the ox, and it is known that he left it in Madison. We may therefore assume that the Governor, confronted with such generosity, would "set them up" with a hearty hand. Only this can explain the befuddled condition of Didrik, who, instead of returning the way he had come, took a northwest course, and did not discover his error until he reached La Crosse, two hundred miles off his way home. Eventually he reached home, a much travelled man. If the Governor made him any promises, he did not make good on them, which, unfortunately, is the way of politicians the world over.

Didrik was much disappointed when he reached his home. He found that his neighbors no longer looked upon his boastful defiance of the court as staunch independence, but as plain stupidity. He therefore rigged up a 'prairie schooner' into which he loaded his most necessary possessions and his wife and children. Thus, with two oxen in front and two cows behind, he set forth toward a nebulous region called Dakota.

chapter nineteen

THE CHRONICLES OF LIBERTY GROVE

A land of Heart's Desire
Where beauty has no ebb, decay no flood,
But joy is wisdom, time an endless song
WILLIAM B. YEATS

THE earliest event in the history of Wisconsin of which we have any record or tradition took place at 'The Door,' north of the town of Liberty Grove. It probably antedates the visit of Jean Nicolet by a few years and was a very vivid memory among the Potawatomi. Father Allouez alludes to it, and it is mentioned by some of the earliest pre-settlement travelers.

To the savage youth of the Winnebago, the first mark of distinction was an enemy scalp. He who did not have one was a 'sissie' without honor. Knowing nothing of art, culture or riches, their only standard of greatness was the number of scalps they could call their own. Their outlook was therefore much the same as that of the tiger and the wildcat.

Impelled by this bloody aspiration for honor among the youngsters, the Winnebago set out from their village at Red Banks near the base of the Peninsula, to exterminate the Potawatomi. They encamped on the extreme end of the Peninsula to lay plans for finding the Potawatomi who had their village somewhere on the islands beyond.

The Potawatomi were early apprised of the coming of their enemies. After hurried deliberation, the chiefs decided that their only hope was to take the offensive and attack the Winnebago in the rear at such a time when they might be unprepared for attack. Three spies were therefore sent across the strait with instructions to build a signal fire at a certain spot, by which the Potawatomi would be guided at the right time in making a landing in the night.

Unfortunately these spies fell into the hands of the Winnebago, who subjected them to torture. Rather than reveal their mission, two of the spies perished at the stake. The third was finally bribed to reveal his secret.

With great glee the crafty Winnebago now prepared to turn this stratagem to the destruction of their enemies. The next night the signal fire was lit and the Winnebago took their stations in a semicircle a few feet back from the beach. The Potawatomi came, not expecting any attack here, and their destruction would have been complete if the young hell-hounds had restrained their eagerness. But so eager were they for the precious scalps that they attacked too early. The Potawatomi now saw that they had been led into a trap and most of them escaped in their canoes.

Much disgusted with this turn of events, almost the entire force of Winnebago set out in their canoes as soon as daylight came. Their purpose, no doubt, was to pursue the Potawatomi until the last man was killed. But they knew nothing of the dangers of this strait. Here, frequently, the current runs in one direction while the wind blows from another, making a choppy sea in which the round-bottomed canoes become unmanageable. For a whole day the old men of the Winnebago stood on the bluff, seeing one canoe after another turn over, their occupants struggling in the water. Not one returned. They took this an an omen that they must never attempt to cross that Door of Death, which it was afterward called.[1]

Evidently this great event in the history of the Potawatomi urged some artist among them to paint a pictorial memento of this bloody encounter. Col. Stambaugh, in his *Report to the Federal Government*, says that in 1831 he saw "on the face of Table Bluff, fifteen or twenty feet above the surface of the water, figures of Indians and canoes painted in Indian fashion, which must have been done with much difficulty."[2]

In 1856 this old painting was repainted by a man named Charles Schulten who lived in a house on top of the bluff. Two years previously a group of Green Bay promoters believed they had discovered a rich marble deposit in the bluff, and they hired a number of men to open a quarry. A large pier was built, a village was laid out, and the quarrying proceeded. But their hopes faded within a week—the marble proved to be in too thin a layer to make the quarry profitable. Schulten was one of the few who remained there. He had a small sailing vessel and did some trading among the fishermen on Washington Island. Finally he, too, departed.

The real founder of Liberty Grove and its first permanent settler was a Norwegian named Jasper Morefield who is described in the preceding chapter. He was a member of the first group who settled at Ephraim in 1853, and his farm was two miles due east from the village. Pietistic, stern and domineering, he was a terror to evildoers because he was Justice of the Peace, which was the most profitable town office in those days. While he had plenty of trouble with the people of Ephraim, this was not of a legal nature. But the boundaries of the town of Gibraltar, of which Ephraim was a part, took in all Door County north of Sturgeon Bay except Washington Island, and there were many malefactors because whiskey was very cheap, and Morefield was righteous but very stern, and he hated sinners of all descriptions.

But Morefield was far from happy even if he wielded the rod. He was convinced that he was the best qualified man to hold the office of Chairman, Clerk, Assessor, Treasurer, et cetera, but did the people appreciate his willingness to sacrifice his time and talents for their good? No, indeed! There were always some simpletons who wanted to crowd in and handle affairs they did not understand. Stupid ingratitude, that seemed to be the most common characteristic of his neighbors. Even his own fellow members of the Ephraim congregation lay awake nights conspiring against him. His disappointment grew from day to day, and then came that aggravating wife-beating case—

What should he do now? That was a difficult question, but he was fully resolved about what he would not do: he would have nothing to do with that illiterate mob known as the town of Gibraltar, where there was no respect for law and order. But here he was, tied down by his farm.

Then a bright idea struck him. Why not create a new town of which he would be the father, counsellor and chief magistrate? North of him for ten—fifteen miles stretched a vast and nameless area of timbered land without a living soul, but which no doubt would soon be settled. There was an idea!

But could a municipal township be organized without inhabitants? Morefield feared not, but then it was not entirely without residents. He lived there, and if the boundary line was drawn right up to Ephraim's back yards, the new town would include three Norwegians who could perhaps be persuaded to join on the promise of becoming officeholders in the new town. There were also two or three Germans south of him, but they were not citizens and therefore had nothing to say.

Morefield succeeded in carrying out his plan although it took much time and there was one big fly in the ointment. The three Norwegians were obstinate and threatened to wreck the whole plan unless they, being the majority, could write the slate. This was a bitter pill for Morefield to swallow; but he had to take it. The result was that the three Norwegians took all the offices except that of Justice of the Peace, which was of no value as the town had almost no inhabitants. However, they accepted his name for the new town—Liberty Grove—by which he meant that liberty, the Morefield brand, had here found a home.

The first chairman was Ingebret Torgerson who preempted the flat just south of Sister Bay where now is the County Convalescent Home. As this is now a part of the thriving village of Sister Bay, he thus became the first settler within its limits. His son, Hans, was educated to become a missionary among the Eskimo in Alaska. In 1885, shortly after he arrived at Bethel, near the mouth of the Kuskokvim River, he was drowned, but his body was recovered and buried in the frozen ground. Fifty years later the mission chose a new cemetery, and the body of the first missionary was moved to this location. On opening the casket it was found that the dead man looked as natural as if he had just died.

Contrary to Morefield's expectations, the town had a very slow growth. This was because of the Civil War, during which time there was no immigration.

In the first company of Moravians who settled in Ephraim in 1853 was Gotfried Matthe, from Bavaria. In 1857, when he with the other members of the congregation went to Green Bay to sign the contract with Mr. Gray (see page 111), he met some German immigrants from East Germany who were looking for land. They were Wilhelm Dorn and Christian Hempel and they settled near Morefield in the future Liberty Grove. These two were the cause of a large immigration of people from Hinter Pomern who after the war settled in Liberty Grove. These people came from a section in Prussia which was chiefly occupied by big estates. Here they worked as laborers, and were slaves in all but the name. The girls received three dollars per year and board, while some of the able bodied men received as high as twenty-four dollars a year and board. The board was largely potatoes, with meat twice a week. Water or buttermilk was their drink, with black coffee on holidays. The married men were paid twenty cents per day and boarded themselves. The day's labor started at three o'clock in the morning. If they had a piece of land, it was unlawful for them to kill a rabbit that might be nibbling their garden truck. The rabbit must be protected while the Graf and his guests at intervals galloped proudly over the tenant's small field on a hunt. If at such a time the laborer's dog barked at the passing horsemen, he was shot down at once, while the laborer stood by humbly, his cap in hand.

The greatest trouble that these early settlers had to contend with was a lack of water. They could not dig any wells because the ground a foot below the surface was a solid mass of limestone. Nor could they drill a well because there was not yet any drilling machines. Those who had no cattle got along by help of the rain barrel, but those who had cows were obliged to fetch water from the bay. Among the early German settlers was Carl Seiler, a son-in-law of Gotfried Matthe, the first German on the Peninsula. His farm was high up on the ridge a mile and a half from the Ephraim harbor. Carl Seiler, Jr. whom I knew well told me that he made a rough wooden wheelbarrow on which he placed a half barrel. This half-barrel he trundled up the steep hill through the woods every day with water from the bay. On washdays he made two trips.

After the end of the Civil War there was a big upswing in business which created a market for cordwood. In Marinette were many sawmills which paid their men one dollar per day (twelve hours). Someone reported that in Door County men were wanted to cut cordwood for a dollar per cord (128 cubic feet). This resulted in a large influx of men, mostly Swedes. They were big strapping fellows, working in pairs, chopping wood from fall to fall, often four cords per day, drinking, fighting and eating. Among them was a Swedish giant by the name of John A. Johnson, but commonly known as Long John. He was doubly famous, being not only the champion woodchopper, but also the biggest eater ever heard of. James Hanson, a storekeeper in Sister Bay, once had a case containing five dozen eggs standing on his counter. To test Long John's appetite he wagered five dollars that Long John could not eat them up in one meal. Long John thoughtfully surveyed the big box of eggs, examined the five-dollar bill critically and accepted the wager on condition that he be allowed a pint of whiskey. This was granted. Methodically, like a machine, he consumed the entire lot of sixty eggs, drank his whiskey, pocketed his money, and then went home. It is said he finished the day with a loaf of bread and a pan of milk.

Long John lived north of Sister Bay, near the place where Professor J. C. M. Hansen later built his house. The cliff at this point is more than two hundred feet high above the bay and its upper half is perpendicular. Here, in the water, outside, Long John had a pound net, and one night as he was returning home he went out to the edge of the cliff to see if the lantern on his net was burning properly. As usual, he had had a few drinks more than the proper limit, and this caused him to take one step too many—into open space! Down he hurtled and his end on the jagged rocks below seemed certain. But luckily he hit the top of a tall balsam. His descent was so swift that he broke all the limbs on one side of the tree. This checked his fall and he reached the bottom without broken bones. His hat was still tight on his head, but his clothes were in rags and he had many bruises. Painfully Long John made his way home, firmly resolved to cut out whiskey forever.

However, these roisterers were not many, nor continued long in that role. The earliest of these Swedish settlers, or at least one of the earliest, was Andrew Seaquist from Dalarne who is commonly considered the father of the settlement. The little church at Ephraim and its resident pastor was the magnet that drew many pioneers to northern Door County. Seaquist also took land here in 1868, a mile east of the Anderson pier. But the land he had chosen was found to be too shallow for successful farming, and after eight years he took a homestead two or three miles north of the present Sister Bay.

Seaquist was a model pioneer. Cheerful, intelligent, helpful and deeply religious, he was highly respected. He was also famous for his strength. Once, he and two other men were cutting logs, and the talk turned to feats of strength. It appeared from the boastful talk of his two companions that they were both tremendously strong. To settle the question of who was the stronger, Seaquist suggested that they lift one end of the large log they had just cut. However, neither of them was able to lift it. Then Seaquist told one of the men to sit upon the log, whereupon he raised the end with the man astraddle of it.

Seaquist was also very ingenious and he spent his spare time in contriving various labor saving machines. Like everyone else he begrudged the time spent in carrying or hauling water from the bay. To lessen this waste of time, he built a wooden railway which ran down a steep incline from his house to the beach about a hundred feet below. The tracks were wooden poles laid lengthwise on cross-arms attached to posts set in the ground. The 'car' was a large water-tight box on wheels with an automatic valve in the bottom. When the box reached the bottom of the track it quickly filled with water and was then hauled up by a rope attached to a vertical windlass operated by a man pushing a capstan bar.

Seaquist had a friend from Sweden named John Anderson. He was a lay preacher and held religious services in many log cabins, and through the efforts of these two men a Baptist congregation was organized. This proved successful and the Swedish baptist church at Sister Bay became one of the leading churches on the peninsula. Their Men's choir is famous far and wide.

When the above mentioned John Anderson came to Green Bay to join his friend Andrew Seaquist, he had no other instructions than to follow the west shore of the Peninsula until he came to Ephraim. All his material possessions were packed in a small box or trunk, twenty-six inches long, and with this on his back he trudged on, foot-sore and weary. When he reached Little Sturgeon Bay he got into trouble with the Indians and thought his end had come. Happily, no blood was shed. He made the circuit around the ten-mile-long Sturgeon Bay and continued northward and eventually reached Ephraim, very glad at last to drop his chest on the ground.[3]

The northern part of Liberty Grove is inhabited mostly by people of Norwegian ancestry and is also an outgrowth of Ephraim. Ellison Bay is named after John Eliason, an early Ephraimite who settled here about 1860. In that year or possibly earlier came Elias Gill whose memory is preserved in the name of the village Gills Rock. His deed from the Government is dated 1860. He appears to have been connected with the group which started a marble quarry at Door Bluff, but very little is known about him. In 1902 Gills Rock had a post office which continued for more than thirty years.

The first farmer in the Gills Rock area was Avli Simonson from Lille-elvedalen in eastern Norway. He was one of the employees of the marble quarry company, and when that came to a sudden end, he settled on a tract of land just east of Gills Rock. Here he lived practically a hermit for twenty years until his tragic end in 1877. One morning in February, a young woman from Sturgeon Bay came to him with the request to be taken across "the Door" to Washington Island where she was to teach the newly started school. She had expected to drive across on the ice, but this had broken up, and the strait was now open. As Simonson was a fisherman as well as a farmer, he set out with her, accompanied by his son Alfred. They arrived at the island about noon, and as the wind was favorable, they immediately started on their homeward journey.

They had not gone far before a heavy snowstorm out of the northwest descended upon them, shutting out all vision except immediately around the boat. Soon they found themselves surrounded by huge ice floes. They lowered the sail and, bending to the oars, they attempted to extricate themselves from the grinding ice cakes, two feet thick. again and again they found long lanes of water which promised escape only to find they were blind pockets.

So often had they turned and twisted in the blinding snowstorm that they no longer knew in which direction they were going. The storm seemed to buffet them from every quarter of the compass. They remembered, however, that the wind, upon leaving the island, was from the northwest, and that should bring them out into Lake Michigan, where the ice floes would open up. They did not know that the wind had changed into the northeast. Finally came night with bitter cold, and, after many hours of struggling with the oars, they were powerless to handle their ice–laden boat any longer. They could only stare through the darkness hoping to see a headland or hear the surge of the waves upon some beach. And while they drifted and stared, the numbness of death stole upon them, until it changed the keen look of their eyes into a glassy stare.

About six weeks later, the ice began to break up and was driven southward into Lake Michigan close to shore. One day, William Sanderson, the lightkeeper at Cana Island, chanced to look out and saw a boat drifting by imbedded in an ice floe. In the boat sat two men, and their positions were so natural that he at first thought they were alive. Taking his binoculars, he saw that they did not move, and soon he realized that the two mariners were dead. In the stern sat an old man, slightly bent forward, with his arms folded, resting on his knees. His face, with the expression of one straining every nerve to see or hear something, was turned toward shore. On his cap was frozen snow, and from his gray hair and beard hung icicles. The young man, like his father, sat huddled up, waiting for the morning light. They had abandoned the oars, but not hope. The boat drifted by, and the occupants were never seen again.

In this extreme northern corner of the Peninsula there lived a man who through his inspiring personality and appreciation of nature had a strong influence on many men and women in Wisconsin. This was Jens Jensen, the Henry Thoreau of the West, but a greater interpreter of nature than the latter. He was not among the pioneers but came here in the 1920s. Previously he had gained a high reputation as Superintendent of the West Chicago Park Commission and as a landscape architect of several big estates. In this capacity he introduced a new line of landscaping: he rejected the use of exotic plants, and his preference for natural rather than formal design was a highly pleasing innovation in landscape planning. He was the founder and chief promoter of a society of nature lovers with the name of "Friends of our Native Landscape" which held many inspiring and profitable open air meetings in the northern end of the Peninsula and elsewhere in the State.

One of Mr. Jensen's chief desires was to create a school of domestic arts and handicraft, and to this end he erected several large and pleasing buildings. But old age was coming on and in 1953 he died, 91 years old, without seeing the fruition of his hopes. The Wisconsin Farm Bureau has now leased his buildings and they have become a small summer academy of learning for people interested in the humanities.

Liberty Grove is the largest municipal area on the Peninsula, and although it was the latest to be settled, it will not be long before it will also be the richest, with the exception of the city of Sturgeon Bay. Most of its area is excellent farming land, and it is the most favorable part of the Peninsula for growing cherries and other fruits. In addition it has twenty–five miles of water front which makes it most attractive for the summer cottagers.

---

[1] This catastrophe is first mentioned in print by Samuel A. Storrow in 1817, see Wis. His. So. *Collections*, VI, 166; also by Col. C. Stambaugh in 1831, *Collections* XV, 423-4; and John Brink, a government surveyor in 1834. He gives a detailed account of it about as told above. See H. R. Holand, *History of Door County*, 1917, pp. 39-40, note 6. These men must all have gotten this information from the Indians, because their reports all antedate the coming of the earliest settlers.

[2] "Report on Wisconsin Territory," Wis. His. So. *Collections*, Vol. XV, p. 424.

[3] This little trunk is still in the possession of his grandaughter, Mrs. Gustav Carlson.

chapter twenty

THE RISE AND FALL OF ROWLEY'S BAY

I am monarch of all I survey;
From the center all round to the sea
My right there is none to dispute;
I am lord of the fowl and the brute.

WILLIAM COWPER

FAR away, in the most obscure corner of the Peninsula, lies Rowley's Bay. It is the last little cove of Lake Michigan to the northward, dipping deep into a land of reeds and rushes, of mink and muskrat, of marsh, marigolds and fragrant balsams. At the head of the bay is a sluggish lagoon, masquerading under the name of Mink River. Here the pickerel in June are reckless, and the black bass bite with abandon. Aside from these annual piscatorial activities, Rowleys Bay is as quiet and secluded as the North Pole, as indolent as the sunrise of a June morning.

But the name of Rowleys Bay has not always been the synonym of peace and pickerel. There was a time when the commercial possibilities of Rowleys Bay were eagerly discussed from Chicago to Tacoma, and glowing lithographs eloquently describing financial investments at Rowleys Bay, possible and impossible, were scattered by the tens of thousands. But we are anticipating.

Away back in the early morning of Door County's history, there was a querulous old man by the name of Peter Rowley. He was one of that eccentric tribe of western pioneers who feel themselves crowded to suffocation if they have a neighbor within a day's journey. In 1836 he became oppressed by the imaginary congestion of the little frontier post at Fort Howard. He packed his possessions into a boat and fled northward past an uninhabited wilderness. Forty miles away he came to Sturgeon Bay, as quiet and undisturbed as the morning after creation. Here at the mouth of the bay, on the west side, he pitched his tent, thinking he had left civilization behind forever.

But an evil fate pursued him. After a few years other eccentric pioneers followed his trail and settled in secluded coves not many miles away. On a clear day he could see the smoke from their cabin chimneys rise above the tree-tops of the distant horizon. This was intolerable. Once more he fled from congestion.

He followed the shore of the Peninsula to its extreme northern point. Not a living soul of white origin had settled here in this north end of the peninsula, and Peter Rowley grew hopeful. Then, as his boat was bobbing on the waves of Death's Door passage, his keen old eyes discerned the boat of a lonesome fisherman who lived at Detroit Harbor, five miles away. Sadly he rounded the point into Lake Michigan.

Where should he go? To the south of him lay Chicago and the pioneer camps of Milwaukee and Sheboygan. Restless fellows would soon push up the shore. In that direction lay no hope of peace. To the north was the impertinent fisherman on Washington Island. Where should he go?

Then he discovered Rowleys Bay. He examined it carefully and believed he had discovered an oasis in the desert of civilization. Swamps to the north of him, swamps to the south of him, the great lake in front of him. Here surely was a spot where he might live and die in peace. Contentedly he reared his cabin on the shore and ate his venison and his fish. As far as we know he lived and died contentedly, his name preserved to posterity as the discoverer of Rowleys Bay.

Strictly speaking, Rowleys Bay was not discovered by Peter Rowley. A few years before he began to fish in Mink River, other white men camped there for several weeks and ate of its fish until they loathed the sight of it. The story of this adventure is as follows:

In 1834 northern Door County was surveyed by a man named John Brink and his assistants. At one time in the fall of that year he found that provisions were running low, and a messenger by the name of James McCabe was sent to Hamilton Arndt's trading post at Green Bay for supplies. Mounted on a trusty pony, named Polly, the messenger started off with instructions to join Brink and his men at a certain place near Death's Door in three weeks.

The trip to the Indian trader's was made without incident, but on his return, when not far from the surveyor's camp, he was taken prisoner by a band of Indians, who thought he was a deserter from the army. McCabe was about one hundred yards from the pack horse at the time, having stopped in a grove to camp overnight. When the Indians seized him, they did not know that he had a horse with him, and they would not, or rather could not, let him explain, as he did not understand their speech.

The Indians were sometimes called upon to assist the soldiers in running down deserters, and when they were of any assistance, they were always supplied with a little whiskey for their services. With the prospect of getting some "fire-water" for the return of McCabe to the government fort, they watched him carefully. The more he remonstrated, the more the Indians believed he was a deserter.

McCabe, therefore, not knowing how soon the red men intended to burn him at the stake, was compelled to go with the Indians, while Polly, with the pack of provisions was left grazing in the little grove. Brink writes:

> "Those fool Injuns actually made McCabe carry a canoe five miles across the peninsula, and he was taken to Hamilton Arndt's headquarters, where the Injun trader had some difficulty in making the varmints believe that McCabe was not a deserter from the army.
>
> "All this time, we of course, were waiting for the packman at the place appointed, and were without anything to eat, having waited two days more than the time appointed and lived during that time on nothing but hope. Still no packman, and we had no firearms to kill game, even if any could have been found. At the expiration of two days you can imagine that we were pretty hungry. We concluded to get something to eat when the third day rolled around, and we moved on toward the lake and discovered a little creek running into it.
>
> "As luck would have it the stream was full of fish, and we had no trouble in catching all the big fellows we wanted. There was one man in our party who was so hungry that he didn't even wait to cook the fish. He just scraped off the scales and chewed the stuff up almost before the finny creature was dead.
>
> "For eleven days we lived on nothing but roasted fish. It was fish for breakfast, fish for dinner, and fish for supper, and you had better believe we were sick of fish before we got through with our experience. We had no salt or anything to flavor the stuff with. It was simply roast fish day after day. It sickened me of fish and I haven't eaten any since. It kept life in us, however. When relief did come it came unexpectedly.
>
> "The twelfth day, when we arose to begin the day

with a fish breakfast, we heard the tinkling of a bell, and on the crest of a little hill we saw old Polly. As soon as she discovered us she came galloping up, neighing as if overjoyed to see us. She was so pleased to see us that she actually laughed. I could see her eyes blaze with delight, and as she rubbed her nose against my shoulder she appeared to be brimful of happiness.

"The pack containing the pork and beans and flour was still strapped to her back, and you can bet all you have got that we had a good square meal that day. As far as we could learn, Polly had gone back to the place from where McCabe had started with her, and, not finding us there, had wandered around the country following our trail, and finally discovered us.

"The next day McCabe appeared, having been released as soon as the Indian trader explained matters to his captors. He expected to find a rather sickly looking lot of men, and if he didn't find what he thought he would, he certainly did find a fishy crowd, for we were covered with scales and smelled like the inside of a whale."

The history of Rowleys Bay for the next twenty—thirty years is a blank as far as human interest is concerned. Then the lumber companies found their way thither. Camps were built where the men sat in their bunks and swapped stories of the woods. A pier was built, and huge cargoes of telegraph poles, ties, and cordwood were shipped. The work of destruction pursued the even tenor of its ways.

In 1876 S. A. Rogers arrived from New York. He had a farm in Illinois which, through the medium of a real estate agent, he traded off for a vast acreage of land and water at Rowleys Bay. Unfortunately, the land and water were mixed together after a somewhat haphazard formula, constituting a 4000-acre tract of swamp land covered with a pretty good stand of cedar. Being a man of energy, Mr. Rogers built a large sawmill which sometimes scaled a run of seven or eight million feet of lumber in a season. He built a commodious pier along which nearly always lay a vessel or two loading. He also built a store and other buildings for the accommodation of the growing business of the place.

All this business centered in the cedars which were large enough to cut. But there were millions of cedars too small even to make a fence post. Of what use were they? Much cogitation on this subject followed.

About 1885 a man was found who solved this puzzle. This was
J. H. Mathews of Milwaukee, who understood the process of
making cedar oil. He built a factory on the northeast side of
Rowleys Bay, where he employed about twenty-five men. Cedar
twigs were cut and placed in a tank or retort. The dimensions of
this retort were four by twenty-two by eight feet, the top being
convex. The steam from this retort was taken up into a four–inch
pipe and cooled and conducted through a succession of pipes of
decreasing diameters placed zigzag fashion in a bed of a small
creek fed by cold spring water. After the steam had meandered
through these cold pipes for a distance of about two hundred feet,
it trickled into a receiving tank in the shape of limpid oil which
sold at eight dollars per gallon. For two years the business was
pushed and paid well.

Mr. Mathews was a man of enterprise and ambition. He
reasoned that if good money could be made out of waste timber
products in such an inaccessible place as Rowleys Bay, much more
could be made if the business was enlarged and established in a
more central place. Accordingly, he pulled up his cooling pipes and
moved to Marshfield, Wisconsin, where he undertook to make
wood alcohol. He promptly failed in business, and with this his
part in the history of Door County is finished.

About 1892 Mr. Rogers found an opportunity for trading off
several hundred acres of his swampy estate for a farm in Missouri.
Through another trade this tract of swamp land was transferred
to a Mr. Ditlef C. Hanson, a thrifty little Dane of Tacoma,
Washington. In the course of time Mr. Hanson came to inspect his
purchase.

He found the land too low for farming, too high for fishing. The
timber was all gone. It was too inaccessible for a frog preserve, and
muck was drug on the market. What was it good for?

Mr. Hanson had one great ambition in life. He had seen and
heard of other men laying out townsites, waxing rich by the sale of
building lots, and famous by having the town named after them.
He reasoned that since his Rowleys Bay possession was fit for
nothing else, if it was not created in vain it must have been
intended for a townsite. True, it was wet, but Mr. Hanson, being a
man of reading, recalled that a wet foundation was no barrier to
the most shining successes in city building. Chicago was built in a
marsh. Venice was built in a lagoon, and Shanghai was originally
a frog pond. A townsite then it was to be, forever to immortalize its
founder, Ditlef C. Hanson. He debated whether to call it "Ditlef's

Hope" or "Hansonburg," but finally rejected both as lacking in
resonance and dignity. Instead, he named it Tacoma Beach, which
was both resonant and reminiscent of the city of his home. This
important point being settled, he immediately sought a printer.

Townsite lithographs are wonderful things. In 1836 a city was
platted about where the present city of Kewaunee now is, and
large fortunes were made and lost by means of an eloquent
lithograph. A nomadic fur trader had shortly before picked up
something in the swamp at the mouth of Kewaunee River, which
his imagination had transmuted into gold. Rumor reached the
ears of some enterprising promoters who proceeded to lay out a
townsite. Not a settler at that time lived within thirty miles of the
place, but that did not prevent the project from becoming a great
transient success. A number of men of national fame became
interested, among them being such men as John Jacob Astor,
Governor Doty, Governor Beals, Judge Morgan L. Martin, Hon.
Sanford E. Church, General Ruggles, Colonel Crocker and Salmon
P. Chase, later Chief Justice of the Supreme Court of the United
States. For a while there was much debate in the minds of great
financiers whether to invest in Chicago or Kewaunee real estate.
In April 1836, a forty-acre tract in the swamp was sold to
Governor Doty for $15,000. Judge Martin had entered a tract of
eighty acres in the swamp from the government. This he sold
within a few days to his distinguished colleague, Chief Justice
Chase, for $38,000. These and other lands were subdivided into
lots and on September 2, 1836, a grand auction was held in
Chicago. There was a great rush for the lots, some selling as high
as a thousand dollars, and the promoters reaped barrels of money.
For a while there was much slushing around in top boots in the
Kawaunee swamp in search of gold. Nothing was found, the
investors went sadly away, and the land reverted into an untaxed
and unsettled wilderness for the next thirty years.

Our Ditlef C. Hanson had no such rosy dreams of success. He
did not know any Governors or Supreme Court Justices. But he
did his best with the material in hand. He got out a stock of
splendid lithographs. These showed a townsite plat more than a
mile long with wide streets and curving avenues. No such common
names as Pike Street or Billing's Avenue were here permitted.
They were all sonorous street names, reminiscent of the glory of
the republic, such as Arlington Avenue, Columbia Street, Potomac
Boulevard, etc. Along the shore a beautiful park was shown,

enlivened by smart carriages and gay children dashing around on roller skates. Some streets were marked with street car lines, and certain corners were marked as occupied by a public library, post office, sanitarium, bank, or other institutions of importance. Even sluggish old Mink River, as if taking new life by this activity, was pictured as a dashing stream, leaping over boulders and plunging at last into the lake by means of an inspiring waterfall. All in all it was the most imposing document ever published setting forth the charms of Door County.

Armed with these lithographs, Mr. Hanson returned to Tacoma and opened the campaign. He showed them to friends and foes who were duly impressed and sometimes bought. He discovered, however, that the vastness of the American continent lying between Tacoma and Tacoma Beach deterred many who would otherwise have invested. Because of this, and because, like Moses, he was slow of speech, though of great resource, he determined to go to Chicago and sell out. He went to Chicago where he met a man with a name something like Rosenstein. To him he sold his entire stock of lithographs, with the townsite thrown in.

Mr. Rosenstein was enthusiastic about his purchase. He went out into the highways and byways of the city and explained the lithographs to all who would listen. He showed them how they could live happily at Tacoma Beach, or, if not, how they could die, secure in the faith that their money was well invested and that their widows would bless their memory. His arguments were irrefutable.

In due course of time many of these investors came to view the paradise of their purchase. Among them was a semi–invalid who came with a full equipment of paints, pots and brushes. He planned to get the job of painting the cottages of the new city. Some went as far as Sturgeon Bay, others went on to Fish Creek and Sister Bay, while still others persisted in pushing on to Rowleys Bay, before they were disillusioned. Alas, they each and all discovered that they had forgotten the most important part of their equipment for viewing the new city—top boots.

We will not linger over the gnashing of teeth or the bitter recriminations heaped upon old Rosenstein. The lots were sold and the lithographs used up, so he merely shrugged his shoulders and turned his thoughts to other things. So, also, after a while, did the dupes. Their money was gone, so they wasted no more in paying taxes on their submerged lots on Potomac Boulevard. It remained now for the long-suffering county board to unravel the tangle. Finally the "streets" were vacated and the land sold for taxes. The affair cost the county about five thousand dollars.

After eight years' flight in financial circles Rowleys Bay returned once more to its undisturbed seclusion. In the parks of the new city the frogs croak by day and the crickets chirp by night. Even frisky old Mink River has ceased from its gambols and settled into its sluggish solitude where the pickerel in June are reckless and the black bass bite with abandon.

chapter twenty-one

JACKSONPORT

—But who in this wild wood
May credit give to either eye or ear?
From rocky precipice and hollow cave,
Come burst of spray and thund'ring wave.

JACKSONPORT was the last district to be settled in Door County, but its roots go back almost three hundred years. Here, in the spring of 1653, was fought the battle between the ferocious Iroquois from New York on one side and the remnants of several refugee tribes from Lower Ontario and Michigan on the other, as briefly told in Chapter Two. These refugees had found shelter in the newly built Potawatomi village of Mechingan which stood on the lake shore, enclosed by heavy palisades, a half mile north of the present village of Jacksonport. The Iroquois were defeated and their insolent power was temporarily broken. Even now old men among the Potawatomi relate vague legends of this battle. The site of this great Indian village, which housed several thousand Indians, is said to be one of the richest archeological remains in the state. In the Neville Museum in Green Bay, may be seen hundreds of relics which Mr. J. P. Schumacher found at this site and donated to the Museum, and local collectors have hundreds of other specimens picked up there.

Radisson and Groseilliers were the first white men to penetrate into the West after Nicolet's visit in 1634. They spent the winter of 1654–55 in this village, and brought back much information about this region when they returned to the French settlements on the lower St. Lawrence. The narrative which they gave to the Catholic Fathers in Quebec about this village is among the most interesting that are recorded in the seventy volumes of the contemporaneous Jesuit Relations.

The defeat of the Iroquois at Hibbard's Creek, just north of the present village of Jacksonport, as related by Nicolas Perrot who heard about it first hand from the surviving participants among the Potawatomi, was one of the most important events in the

history of the western Indians. And the veneration with which the
present day Potawatomi speak of their ancient village of
Mechingan, is also proof of its great importance. Here great chiefs
made stirring speeches inciting their people to war and conquest.
Here they schemed and struggled, fished and farmed, fought and
played. But of the succeeding generations of red men who lived
here we know nothing because the door to the West was closed for
almost two centuries.

The history of white man's occupation of the Jacksonport area
covers only the measure of one lifetime. It is a history which deals
with cordwood, corn and cattle. The first pioneers came here
drawn by the lure of cordwood, and some of them remained for the
sake of corn and cattle. But while the pioneers of other parts of the
Peninsula came to make a living by fishing and farming, the first
white men in Jacksonport came prompted by a business
speculation.

In the winter of 1867, three men in Madison, Wis., were busy
planning the future of Jacksonport. It was a nameless lakeside
wilderness, but they had high hopes of making it an El Dorado.
These men were Col. C. L. Harris, John Reynolds and Andrew
Jackson. The last was connected with the Federal Land Office in
Menasha and told the others that up there (where now is the
village of Jacksonport) was a large area of valuable timber on
which no one had filed a homestead claim. Its location on the
shore of Lake Michigan made possible a minimum expense for
transportation of its forest products to Chicago and Milwaukee.
This land could be had for only fifty cents per acre, and each acre
should conservatively yield a return of a thousand dollars gross. It
was in short, a bonanza of boundless promise.

The two others agreed and a company was formed. Harris and
Reynolds each put in $7,000, while Jackson, who had showed
them the way to this pot of gold, was given as equal share without
being required to put up any part of the capital. As the plan also
included the creation of a townsite with the sale of lots for
prospective homeseekers, the name of their embryo city came up
for discussion. One suggested Harrisport, another Reynoldsport, a
third Jacksonport. As Jackson was the father of the enterprise,
the last name was chosen in honor of him. These details disposed
of, a crew of thirty-seven men were hired; axes, saws, blankets and
other necessary equipment were purchased, including a team of
horses and a sleigh which were entrusted to Thomas Reynolds, a
brother of John, who was to be teamster.

The thirty-seven woodchoppers were sent by rail to Green Bay. From here Tom Reynolds was to carry them to their destination, about sixty-five miles farther on. But Tom's sleigh was fully loaded with needed supplies, so there was no room for riders. However, the woodchoppers were hopeful of good wages and happy in the possession of at least one pocket flask per person and plenty more on the sleigh, so all went well until they got north of Sturgeon Bay. Here the road ended and dubious trails with stumps barely covered by snow led hither and thither. Every little while the low bumpers of the sleigh would fetch up with a terrific jar against a green stump which threatened to smash the sleigh, but with the help of good luck and thirty-seven pairs of hands, the sleigh was gotten under way again. Finally even the trails ended, and they had to chop their way through the remaining miles.

At that time there was only one lone settler on the lake shore south of Baileys Harbor. This was Perry Hibbard after whom Hibbard's Creek is named. He owned the site of the Indian village of Mechingan, and his land also included the best site for a pier. The new company had paid him a good price for this pier site, and in return he permitted the thirty–seven Madisonians to use his log barn for sleeping quarters. It was a bitterly cold place to spend the winter nights, and the men complained loudly, but after a few weeks better quarters were provided.

When the woodcutting began, it was the Company's turn to complain. The men had been hired with the understanding that they were all expert woodsmen, but it was soon found that most of them knew nothing about felling trees. When they became more familiar with the use of an axe, they discovered that some trees split more easily than others. They made constant disgressions into the woods to find such easy trees so as to make a cord of wood with the least exertion. This made necessary so much extra cutting of roads that the profit was lost in the extra expense of getting the wood hauled out. They also sought to save labor by cutting fence posts a few inches short. When the posts were delivered in Chicago, these posts were heavily docked, and here, too, the profit was lost. The friction between the employers and the crew therefore grew worse steadily.

Finally a small animal, about the size of a cat, caused a catastrophe which disrupted the crew completely. One morning the cook entered the storeroom and found that a skunk had made his way into it. At first he was disposed to treat the visitor with proper caution and permit him to take his departure at his own

pleasure. However, some of the hungry boarders insisted that the
skunk be expelled at once before the food supplies were spoiled.
The cook therefore seized a shotgun, marched into the skunk's
retreat, and perforated him with small shot. The skunk slowly
expired, but not before he had delivered himself of every drop of
the fluid with which nature had provided him for his self-defense.
It happened that the industrious teamster, Tom Reynolds, had just
filled the storehouse with a full supply of provisions. There was a
ton of butter, several thousand pounds of pork and beef both salt
and fresh, a huge quantity of flour, and the usual assortment of
groceries. The entire lot was spoiled and had to be thrown away.
New supplies were brought in, but the building was so surcharged
with the essence of polecat, that the new provisions tasted and
smelled as bad as the old. The whole camp was saturated with the
stench, and for years the building was unfit for use. The seventy-
nine notorious and indescribable stinks for which the old city of
Singapore was famous are as nothing compared to the smell of one
full-grown Jacksonport skunk fighting for his life.

That skunk hunt cost the Company several thousand dollars,
and what was worse, it entirely disrupted operations. As there
was no food fit for human consumption, the thirty-seven men of
Madison departed, uttering dark imprecations against the skunk,
the cook, the Company, and the whole Peninsula. The Company
advertised for new men and a few came. But the place had a bad
name, and hard luck pursued it. After two or three years the
Company was bankrupt. The $14,000 was used up, and it owed
many thousand dollars to Green Bay merchants. So everyone
went his own way. Only one man remained—Tom Reynolds. He
had acquired 700 acres and became the first permanent settler
and farmer in the township. Forty years later he visited Madison
again, but then he came not as a teamster, but as a member of the
State Legislature.

About three miles south of Jacksonport, in a secluded corner of
the Peninsula, is a scenic phenomenon of unique interest. It is
called Cave Point, now a part of a county park of the same name.
The shore at this place rises from twenty to thirty feet in a most
picturesque precipice. There is no beach whatever, for the cliff
rears up from unknown watery depths. It is seamed with fissures
and indented with caves and recesses, and when the wind is on
shore, an unforgettable spectacle is presented. The big combers,
rolling grandly toward the shore, fling themselves on the black
stone wall with a thunderous roar, only to be shattered to spray,

which is thrown high up. Through this the sunlight is seen, transformed into a small but gorgeous rainbow. The multiform facets of the cliff cause an infinite variety of antics by the rushing waves. At one place is a circular grotto wherein the waves spin around in a wildly tossing whirlpool. At another is a low, wide-mouthed cave of unknown depth into which the big waves plunge heedlessly, only to return after some time like a torrential river. At still another the waves are deflected upward by the sloping rock and find a hole through which they jam and then emerge in another cave in the form of a beautiful waterfall. At the end of the precipice, where the cliff changes from a vertical to an inclined position, there is a succession of waterfalls caused by the vain rush of the waves which return to their element in the form of innumerable pretty cascades. Nowhere can one see water in action in more lively and diverse forms. This incessant and impetuous action explains the absence of any beach. Such rocks as are broken off by frost, erosion or the expansion of roots are permitted no long rest, but are ground into powder by the pounding of the sea. In the midst of this turmoil can be seen the rock face of the Old Man of the Sea, laughing hilariously at the playful sport of his children.

Such is the display when the wind is of only moderate strength. But when a storm is blowing, the scene is terrific. The picturesque details are then obliterated in a cloud of spray. Huge geysers spout up off shore among the roaring whitecaps, marking the site of hidden reefs. The waves pound the cliff with annihilating force, and the limestone foundations of the land quake in terror.

Into this raging tumult of sea and rock was once flung a well built schooner carrying a crew of nine men and 30,000 bushels of corn. She was the D. A. Van Valkenburg under command of Captain Andrew L. Keith, a navigator of forty years' experience. In the fall of 1881 she left Chicago bound for Buffalo, heading diagonally northeast across Lake Michigan. On the second night when a storm drove the vessel up on a reef, it was thought that they were close to Manitou Islands. But there was something wrong with the compass, and instead of being near the Manitous, they were fifty miles to the west, on the other side of the lake. As there was no way of getting off the reef, and as the vessel was beginning to break up, the yawl was lowered, and all the members of the crew disembarked. It was in the middle of the night, but they could see land close by—a forbidding cliff, on which the waves dashed furiously. No landing seemed possible there, so they started off into the lake. But they had taken only a few strokes beyond the lee of the schooner, when a big roller crashing over the reef rolled the yawl bottom side up. Four men were washed away and were not again seen, but the remaining five swam to the boat and clung to it. This was only for a few moments, however, when they were again swept away. This time another man was lost, but three men regained the capsized boat. On being instantly washed away again, these three men struck out for shore, but two of them were dashed against the cliff and killed. The last man, whose name was Thomas Breen, was tossed back and forth by the waves and the undertow, but eventually managed to fling his arms around a rock just beyond the precipice, where the shore begins to slope. Bruised and bleeding, he painfully worked up the incline in the momentary lulls between the breakers, and got behind some large rocks where he fainted from exhaustion.

The next morning he followed an old road near the shore to Jacksonport which he reached in a dazed condition. On learning of the shipwreck, the men of Jacksonport dropped their work and hastened to the scene of the tragedy to see if they could be of any help. Four of the dead sailors were found, but the other four, including the captain, were never found. The men were greatly surprised on looking out to see no signs of the wreck. How could a large, fully loaded, schooner take itself off a reef and sail away? But it had not sailed away. Shortly after the crew left the Van Valkenburg, the vessel had split apart from stem to stern, and its sides and tackle now lay awash on the reef practically invisible. This rending asunder of the vessel was caused by the swelling of the corn—30,000 bushels—with which she was filled right up to the hatches. This corn was soon washed up and lay knee deep along the shore for miles. Everyone now got busy salvaging corn. The old buildings of the Reynolds–Jackson Company were filled to the roof with soggy corn, and every spare room in the village was turned into a granary. But there was plenty left, and men came with wagons from all over the county to get cheap pig feed.

This was only one of the numerous shipwrecks that had happened in this vicinity.

About a half mile southwest of Cave Point is the northern end of a belt of sand dunes which stretch along the shore down to White Fish Bay. Here is a region of impressive and charming scenery. The dunes are the largest on the west side of Lake Michigan, some of them towering more than a hundred feet above the lake. The largest are now destitute of any vegetation, but the smaller dunes are rich in spruce, balsam, cedar, and white pine, with large carpets of prostrate juniper interspersed. Many years ago, a Mr. Glidden bought most of the shore property from the canal to Jacksonport and built a meandering highway through this woodland. Unfortunately, he failed in business, and his grandiose plans came to naught. The part of this highway leading through the sand dunes is now partly buried by drifting sand, but it still makes an ideal path through a most delightful scenic tract, unlike any other on the Peninsula or in the State.

chapter twenty-two

A VERY OLD HIGHWAY

*The noblest prospect that a Scotchman ever sees
is the high–road that leads him to England.*

SAMUEL JOHNSON

THE world is full of roads running hither and thither, criss-crossing each other, leading nowhere in particular.Like the minor streets of a great city they are of no special interest except to the people who live upon them. But there are other highways of such compelling interest that, like the occasional superman, they compel all their surroundings to do them service. Such roads have a forceful identity of their own, and without them history would not have been the same.

Recorded history began so late here in America that we know little or nothing of the strategic highways of ancient America or of the people and expeditions that have wended their way over them, although it is possible that they may have played quite as impelling a role as the famous travelers of European highways. Moreover, the pioneer's plow has obliterated the traces of practically all our ancient lanes of travel, so that they can no longer be definitely traced. There remains, however, in Wisconsin, one important trail which has probably been used for thousands of years. And while this trail is humble both in size and significance compared to the great thoroughfares of Europe, it has one merit in which it excels those historic highways. These have been rebuilt so many times that their physical character is no longer the same as in the ancient noon-day of their historic traffic. This Wisconsin trail has never been changed or repaired, but is today the same, in all likelihood, as it was a thousand years ago. The deep furrows hollowed out by the feet of countless thousands in remote ages may still be seen. As it is now, so it was long before the white man crossed the Atlantic and glimpsed the mysterious land of the West.

This oldest of highways in the West is the trail that crosses the Door County Peninsula from Sturgeon Bay to Lake Michigan.

The topography of this part of Wisconsin is such as to make it reasonable to assume that this trail has been used as long as the region has been inhabited by human beings. On the east lies Lake Michigan, stretching hundreds of miles to the southward; on the west lies Green Bay. Between the two extends the rockbound peninsula a hundred miles long. On the shores and rivers of these big bodies of water dwelt many Indian tribes, between which was much intercourse, for the Indians were energetic travelers. In those days the birch bark canoe was the favorite means of transportation. To go around the shore of the long peninsula entailed a toilsome journey of two hundred miles, with the serious danger of destruction in the treacherous currents of Death's Door. But this long journey was made unnecessary by the discovery of the short portage between the head of Sturgeon Bay and Lake Michigan. Here was a neck of land only about two miles wide. This trail therefore became the great highway between the tribes living around the southern half of Lake Michigan and those living on Green Bay and west and southwest of it. The trail runs through an almost flat and sometimes swampy region where once grew giant pines and cedars. These have long since been cut, but as the forest has never been cleared, the course of the trail may still be plainly followed. Abundant Indian remains at both ends of the trail show that here are sites of ancient villages.

If this historic trail could whisper to us its memoirs of the countless caravans that have worn down a path like a deep plowfurrow it is probable we would hear many stirring tales of valiant endeavor. No doubt the warlike Winnebagos of the Green Bay region used it on their marauding expeditions southward along Lake Michigan. We know also that the prowling Iroquois ventured as far west as this from their palisaded towns of western New York. But most of the time it was presumably used on more peaceful excursions of hunting and trading; braves and squaws alike toiling under their burdens of canoes, pelts and movable tepees, busily plodding along the forest aisles on trivial business which to them seemed all–important, quite in the way of man generally.

Coming down from that long period of unrecorded history, we know of many famous white men who have used this highway hundreds of years ago.

Among these were the zealous missionaries carrying their

message of salvation to the most distant tribes; great explorers animated by visions of empire building; and tireless furtraders seeking adventure and riches among strange tribes.

The first white men known to have crossed the portage were Father Jacques Marquette and Louis Jolliet, and their crossing marked the finish of one of the greatest exploration expeditions in American history—the discovery of the Mississippi River. In 1672 Louis Jolliet was ordered by the French government to seek and follow the Mississippi River in order to learn where it debouched. Vague rumors about the great river had reached the Governor in Quebec, and it was hoped that it empties into the Pacific Ocean, in which case it might prove a gateway to the riches of China and India. At Mackinac Jolliet was joined by Father Marquette who was a missionary there. Together they set out the 17th of May, 1673, in two birch bark canoes, accompanied by five white men. They paddled their way along the shores of Lake Michigan and Green Bay to the mouth of the Fox River, ascended this stream to the portage where it almost joined the Wisconsin, then followed this stream until its junction with the Mississippi and then onward for a thousand miles to the mouth of the Arkansas. They now learned that the great river did not empty into the Pacific as they hoped, whereupon they began their return journey up the Mississippi and Illinois Rivers, crossed the portage at Chicago and followed the shore of Lake Michigan for 250 miles. They reached the Sturgeon Bay portage about the 25th of September, 1673. When they crossed this portage their great circle of 3000 miles through unexplored waters was completed. They were once more in familiar waters. Not a man had been killed or lost and the two canoes were still intact.

The second known crossing of the portage by white men was also made by Father Marquette. On October 25, 1674, he left the mission of St. Francis Xavier, at the present city of DePere, to get on a missionary journey to the Illinois Indians. He was accompanied by a number of Potawatomi and Illinois Indians who were going south to the country of the latter. The party reached the portage on the 27th and Father Marquette slept that night at the Lake Michigan end of the portage. It took them more than two days to carry their equipment across. On October 30th Father Marquette launched his canoe on Lake Michigan on that last journey of mercy from which he was not to return alive.

Two years later Father Claude Allouez took up the work as missionary among the Illinois Indians. He started out in winter time, sailed his canoe over the ice of Green Bay like an ice boat and crossed the portage March 28, 1677. By this time his work as a missionary in the Green Bay region had made good progress and hundreds of Indians had been baptized. Father Louis André, later Superior of the College of Quebec, was therefore sent to him as an assistant. Father André crossed the portage many times, for his parish consisted of all the tribes dwelling on the shores of Green Bay and Lake Michigan south of the portage. He was followed by Fathers Silvy, Albanel, Chardon, and others who carried their canoes over this ancient trail. Sublime in their devotion to the Indians they counted no toil or sacrifice too great if they could but win one red man of the wilderness to a better faith.

In 1679 Robert La Salle set out on his great enterprise of adding the bulk of America to the French dominions. He reached the vicinity of Ottawa, Illinois, when the desertion of his men and a sudden attack by the Iroquois of New York brought ruin to his expedition. La Salle made a magnificent journey straight eastward through the wilderness to Montreal, leaving to his trusty lieutenant, Tonty, the task to bring the remnant of his force back to Mackinac. Toiling northward along the stormy shore of Lake Michigan without food or ammunition, Tonty by accident discovered the Sturgeon Bay portage. Almost dead from hunger, sickness and wounds, Tonty, accompanied by Father Zenobe Membre and three other Frenchmen, barely crawled across the portage November 15, 1680, wishing only for a warm campfire by which to die. Happily they were discovered by some friendly Indians and brought back to life. Tonty and his party spent the following winter in the vicinity and lived to firmly establish the power of France over the entire Mississippi valley.

Only a few of the indomitable men of early western history who have dignified this trail with their campfires have made mention of their presence, but their number was no doubt large. It was one of the great gateways of travel, a necessary stopping place in the work of winning the west for white men.

Among these picturesque characters was the resourceful Nicolas Perrot, the first commandant of the Indians of the West, with headquarters at Green Bay. In his forty years of life in this region he doubtless crossed the Sturgeon Bay portage many times. There was also old Ducharme, the intrepid furtrader of Green Bay, who with his own resources raised a considerable army and led it to war against the Spaniards of St. Louis. And last but not least was the gallant Charles Langlade, the reputed father of

Wisconsin, who several times gathered the Indians from Mackinac to Milwaukee to go to war for the defense of the French dominions.

When finally Milwaukee in the course of time got its first settlers, their supplies for more than a generation were laboriously toted over this portage trail. Green Bay was then the distributing point of the West and periodic schooners from Buffalo went no farther. Old Jacques Vieau, the first permanent settler and merchant of Milwaukee, brought his freight from Green Bay by way of the portage. So also did his more distinguished son–in–law, Solomon Juneau, "the founder of Milwaukee," who carried unknown tons of supplies over this trail for the first settlers of the new metropolis.

Even Chicago's first traders received their early freight by way of the Sturgeon Bay portage. Col. Abram Edwards, who had a trading post at Chicago, tells of a journey he made there in 1818, the same year that Juneau settled in Milwaukee. This journey is of particular interest because it was probably the most rapid canoe journey in the history of the lakes. Col. Edwards was returning from a journey east and was accompanied by the army paymaster, James Phillips, and Inspector General Wood. In Green Bay they purchased a large bark canoe, and Major Zachary Taylor, later President of the United States, who was commandant of the fort, furnished them with seven expert canoe men, making ten in the party besides considerable freight.

"We left Green Bay garrison," writes Col. Edwards, "after dinner, and went to the head of Sturgeon Bay, 40 miles, and encamped for the night. The next morning we carried our canoe, two and a half miles over the portage to the shore of Lake Michigan, and, after getting the baggage over, we were willing to encamp for the night. The next morning found us in our canoe afloat on the waters of the Lake, paddling our way to Chicago, where we arrived the third day from our lakeshore encampment. On our passage, although we frequently landed, we did not meet with a white man—we were, however, informed one was trading with the Indians at Milwaukee. At Twin Rivers, Manitowoc, Sheboygan and Milwaukee the shore of the lake was lined with Indians; near Manitowoc many were out in canoes spearing white fish."[1]

We think of this ancient highway as a unique memorial of the past, which is quite correct. But it is much more than that. In one sense it is a greater thoroughfare than ever and carries a traffic far greater than in ancient times. As the old travelers toiled along the woodland path, burdened by their packs, the thought probably occurred to most of them that their lot would be much easier if this path across the low-lying isthmus were a ditch through which their canoes might glide. Eventually their dream was to be realized. About eighty years ago, when more than seven thousand schooners annually sailed between the ports of Green Bay and those of the lower end of Lake Michigan, enterprising citizens of Sturgeon Bay determined to change the path into a canal. A company was organized to cut the isthmus on the route of the old trail. As it was found that this was underlaid by a ledge of rock, it was found necessary to locate the canal a short distance to the south. Eventually the canal was completed, and large vessels now sail where formerly the Indians and the pioneers carried their canoes.

It was the hope of the Door County Historical Society to preserve this unique trail for posterity. It was planned to acquire a hundred foot strip of land on each side of the trail, clean up the rubbish and leave it as a forest park to be known as Marquette Memorial Park.

---

[1] *Wis. His. Collections*, V. 158,159.

chapter twenty-three

THE GOLDEN AGE OF LITTLE STURGEON BAY

A wizard he was both keen and bold.
Whatever he touched became silver and gold.
A market for timber and stone he found
And raised the standards of all around.

HAVE you been to Little Sturgeon Bay? No? Well—then you can look forward to an interesting trip. It lies about ten miles west of the bridge in Sturgeon Bay, and with its sloping meadows it looks more like an inland lake than a bay. Here, at its mouth on the west side, is the spot first chosen for occupancy on the entire Peninsula by white man (see Chapter Six). The site of his home is marked by a bronze tablet on a big boulder.

Here, later, was the first big shipyard on the Peninsula, and for a time there was quite a contest between Little Sturgeon and Sturgeon Bay as to which was to become the business center of the Peninsula.

A short mile west of Little Sturgeon Bay the shore rises boldly from the water's edge in a perpendicular cliff about seventy-five feet in height. This cliff is a conspicuous landmark overlooking nearly all of Green Bay. On the right lies Sturgeon Bay, deeply indenting the land. On the left is Green Island and the cities of Marinette and Menominee. Straight ahead stand headland after headland that mark the bold shore of Northern Door County.

Backed up against this cliff formerly stood two huge cylinders, resting upon a massive masonry foundation about seventy-five feet long. These cylinders were forty feet high and fifteen feet in diameter. It took very little imagination to see in them two huge howitzers, uptilted against the sky, ready to pour out their burden of destruction as soon as an enemy appeared on the waters of distant Death's Door. Thus they appeared to me forty-five years ago when I first saw them.

But these ominous-looking cylinders were not engines of destruction but of construction. They were erected to help rebuild

Chicago. When the Chicago fire turned that city into ashes, there was a great demand for material to rebuild it. Stone, brick, lumber, and lime were needed. It was to partly fill this last want that these cylinders were erected.

One day in the Fall of 1871 a steam yacht carrying a party of Chicago businessmen floated by this cliff. They were the guests of F. B. Gardner, Little Sturgeon Bay's lone businessman. As they came abreast of this sturdy headland, a big contractor who was a member of the party exclaimed:

"See what waste of good material! Here is a mountain of limestone and in Chicago we are at our wits end to get lime!"

"No waste at all," replied Mr. Gardner. "This cliff stands here in reserve, awaiting your need. If you need lime, I will send you 1000 barrels a week. I own that cliff."

The price was quickly agreed upon, and Mr. Gardner at once proceeded to erect a modern process lime kiln. This stood close to the cliff and almost reached to the top of it so that only a short ramp was needed to enable the teamsters to drive their loads right down to the top openings of the kiln. At the bottom of these were other openings, through which the lime was drawn every six hours. Immediately below the kiln a substantial pier was built, 75 by 300 feet in size. Here the lime was barrelled and loaded into a vessel. For many years vessels made weekly trips from here to Chicago with cargoes of lime, 160 barrels being produced daily. As most of this work was done by gravity, the operation was not as laborious as expected.

It is long since these huge kilns ceased their labor. Their very existence is unknown to almost all the people in Door County. The big boarding house on top of the cliff has mouldered away, and all that is left of the old pier is a shallow spot of rocks, marking its former outer end.

This Mr. Gardner who built and operated these lime kilns was one of the most remarkable men who have come to this Peninsula. He came here in the early 1850's and bought the old Increase Claflin homestead October 18, 1854. No doubt he was proud to be the owner of this beautiful spot, but what could he do with it?

Presumably it was the well protected harbor which caused him to invest his little capital here. A good harbor meant a promising shipping point, but what was there to ship? The answer was: thousands of acres of virgin timber. Only one thing was needed to turn that timber into forest crops. This was cheap labor.

He did not have to wait long. In the middle of the 1850's there was a vast emigration of people in Belgium to America. Many thousands of them settled in the southwestern corner of the Door Peninsula, and as most of them preferred to be near the bay with its promise of good fishing, it was not long before these early pioneers reached the vicinity of Little Sturgeon Bay. As the land was all covered with big timber, no crops were possible until this was cut. In the meantime the only way to keep the family alive was to get a job in a sawmill. Thus Mr. Gardner got all the labor he needed. He could not understand Belgian, and they knew no English; but as both employer and employees were eager to please, they got along very well. Before many years he had about 400 men working for him.

Mr. Gardner's first venture was a sawmill which employed about fifty men, and a grist mill. This was the first grist mill on the Peninsula, and it was a great boon to the farmers. Sometimes forty or fifty farmers came through the timber with their slow oxen from Red River and Forestville to meet at the mill the distant pioneers from Fish Creek and Washington Island who brought their grain in pound boats. To accommodate these men, Mr. Gardner built a roomy house where they could cook and sleep while waiting for their grist. He also built a three-story store building with basement, filled with all manner of implements, merchandise and machinery needed in a new county. All kinds of produce were taken in exchange. Up to within recent years, this was the largest mercantile establishment on the Peninsula. A storehouse, 425 by 40 feet and a number of other buildings were also erected.

Mr. Gardner was the first shipbuilder on a large scale in the county. For a long period he employed about a hundred ship carpenters besides many other workers needed in a shipyard. Among the vessels built at Little Sturgeon were the *John Spry*, the *Ellen Spry*, the *Halstead*, the *Norman*, the *Ozaukee*, the *Pensaukee*, the *F. B. Gardner*, and the *J. W. Doan*.

After the Chicago fire (1871), there was a big boom in business, and freight rates were very high. It took about ten days to make a round trip to Chicago, and Gardner needed many vessels to carry his forest products and lime. Shipbuilding was therefore pushed with all possible speed. When the keel of the *J. W. Doan* was laid, Gardner half jestingly told his foreman, Tom Spear, that he would give a thousand dollars if the ship could be launched in sixty days.

"I'll take you up on that if you mean it," said the foreman.

"Do you think you can do it in sixty days?"

"Yes."

"Well if you can launch her in good shape in sixty days, the thousand dollars are yours."

For two months there was a whirlwind of hustle at the shipyard, infecting all from the boss to the water boy. Finally came the fifty–ninth day, and the new vessel slipped into the water, ready to be towed to Chicago to be equipped with rigging. But she did not go empty as she carried 700,000 feet of lumber on board, for which Mr. Gardner was paid $7.00 per 1000 feet in freight charges or a total of $4,900.00 for less than a week's rent.

The *J. W. Doan*, in spite of the record–breaking speed in its building, proved to be one of the smartest schooners on the Great Lakes. At one time she was loaded at Buffalo, ready to sail to Chicago at the same time as the *Annie M. Peterson*—a boat famous for its fast trips. The captains wagered $200 apiece on the speed of their boats and started from Buffalo at the same time. All through the voyage it was nip and tuck, the vessels passing each other several times due to skillful maneuvering. Finally, the *J. W. Doan* pulled into Chicago two hours ahead of the *Annie Peterson*.

With all this business Little Sturgeon was a most active place. For years, at least one vessel per day took on her load of lumber, lime, or produce and sailed off. In 1862, when Joseph Harris started the Door County Advocate, it was seriously debated whether the printing place should be located at Little Sturgeon Bay or at the county seat.

But Little Sturgeon Bay was only a small part of Mr. Gardner's business activities. At Pensaukee on the west shore of Green Bay he was operating the largest sawmill in Wisconsin. Charles Scofield, the father of Sturgeon Bay's H. C. Scofield, was in sole charge here for a number of years while Mr. Gardner traveled in Europe.

He had another big sawmill in the Menominee River. All the river frontage in Marinette and Menominee had been bought up by the local lumber barons in order to keep Gardner out. It was therefore impossible to buy a foot of land. But Gardner sank a number of mammoth cribs in the river and upon them he erected his sawmill. This is now the site of the mammoth million dollar beet sugar factory.

Besides mills and shipyards, Gardner was also interested in building hotels. In Chicago he built the finest hotel of its time and place. It was the Gardner, later known as The Leland, which on Michigan Avenue long survived. At Pensaukee he built another which was even more of a marvel. This little town in the wilderness was very dear to him as being the place of his first great success. He therefore determined to build a hotel there which would be an honor to Pensaukee even after it should become the city he dreamed of making it. He spent more than a hundred thousand dollars on it, which eighty years ago was a lot of money. It had marble fireplaces, porphyry pillars, and other wonderful trimmings, scarcely equalled in the entire state. But this amazing hotel, the talk of all travelers, met a sudden and disastrous fate. Hardly was it completed in 1878 when it was struck by a cyclone and completely demolished. A 6000 pound safe went spinning over the ground disgorging money, papers and account books, some of which were carried by the wind across Green Bay and later found in the fields near Sturgeon Bay. Planks from the mammoth lumber yard in Pensaukee were picked up in Joseph Dalemont's field near Little Sturgeon. A big store building belonging to Mr. Gardner was picked up in one piece, whirled away and never seen again.

Mr. Gardner was a pleasant, congenial man, easy to get along with and generously helpful. Because of this he was very popular with the Belgians who completely dominate that part of the county. When the town was organized in 1862 it was therefore given the name of Gardner without a dissenting vote.

With the exception of this name, there is now nothing to remind the visitor of Mr. Gardner and his dynamic energy. The big piers built of huge pine logs have crumbled down. The stones of the old grist mill that fed our first pioneers have been chipped up and carried away by relic hunters. Scarcely a bolt or a board remains of all the equipment that once made Little Sturgeon famous as the busiest place on the Peninsula. The peace and quiet of a charming summer resort has descended upon it, and it lies almost as tranquil as the day when Increase Claflin settled on it in 1835.

chapter twenty-four

THE BELGIAN SETTLEMENT

Where resounds the Belgian tongue,
Where Belgian hymns and songs are sung;
This is the land, the land of lands,
Where vows bind less than clasped hands.

BELGIUM is a compact little country with the densest population of any in Europe. In spite of these crowded conditions, the Belgians have been content to stay at home, and comparatively few have emigrated to the open spaces in America. Aside from a number of small groups in various cities, particularly in Detroit and Rock Island, Ill., there is in fact only one large rural settlement of Belgians in America. This lies on the Door Peninsula between Sturgeon Bay and Green Bay and numbers about fifteen thousand people. When the Belgian pioneers came, the locale of this settlement was a dense forest with many tangled swamps. Now it is a well-tilled open country, thickly settled, one of the most productive in the state. Although the settlement is three generations old, it is still distinctively Belgian with French speech and many customs characteristic of the homeland.

The settlement had its beginning in 1853. Early in the spring of that year a small farmer by the name of Francois Petiniot made a trip from his home in the province of Brabant to the city of Antwerp. In the tavern where he lodged, he found a small pamphlet written in the Dutch language concerning an unknown place or country called *Wisconsin*. Petiniot was only moderately acquainted with Dutch, and it was slow work to apprehend the meaning of the words on the printed page. But their message was of absorbing interest for they told of fertile farming land that could be purchased from the government for only a dollar per acre, and of new cities where work was abundant at unbelievably high wages. The climate was described as excellent. Here, too, every man could vote, whereas in Belgium only five percent had the right of suffrage.

Vastly interested, Petiniot took the pamphlet home with him and showed it to his neighbors. Then followed many conferences and inquiries. The whole *Commune* was stirred to its depths. Finally ten men sold their little five-acre farms and went to Antwerp and bought tickets to "Wisconsin" for themselves and their families.

Eventually they reached Milwaukee, full of wonderment that the world was so big. But they did not linger here for they had become acquainted with some Hollanders while crossing the Atlantic who were going to Sheboygan where they had relatives. Thither also the Belgians went, only to realize suddenly that they were homeless strangers in a strange land. There they stood, speechless and forlorn, with no place to go.

In this dilemma they met a man who understood their predicament. With many signs and loud words he managed to tell them that in Green Bay were many Frenchmen. He bundled them on board a little steamer, and after three days more of sailing they arrived there. This seemed like coming home, for in Green Bay their mother tongue was a familiar sound. To climax their joy they accidentally met a young Belgian priest by the name of Edward Daems who was in charge of the last frontier parish in northern Wisconsin, about ten miles northeast of Green Bay. He persuaded them all to come with him.

Ten miles back in the primeval forest from Bay Settlement where Father Daems was building his church, the Belgians found lands. This place, four miles south of Dyckesville, is now known as Robinsonville, but for many years it was called *Aux Premiers Belges.*

Delighted with finding themselves the possessors of tracts as large as those of the landed gentry in Belgium, the pioneers tackled the problem of clearing the wilderness with enthusiasm. They were young and used to hard work and had enough to live on for a while. The cost of postage was prohibitive, but a few letters were nevertheless sent "home" by the most optimistic. These enthusiastic letters were read and preserved like sacred writings by those at home, and in a couple of years they resulted in a veritable exodus of small farmers and laborers in the province of Brabant.

It was a great pleasure for the pioneers in *Aux Premiers Belges* to receive the new immigrants in their little log houses. Friends and relatives were united and there was much news to tell. But, unfortunately, some of these newcomers brought with them the deadly germs of the Asiatic Cholera, and soon the little forest cabins were filled with tears and terror. It was a sudden and generally unconquerable disease. Strong men, apparently well at night, would be found dead in the morning; the skin on their faces turned almost black, and their eyes sunk far back in their sockets. Many of these immigrants died, and some of their hospitable hosts. Father Daems' parish was so large that he could attend to only a few. Most of the victims were therefore buried back in the woods, usually without coffins and without the rites of the church or the sustaining presence of the priest.

Meanwhile the Belgian immigrants kept pouring in, thousands every year, for the news of the pestilence had not yet reached Belgium. They took all the available land in many townships in Brown, Kewaunee and Door Counties, until a tract forty miles long and six miles wide was settled exclusively by Belgians. The bulk of the immigration took place in 1855 and 1856. In the latter year, news of the cholera reached the relatives at home, painted in most terrible colors. This brought the emigration to a sudden stop. Evidently it was tempting providence to thus plunge into a foreign wilderness. Comparatively few Belgians came after 1856.

Very few of these immigrants had any conception of the gigantic struggle that awaited them before they could turn the wilderness into productive farms. Most of them were penniless, but during the first winter they made a precarious living by hunting and fishing. They also cleared some land, but in the spring it was necessary for them to strike out on foot to distant cities and there seek work. In the meantime the women and children remained at home, harassed by loneliness, and frightened by the wolves that often howled around the cabin at night.

In the fall of 1857 a severe financial crisis paralyzed most industries, and the Belgians were unable to get any more outside work. They therefore gave renewed consideration to the possibilities at home. Their future farms were covered with big timber containing thousands of logs. Pine logs, the most valuable, were selling for a dollar and a half per thousand feet of board measure, but they had no horses or oxen, and the logs could not be carried out. But if the pine logs could not be gotten out whole, they could be cut into shingles and carried to the waterside by hand. Pine shingles, eighteen inches long and a half inch thick, were worth a dollar and a half per thousand in Green Bay. Here was a chance to make a little money, and all, young and old, became shingle makers. Father and mother sawed the trees into

eighteen–inch bolts, the children split them, and father shaved
them and bound them into bundles. Then they were carried to the
shore, miles away, sometimes on the back, but better still on two
bars by two men. From time to time a schooner came and carried
them to Green Bay, but it was necessary for the pioneer to get a
small boat and carry his shingles from the shore to the schooner. A
day's wage was very little, but by everlastingly keeping at it the
Belgians made enough to keep their families alive. Very little was
needed for clothing, for gunnysacks were cheap, and wooden
sabots were used instead of leather shoes.

The worst trouble was to keep the household supplied with
bread. Wheat was sowed among the stumps, and cut and threshed
by hand. But there were no mills nearby to grind it. While the
husband was busy with the shingles, it therefore became
necessary for the wife to take a bushel of wheat on her back and
tramp off ten or fifteen miles to the nearest mill to get it ground.
She readily carried it on her head. To an American of today it
would be quite impossible to carry even a half bushel of wheat on
his head for any considerable distance, but the Belgian women
had strong necks, being accustomed to carry heavy burdens that
way. The wheat was put in a bag which was securely tied at the
opening. Then the bag was turned upside down and one corner of
the bag was pushed back into the other corner so that this formed
a rough hood. This hood was placed over the head, while the other
end of the bag was tied securely to the back by means of a rope
under the arms. This left the hands free, and with this burden on
her head and back she trudged on indomitably all day through the
forest lanes, her feet bare, and her *sabots* dangling from another
rope so she could make a decent appearance at the mill.

About this time something happened, which seemed to the
humble pioneers in the wilderness like a heavenly benediction.
Indeed, it was a veritable miracle.

When the early French pioneers of Beau-Pre settled in the
wilderness of the St. Lawrence valley, they were much comforted
by the report that the Holy Virgin had appeared among them in a
vision. This was taken as a divine assurance that, although far
from the altars and churches of the homeland, they were not
forgotten by Heaven, but the Mother of God was with them,
solicitously interested in their welfare.

As it was in the woods of Beau-Pre, so also was it in the
Wisconsin wilderness where the Belgians had sought a home.
There, too, it is said, the Holy Virgin appeared in person, and the

first house of worship was built on the spot blessed by her visual presence. This is said to have happened August 15, 1858, in the heart of *Aux Premiers Belges* and until recently there were still some who remembered with what grateful exultation the people received this wonderful testimony of the Virgin's favor. The following is their account of what happened.

On the 15th of August, 1858, the feast of Our Lady's Assumption, Adele Brice (a young girl of eighteen) was on her way to church at Bay Settlement, about eight miles away. As she passed through the woodland there appeared between two trees a blinding white light which paralyzed the poor girl with fear. She cowered before it and prayed rapidly and breathlessly. Meanwhile the light took definite form, and between the trees stood a marvelously beautiful lady clothed in dazzling white garments. Around her waist was a yellow sash or girdle. Her eyes were deep and dark, and she bore a radiant and kindly smile. Adele trembled with fear, whereupon the vision gradually faded away.

The girl told her mother about this vision and the latter suggested that it might have been a departed relative who wanted prayers. The following Sunday Adele, still fearful, was accompanied on the long journey to church by her sister Isabelle and a friend. As they came to the little knoll between the two trees, Adele was about to describe the apparition when suddenly she screamed and fell to her knees, turning deadly pale. Again she beheld the vision precisely as she had seen it on Assumption Day. Deeply agitated Adele hastened to the church and narrated her strange experience to the missioner of the order of the Fathers of the Holy Cross.

The missioner was impressed with the earnestness of the young woman and advised her to take courage and speak to the apparition if ever she saw it again. "Speak up," he urged, "and say: 'In the name of God, who are you and what do you wish of me?'"

On October 9th the girl wandered through the woodland again with two companions. When they arrived at the spot mentioned they saw her drop to her knees, and they did likewise, though they saw nothing strange. Adele took heart and slowly repeated the words her pastor had taught her.

Then the lady of the vision spoke: "I am the Queen of Heaven who prays for the conversion of sinners. Do you the same." In amazement Adele's companions watched her as she stared and listened. Then the blessed Virgin instructed Adele to withdraw from the world for nine days and devote herself to prayer.

Thereupon she was to go forth and labor for the souls of the settlers who were failing in their religious duties and for their children who were growing up uninstructed.

Adele took the message literally. After the prescribed period of devotion, she went from home to home, from neighborhood to neighborhood exhorting the parents and instructing the children. People were amazed to listen to this formerly ignorant and bashful country girl, who now spoke with power and conviction. Soon she was joined by other sisters and a religious revival followed.[1]

The news of this vision soon reached the most distant parts of the settlement, and everyone was discussing it. Some felt greatly exalted at this sign of divine guidance, while others sneered at it as the invention of an excitable and imaginative seeker of sensations. But this latter view did not seem reasonable to many. They had known the young girl from her childhood, and there was nothing remarkable about her except her gentle modesty and her deep religious temperament. She had read no books of fiction; where could she have conceived the revolting idea of using the name of the Mother of God for the purpose of deceiving her own people? No, it seemed better to take the story as it was told. Their children needed to be taught, and no one was better fitted to teach them than this devout young woman.

And this view quickly became dominant. From far and near, from Green Bay and the distant cabins in Union, Brussels and Gardner in Door County, came people to look on this holy ground. The same fall a chapel was built on the spot and a schoolhouse close by. But the bishop was not among these that believed. He declared that the alleged vision was a myth and an imposition. As Adele Brice continued to affirm the truth of her story, she was even denied the holy sacrament, and for a time was treated as an outcast of the church.

But this made no difference to the Belgians. They did not waver in their faith, but gathered in large numbers to worship at the "Chapel of the Holy Virgin" as it was called. No priest came near, but on certain days, under the direction of Adele, she would lead in prayer. Within five years a large chapel was built on the spot and a church close by. A convent and a large schoolhouse were also erected in which the boys and girls were boarded and educated for a nominal sum.

Thereafter on each fifteenth of August thousands of worshippers came to this sanctuary to offer their devotions. Pilgrims from distant states and cities came here to pray. Many cripples also came and, with a triumphant faith gained in that sacred place, were able to walk out whole, leaving their crutches behind. Then, finally, the church authorities could withhold their blessing no longer.

It would seem as if Sister Adele's institution was indeed under the special protection of Heaven.

In 1871 a great forest fire laid waste the entire Belgian Settlement, and hundreds of people perished while the survivors fled terror–stricken. The chapel and the school were directly in the path of the flames, and its hot blast was almost suffocating the inmates, but Sister Adele would not listen to any suggestion of safety in flight. Instead she arranged a sacred processional in honor of the Virgin. While the flames were scorching the rail fence that surrounded the frame buildings, she led the sisters forth with a song of prayer that the school might be saved. Then the flames divided, passing on either side, leaving untouched the chapel and school in a sea of charred desolation.

Eventually the schoolhouse became too crowded to accommodate the many children that came there. Then Sister Adele went out on a long pilgrimage to distant places soliciting funds. In this way she obtained many thousands of dollars, and a large brick building was erected.

Above the altar in the Chapel of the Holy Virgin is a beautiful painting. At the top is seen a painting of a woodland scene in which the Madonna appears before Sister Adele, while her two companions are watching her uncomprehendingly. Above in the semi–circle is printed the Virgin's message. Many crutches left by former invalids adorn the rear wall of the chapel.

During the first years, the Belgians were treated contemptuously by the other settlers who thought themselves better because they could speak English. They received no aid in their distress and poverty. Their picturesque customs to which they clung were treated with amused raillery, and, while they always had to pay their full share of taxes, little was returned to them in the shape of highway improvements and schoolhouses.

But this discrimination came to a sudden end. Xavier Martin, a promising son of one of the original ten Belgian pioneers, had remained in the East where he acquired a fair education and familiarity with American ways. In 1858 he came to Wisconsin for the purpose of becoming a school teacher among his people. After seeing the condescending indifference with which his countrymen were treated by the older American, Irish and French settlers in the district, he went around among the leading Belgians and explained how they could put a stop to this. He helped them to qualify as voters and told them that by voting unitedly they could take control of local affairs. This was welcome news and a slate was drawn up. Mr. Martin was a modest man and did not ask for all the offices. But he was not too modest. The offices of chairman or supervisor of the town he rejected as being thankless jobs full of criticism. Nor did he care to be assessor or treasurer because both of these offices were concerned with the matter of taxes—then as now a sore subject. He therefore contented himself with claiming the offices of clerk, school superintendent and justice of the peace. The first of these was a matter of necessity because he was the only Belgian who could write English; the second he sought because he was a school teacher and interested in education; the third he desired because at that time it was the most dignified and profitable of local offices. The Belgians lived more than ten miles from the polling place, but on the appointed day the other office seekers, lounging at ease, sure of their laurels, were dumfounded to see an army of Belgians approach, two hundred and thirty strong, marching in double file, each clutching a ticket especially printed for them. Needless to say that every Belgian on that ticket (and there were none but Belgians) was elected.

Thereafter the Belgians continued to rule without interruption. On the first day of May of each year, the electors come to do honor to the successful candidates. They bring with them a tall pole, usually a balsam, with a tuft of green in the top and gaily ornamented with ribbons and streamers. After this is firmly planted at his front gate they shake hands with the officeholder who, knowing what is coming, has made a liberal advance on the prospective spoils of office and is provided with generous liquid refreshments.

After the close of the Civil War the material conditions of the Belgians greatly improved. Sawmills were built in various places making a market for their timber. It was no longer a weary burden to clear new land but a joy, for every acre of waste woods yielded money that was invested in cows. Barns were built and oxen and horses were purchased. The industrious Belgians who never tire of work began to ruminate on the possible time when they could assume just as pompous a pose as the great landlords of the mother country, and they no longer doubted that the bombastic letters which had lured them across the sea, after all contained the gospel truth.

But suddenly, in the midst of these happy visions, came a

catastrophe so terrible that no pen is adequate to describe it. This was the great tornado of fire which overwhelmed this region October 8, 1871. Suddenly, in the blackness of the night, a vast torrent of fire descended upon them, like the crash of judgment day, destroying their homes and woods and the lives of their friends and relatives. The tornado swept the entire Belgian settlement and a little fringe beyond, being about ten miles wide and sixty miles long. Here more than two hundred persons were burned to death and almost all—many thousands—were made homeless and destitute.

There are still a few old persons who remember with shuddering the horrors of that night. The terrific roaring of the wind together with the crash of falling trees caused the stoutest heart to faint. The smoke and glare of the flaming trees drove the wild animals into the clearings, seeking refuge among the bellowing cattle. People heard, saw and felt the terror of the lawless elements that had engulfed them and fled, screaming with terror, into the open fields. Even here they were not safe for whirlwinds of flames in great sheets streamed downward from the treetops and snuffed out the lives of many. Almost all, both victims and survivors, had but one thought—"it is the end of the world!"

The greatest destruction of life was in the town of Brussels in Door County. Here about one hundred and thirty persons perished. At Williamsonville, a little sawmill village of seventy people, sixty were burned to death in the middle of a three-acre field. The site of this tragedy is now a county park, known as Tornado Memorial Park, ten miles southwest of Sturgeon Bay on State Trunk Highway 57. The terrible experience of that little village is beyond imagination, but we have a description by one of the survivors.[2] In the town of Union a few miles west was another sawmill where eleven men were devoured by the flames while rushing across an open field to take refuge in the water of a creek.

What sustained these pioneers in their successive battles with a savage nature? In toil, self–denial and loneliness, beset by poverty, hunger and the irresistible ravages of nature, they struggled on. What were the forces that impelled them onward? It is not easy to plumb the reaction to circumstances so strange both to them and to us. Perhaps, first of all, it was the sturdy manhood characteristic of the pioneers; then, probably, it was sanguine hope of ultimate prosperity; finally the fatalism of their religion carried them onward—what happened was foreordained by God, and His will they accepted submissively but not dejectedly.

The people of southern Wisconsin were generous in their aid to the fire sufferers, and this helped the Belgians to rebuild their homes and obtain a new stock of domestic animals. It was a much more laborious process to clean up the chaos of fallen and charred timber which was all that remained of their woodlots. But eventually the cattle grazed and the wheat grew where formerly the forest had reigned. In the Eighties the Belgians partook of the prosperity that made that period the most abundant that the farmers of the west have enjoyed.

With these plentiful harvests came also the revival of the great Belgian festival—the Kirmess. For a few weeks each fall the Belgians at home and here in New Belgium banish all care and think only of having a rousing good time. Kirmess lasts for three days in each week for six successive weeks. Each week a different parish is the headquarters, determined to surpass in hospitable festivity, which makes necessary a vast amount of cooking and baking. It was the demands of Kirmess preparations that called into existence the numerous Dutch–Belgian ovens, many of which may still be seen. In these huge ovens with the accompanying bakehouses, fifteen pies or forty loaves of bread can be baked at once and with better success.

In the earlier days of the settlement the Kirmess dances were very picturesque. A committee of young men gaily festooned with ribbons of many colors was in charge of the community festival in each parish, and Belgian folk dances were danced on the highway to the singing of Belgian songs. But when the automobile came into general use, the highway became unsafe for dancing, and the dancers had to crowd into dance halls. The folk dances also went out of use and were succeeded by the "Fox Trot" and the "Charleston" because the people wanted to be "up to date." There is a growing demand, however, to revive the folk dances.

There are also many other forms of amusements at the Kirmess festival such as climbing a greased pole, catching greased pigs or giving a blindfolded man a scythe with which he is supposed to decapitate a goose. Foot races are a feature, and, most popular of all, horse races, the winner receiving the bridle as a prize.[3]

In different parts of the Belgian settlement may be seen little wayside shrines or chapels, although not as many as formerly, the new state and county highway construction having ruthlessly pushed many of them into oblivion. They are little places of prayer fitted out with an altar and other pious adornment, built in propitiatory remembrance of a parent or departed relative. Here the neighbors go for moments of quiet devotion, especially in the month of May. Many are the loving and reverent touches given to these chapels by the women.

The Belgians are a decidedly convivial people who never let a wedding, a christening or a family anniversary pass without abundant celebration. There is a vast amount of *flux de bouche* with accompanying influx of spirituous beverages. The phrase—*crever on etouffer do rire*—"to split one's side with laughing"—must have had its origin among the Belgians, for they are constantly doing it. But they are also very religious. One way in which they show this is in their church processionals. The most important is held in spring just before Ascension Day. The order of the procession is as follows: First comes the cross bearer in surplice and cassock bearing the cross. Then follow little girls in white strewing flowers along the path. Then comes the priest wearing sacerdotal robes of dignity and carrying the blessed Host in an ostensorium. He is followed by a choir singing hymns. Next come the women and finally the men. In former years the procession started from the church and proceeded to the nearest wayside chapel and then returned. The pioneers were very musical and often used to participate in the procession with diverse instruments on which were played beautiful selections of sacred music. Now, on account of the increased traffic, the procession is confined to the cemetery, and there is very little instrumental music.[4]

---

[1] The above was narrated by the eighty-year-old Sister Pauline who had worked with Adele Bruce for a lifetime.

[2] See next chapter.

[3] Lee W. Metzner has given a vivid account of "The First Kirmes" in *Wisconsin Magazine of History*, 14: 341-53.

[4] A detailed report on the time of arrival of all the early Belgian settlers is given in H. R. Holand, *Wisconsin's Belgian Community*.

chapter twenty-five

THE GREAT FIRE OF 1871

THERE is one event in the history of the Peninsula which in the memory of the people in the southern half of the County lingers like the recollection of a horrible, indescribable nightmare. This is the great fire of Sunday, October 8, 1871, when in the darkness of the night a tornado of fire descended upon them like the crash of Judgment Day. It devastated their forest and destroyed their homes and the lives of their friends and relatives.The pen of a later historian is utterly unable to picture such a cataclysm of nature—only those who went through it and survived that night of hell can have any conception of its horrors.

The year 1871 is outstanding for the havoc that was wrought both on sea and land. On the Great Lakes mighty storms raged at intervals, and hundreds of lives were swallowed up by the greedy waves. In Death's Door passage almost a hundred vessels were dashed on the rocks. On land, forest fires were numerous throughout the fall, burning up scores of small settlements in northern Wisconsin and Michigan and destroying thousands of lives. At Peshtigo more than four hundred men, women and children were burned to death within an hour. Many of these terrible events passed almost unnoticed by the general public because they were overshadowed by the greater catastrophe of the destruction of Chicago which took place on October 9 of the same year.

Williamsonville was a small settlement a few miles south of Little Sturgeon Bay, established by the Williamson brothers. There was a mill, a store, a boarding house, eight dwelling houses, a large barn, a blacksmith shop and a number of small buildings, and the manufacture of shingles was the only industry. About eighty persons lived here and all perished except seventeen. Of the eleven members of the Williamson family only two escaped—Thomas Williamson and his mother. Some time after the fire Thomas was interviewed by Frank Tilton, a Green Bay newspaper man, and the following is part of Thomas Williamson's narrative:[1]

"Ten days before the great fire at Williamsonville, the whole force was engaged in fighting fire. The clearing of about ten acres was surrounded by fire from half a mile to a mile, as we thought it best to set 'back fires' when the wind was favorable, and by so doing, burned all around the clearing. Then we thought we were safe, and that the fire would not burn over the same ground a second time. But not so. That Sunday afternoon, October 8th, at about five o'clock, there was some fire in the potato patch. Father and brother Fred and I carried water and partly put it out. After supper it seemed to kindle up again, so I had the teamster, John Conlon, hitch the mule team to the wagon, and put the tank, which held about nine barrels of water, on the wagon, and we took it to the mill, and my brother John and I filled the tank with water. We took this to the potato patch and put it all on the fire except two barrels. One we left there, and one a few rods distant, in case the fire should start up again in the night. I then had the teamster take the tank to the creek. This time, John, James and Fred Williamson, John Conlon and I filled it, took it opposite the store and left it there in case we should need it. John Conlon unhitched the mules and put them in the barn. I told him to leave the harness on that night. I then told the watchmen where I wanted them to watch most, and I also went all around the clearing. There was fire in spots all around, but not so much as there was two days before. I then went up to mother's house. Sister Maggie, cousin Maggie and Con McCusker were sitting on the stoop at the door. I also sat down and talked with them.

"In a few minutes after that there came a heavy puff of wind, the trees fell in all directions, and I saw the reflections of a big fire south of us. I thought it was a mile and a half off. In less time than it takes to write this, there came another heavy gale, and the flames came rolling through the woods behind the barn. I went down to the store and saw some of the men and told them to wake up all the crew. I went to the mill, got the hose on the roof, and wet it well. Then the sparks came down like a heavy snowstorm. I wet the end and side of the mill and all around on the ground as far as I could reach with the hose. The fire seemed to catch as fast as I could put it out. Some of the men came down to the mill, and one took the hose; the rest helped the men on the pumps. I went to the west side of the clearing. The fire caught in some sap-wood; I told some of the men to put it out, but they could not. I met John Williamson, who had become much excited. He asked me what I thought of the fire. I told him not to get excited. At that time I did not think our lives were in danger. I went up to my mother's house. The fire had caught in the fence of sap-wood, which was three tiers deep and four feet high, and was connected with all the houses, as the families used it for winter firewood. I told the men to make a gap in the fence, and helped them, but we could not get halfway to the ground. The fire drove us off, and we commenced in another place, but did not succeed there. We put water on, but it was no use.

"I then went to the mill. No buildings were on fire yet. I met brother John again and told him mother's house would soon be on fire; he said if we could save our lives he would be satisfied. I left him there and ran up to the boardinghouse; saw some of the teamsters and told them to take the teams out of the barn and shut the door. A few minutes before this I ran over to mother's house and told the women to put on men's pantaloons, as I thought they would be safer than their own clothing. Mother put on woolen underclothes and a woolen dress. Mrs. James Williamson did so, too, but Maggie Williamson and Maggie O'Neil did not. As I came to the boardinghouse as last stated, all the women were there. Joseph Married was on the roof spreading wet blankets. Frank McAdams, a blacksmith, came out of the potato field, went into the boardinghouse and came out bringing one child on his arm and leading another, and his wife followed with a babe in her arms. All the other women and children followed him into the potato patch. Just before they left I told them to take wet blankets, and some did so; I had one, but gave it to my sister and told her to wrap it well around her. She followed the rest. I did not think there was any danger in the potato patch. I saw father carrying things from mother's house, and told him if he could save his life it would be all he could do. He had on slippers, and went back after his boots, but came back with only one.

"By this time all the houses and the mill were in flames. I could not see anybody but Thomas Cryin. He was standing by the well at the door of the boardinghouse. I picked up a blanket and started for the potato patch, and Cryin said to me, 'Here is a good place to go down in the well.' I paid no attention to him, as my sister had left a few minutes before, and I wanted to find her. I tramped through fire, as there was fire almost all over the potato patch, and the smoke was so thick I could not see more than a rod ahead. Thomas Bush rode a pony into the potato field, and in less than five minutes I saw him on foot, and pony having become unmanageable, I came up to where there were thirty–five persons all huddled together, sitting on the ground. The smoke was so thick I could not tell who they were. Some were crying and some praying. I went about two rods from them, and there were six or seven men walking back and forth in the fire. I do not know who they were, as I was so excited I thought of no one but myself. I walked back and forth a few times, and then a thought came to my mind to run. I ran about five rods from there through the fire, and here I saw a space of about a rod square, where there had been a log–heap burned in the spring in clearing this land off. I lay down there on my face. The smoke was so thick that I thought I could not live. I rolled on my back and side and rooted with my face in the ground for air. Every time the wind blew I thought was my last. The trees fell around me every minute, and I thought they would fall on me. One top fell within ten feet of me. My feet were burning, and my vest caught fire: I could feel the fire burning my back. Twice I put my hand on my back and tried to wring the cloth of my vest to put the fire out. Then I thought I would roll into a big blaze and die quick. Still I lay there; I think I became unconscious.

"About three or four o'clock the smoke cleared away, and I thought I was the only one left to tell the tale. I would have given all I ever had for water; I cannot tell you how I suffered for it. I tried to get up, but could not. I lay some time longer, and finally got on my feet. I was so weak I could not stand, and lay down again. I then heard some one halloo, and I did so too. But I could not tell where the sound came from. I lay there some time, and then got to my feet and called again. This time there came an old man by the name of "Cap" Richmond. I asked him to get me some water, and he went away but did not come back. I could not walk. I lay there some time, and then got up, feeling a little better. I walked along in the direction the noise came from when I heard the first call. I staggered like a drunken man, I was so weak, and was almost blind. I could see nothing to tell me where I was, as every building was gone. I hallooed again, and was answered by someone about two rods ahead of me. I went over there and asked for water. They had some that Tom Bush had taken from the well in which Thomas Cryin and a little French girl lay dead. They told me this, but I did not care, I was suffering so, I drank about a quart, but it did not taste like water. Thomas Bush, Con. McCusker, James Donlon and mother were there. They were all lying down, and some had blankets over them. It became very cold in the morning.

"I could see dead bodies close by, some not six feet off. I trembled with the cold. Mother asked me if I saw any of the family, and I told her no. We lay there until daylight and then got up. The bodies lay in all directions. There were thirty–five or so in one heap. I could not recognize any of them, as they were so badly burnt. I got Cyril Jarvis to halloo, as I thought there might be some survivors in the woods. He did so, and someone answered: I thought it was John Williamson's voice. I asked if that was John Williamson, and the person answered no. I then wandered over the potato patch, seeing bodies here and there, and at length found one that I recognized as that of John. He looked natural. Both his shirts were burned off, but his pantaloons were not burned. I went from there to mother; she wanted me to take her away to Little or Big Sturgeon Bay, or to some house.

"The nearest house was three and a half miles away, and the road was so filled with trees that we lost the way a number of times. It was a weary tramp. Before we reached the location of the first house, Mr. Murray's, we suffered fearfully for water. At length we came in sight of the clearing and found that all the buildings were burned. There was a little muddy water at the side of the road, and we drank some; mother drank till I had to pull her away. The next house was Mr. Langley's half a mile away, and we thought if we could reach there we could get him to take us with his team to Sturgeon Bay. But we found that house and all the buildings burned also. We saw two of his horses and took them, as mother could go no further on foot. I led her horse by the halter. B. J. Merrill rode the other as he could not help himself to drive. The next building had been a mill and that and the next house were also burned. The next house was that of Mr. Daly, which we found still standing. It had taken us from daylight until 3:30 P.M. to come here, six miles. We found six families in this house, but they did all they could for us, and we remained there until the next day, when we were taken down to Sturgeon Bay."

There were sixty or more persons who perished in the little village of Williamsonville. A few miles west of this village was a shingle mill just built by Scofield and Company. Fourteen men were at work installing the machinery. When the avalanche of fire swept down upon them these men made a run for a place where a small flume had been built in a creek. This creek had been dry for some time because of the drought, but there was a little water and mud in a hollow. Ten of the men were struck down while running at top speed, and all were burned to death. The four who reached the puddle threw themselves face downward into it, but two of these were scorched to death.

Besides these there were upwards of a hundred farmers and their families who lost their lives. There was a similar number who escaped with their lives, but lost their homes, livestock and crops. Throughout the greater southern part of the county the hurricane of fire raged, and the humble but superstitious people believed that Judgment Day had come. Certainly no judgment day could come more swiftly, more unmercifully. The dreadful warning sound coming from the distance when the sky, so dark just before, burst into great blasts of fire, the beasts of the forest running for succor into the midst of the settlements, and the great consuming, roaring hell of fire engulfing all was an experience never encountered by man or beast. The dreadful scene lacked nothing but the sound of the last trumpet—and indeed, the roaring from the distance supplied even that to the frenzied imagination of the doomed people.

---

1 This is part of small book entitled "Sketch of the Great Fire" which was published in Green Bay and republished by the Green Bay Historical Society in 1926.

chapter twenty-six

THE PENINSULA'S COUNTY PARKS

THIS peninsula might well be called a national park because it has so much of the scenic charm that people seek in going to national parks. But land in eastern Wisconsin is too valuable to be all given up to sightseeing. However, the Peninsula has two state parks, one of which contains about 3600 acres, the other about one-third that much. It also has a dozen or more county parks. In the creation of these playgrounds, the Peninsula has taken a leading part in the State.

In 1927 the Wisconsin State Legislature enacted a provision for the creating of the so-called County Park Commission Plan. This plan provides for the appointment of seven park commissioners whose duty was "to make a thorough study of the county with reference to making reservations and acquisitions of lands therein for public uses, the improvement of such lands for park, playgrounds, forest reservations and parkways. . . .In making such studies, the commission shall give consideration. . . . to the preservation of places of natural beauty and of historic or scientific interest."[1]

Door County was the first county to adopt this plan. On November 16, 1927, the president of the Door County Historical Society (H. R. Holand) presented this plan to the County Board. The plan was unanimously adopted, and the chairman of the County Board appointed the following persons as members of the Park Commission:

H. R. Holand	1 year
W. E. Wagener	2 years
William Jess	3 years
H. J. Teske	4 years
F. A. Krueger	5 years
J. W. Rogers	6 years
G. J. DeKeyser	7 years

The following is part of the secretary's first report:

This commission immediately met and organized, electing
H. R. Holand chairman, and W. E. Wagener, secretary. Later
in the day the commissioners, accompanied by several other
gentlemen, drove out to the proposed tornado park, inspected
the land and made tentative arrangements with the owner
for the purchase of it. The next morning, November 18th,
they presented a report to the County Board recommending
the purchase of the two park sites mentioned above and the
appropriating of $600.00 therefor. This report was
unanimously adopted and the appropriation was made.

In the afternoon of that day the chairman of the
commission secured the services of the surveyor, Mr. E. W.
Odbert, and drove out to make a proper survey of the land by
metes and bounds. With the assistance of the accommodating
owner, Mr. Albert Eichelberg, this was quickly done.

Thus within twenty-four hours after the commission had
been appointed it had met and organized, considered the
merits of proposed plans, inspected the more important of
the two park sites, made satisfactory arrangements with the
owners, prepared and submitted its report, obtained the
necessary appropriation from the County Board, surveyed
and marked the land, and had the deed ready for signing
which was accomplished the next day.

This memorial park is a triangular tract of land abutting
on the principal highway of the county and lies about ten
miles southwest of Sturgeon Bay, It has a frontage of 568 feet
of State Trunk Highway number 42–57. Its other two sides
measure 450 and 542 feet respectively. The land has never
been plowed but is left as it was with its stumps and stones
that terrible night of October 8, 1871, when fifty-seven
human beings vainly struggled against that roaring tornado
of fire that destroyed them. The open well into which ten
men jumped for safety is still there. Two of these men
perished. A little distance away may be seen the spot where
thirty-five men, women and children crowded together, only
to be all consumed by the fire. Ten feet away are the two
stones between which Mrs. Williamson crouched, covered
with a wet blanket. She was saved, but across her feet lay
another woman partly covered by the same blanket who was
burned to death.

The County Park Commission means to keep this spot as
it is, hallowed to the memory of these martyrs of the
wilderness. In the spring a background of cedars and other

evergreens will be planted on the two converging sides. A dignified stone wall will be built along the highway as soon as the County Board appropriates money for it. Later a monument will be erected by the Door County Historical Society.

The Commission appointed a committee consisting of H. R. Holand and J. W. Rogers to survey the necessary land for the Rowleys Bay project and to make arrangements with the owners for the purchase of the same. The land is now being surveyed by Mr. E. W. Odbert.

W. E. WAGENER, Secretary
County Park Commission

The next park area to be acquired was the Robert La Salle Park in the extreme southeastern corner of the county. This marks the site where La Salle in 1679 feared he would be attacked by the Potawatomi, and he therefore threw up some breastworks for defense. However, when the Indians saw the peace pipe which their great chief Onanguissé had given to La Salle, their surly attitude changed to a very friendly one (see page 24).

The third county park to be acquired is what is known as the Murphy County Park at Horseshoe Bay, four miles southwest of Egg Harbor. Here the County Park Board has about seventeen acres with a sandy beach. This is probably the spot where La Salle's lieutenant, Henry Tonty and his starved companions gave up all hope of returning to the French settlements. It was in the end of November, 1679; and all they wanted was to get back to the Indian village at Sturgeon Bay where there was plenty of wood so they could get warm once more before they died (see pages 31-32).

At this place was a crumbling pier, and Mr. Murphy advertised for bids to repair it. One contractor bid $12,500, the other $20,000. The County Park Commission then offered to rebuild the pier providing the land was given to the county. The offer was accepted and the Park Commission built the pier. Cost, $9000. It was built with the aid of the C.C.C. and the Federal Government paid the bill.

Among these county parks there is one which was selected because of its abundance of rare flowers. This is known as The Ridges Sanctuary (see page 62). This contains more than forty acres immediately north of Baileys Harbor.

About three or four miles south of Jacksonport is Cave Point, an amazing scenic spot when the wind is from the south or east (see page 182).

Sugar Creek and Chaudoir's Pier are two pleasant little parks on the shore of Green Bay in the southwestern part of the county.

There are a number of other parks, some of which contain about a hundred acres, and have not yet been opened. These are the Ellison Bluff, the Door Bluff, Meridian Park, Lyle–Harter–Matter Park, and Washington Island Park.

---

1 *Wis. Statutes* of 1927, Section 27.02 to 27.06 inclusive.